SOCIOLOGY OF LAW

by

GEORGES GURVITCH

With a Preface by Roscoe Pound

Routledge & Kegan Paul
London and Boston

First published in 1947
by Kegan Paul, Trench, Trubner & Co., Ltd.
Reprinted in 1973
by Routledge & Kegan Paul Ltd
Broadway House, 68–74 Carter Lane,
London EC4V 5EL and
9 Park Street,
Boston, Mass. 02108, U.S.A.
Printed in Great Britain by
Unwin Brothers Limited
The Gresham Press, Old Woking, Surrey, England
A member of the Staples Printing Group

ISBN 0 7100 7519 7

CONTENTS

CHAPTER II

SYSTEMATIC SOCIOLOGY OF LAW

(MICROSOCIOLOGY OF LAW)

CHAPTER V

GENETIC SOCIOLOGY OF LAW

CONCLUSION

To
ALVIN S. JOHNSON

PREFACE

Along with much that is unhappy, the war in Europe has brought in its train one distinct good for us in the enforced coming to the U.S.A. of so many eminent scholars from the Continent. In law particularly, the course of history in mediæval England, on the one hand, and upon the Continent, on the other hand, led to a deep gulf between two legal traditions—traditions of lawmaking, of law teaching, and of administering justice—which have made it difficult for one-half of the legal world of to-day to understand and make effective use of the juristic development of experience in the other. A more intimate contact is coming about which can only be of advantage to each, if only in that each will understand the other.

Again, the academic water-tight compartment idea of the nineteenth century, which sought to keep each of the social sciences strictly in its place, much as the citizen was to be kept in his place in the ideal city-state of the Greek philosopher, has been giving way before a realizing of the need of team play among the social sciences, or of co-operation among them towards common objectives. Sociology, in particular, has been working with jurisprudence towards a better understanding of what we call "law", and of what lies behind the phenomena of the legal order as those phenomena appear to the lawyer.

In Continental Europe there has grown up in the present century a branch of sociology calling itself sociology of law; whereas in the U.S.A., with our characteristic bent to direct study towards the practical problems of the legal order there has grown up a sociological jurisprudence. The one has been at work upon sociology with reference to the phenomena of group life as involving "law". The other has been at work upon jurisprudence with reference to the adjustment of relations and ordering of conduct which is involved in group life. The emphasis of the one is upon a general science of society. The emphasis of the other is upon a special science of law. Thus the jurist has been looking at the Continental treatises on the science of law as if they were treatises on jurisprudence from the sociological standpoint, while the sociologists have been looking at the literature of sociological jurisprudence as if it were an attempt at a sociology of law. It is good to have a distinguished exponent of the present-day sociology of law set forth the scope and purpose of his science and a critique of sociological jurisprudence.

In introducing a book on sociology of law, which is not a familiar type of book in this part of the world, it would seem to be the best course to explain something of what is meant by the term and of what the author has in mind in his use of the term "law". If we grasp what is being written about, his definition of law and of the scope and purpose of sociology of law, both of which require thoughtful consideration as one reads them—require to be thought through as well as read through —will give a key to what follows, without which the Anglo-American lawyer, unfamiliar with the present-day methodology of the social sciences, may easily become bewildered.

In reading this book, as in reading the translation of Ehrlich's *Fundamental Principles of the Sociology of Law*, the reader, particularly if he is a lawyer, must continually bear in mind what it is that the author means by "law" and that it is not what the lawyer, at least, is likely to have in mind when he comes upon the, to him, familiar word. I have often written in other connections of the difficulties which arise from the multiplicity of meanings of this term, as jurists use it, and the confusions which arise from translation of Continental treatises on jurisprudence in which we employ the word "law" for a word of different import in other languages. Thus we are told that jurists are concerned solely with *quid juris*—what of right—whereas sociologists are only concerned with *quid facti*, in the sense of reducing social facts to the relations of forces. But the English or American reader may be moved to inquire whether the first proposition (at least as to the qualification "solely") does not flow from the term *droit*, *Recht*, *diritto*, *ius*, for which, perhaps fortunately, we have no exact equivalent in English. "What is right backed by law" is about as near to the idea as it can be put in our tongue. The first part, what is right in the adjustment of relations and ordering of conduct, is suggested more by the word used in the languages of Continental Europe than by our word "law". Our word suggests primarily what is backed by the force, or what carries the guinea stamp of politically organized society. Hence, on the Continent natural law has taken a first place in the ideas of jurists, while in England and America what is prescribed and given effect to by the organs of politically organized society has almost excluded the other idea and has led to the dominance of the analytical school in the science of law. Both sociology and philosophical jurisprudence have moved to over-come this separation of the two ideas. But I am not sure that it would not be an advantage if, while we recognized that neither idea could be kept out of relation to the other, our language could make us conscious that there are two ideas.

What, then, do the sociologists mean by law? Clearly they do not mean what the lawyer means. Thus we are told that there are "jural regulations so diffuse as to be unable ever to reach the bench". We are told that "the bench as well as the State itself presupposes a law which organizes them and determines their jurisdiction". This seems like the natural law of the seventeenth and eighteenth centuries, but, I take it, has a different meaning. However, the lawyer is likely to regard any such "law behind laws" as for philosophy and sociology and the science of politics. The law he is talking about is the regime of adjusting relations and ordering conduct carried on through the institutions and agencies of a politically organized society, in accordance with a system of authoritative guides to determination, applied and developed by an authoritative technique, by means of a judicial or an administrative process, or by both. I do not think it a reproach to the lawyer that he stops here, provided he realizes that the postulate of the legal para-mountcy of the political organization of society is only a postulate for the purpose of his subject.

As· Malinowski has shown, the more important regulations that order conduct in a primitive society work without the support of any tribunals. This is true also to-day. Much of social control is quite independent of the force of politically organized society. The legal order, the order of politically organized society, holds these other orderings together, adjusts them to each other, and to the extent that it recognizes them gives them its backing. This is the order with which the lawyer is concerned. The monopoly of force which the legal order claims and has held since the sixteenth century seems to him to set it off from the other orders among which it establishes a harmony. He sees how every activity of any consequence is now subjected to either judicial or administrative regulation and the legal order made to replace the inner order of so many groups and relations. He sees how juvenile courts and courts of domestic relations have superseded to no small extent the order of the household as it was formerly recognized and backed by the law

of the state. But all this does not mean that the legal order
and the body of authoritative materials of determination which
it has developed may be looked at apart from and ignoring the
broader basis of social control with which the sociologist has
to do.

" Socially significant normative generalizations ", i.e. " right-
patterns ", of different degrees of precision and generality are
functionally, i.e. as functioning towards social control, involved
in the very fact of any group. They are implicit in the very idea
of a group. Hence they are implicit also in the very idea of a
politically organized society, and it is those which, from where-
soever they get their content, are established or recognized or
spring up in the legal order, the order of that society, about which
the lawyer is talking. There is that much truth in Austin.

It has been remarked by philosophers of law that in such
things as wills, conveyances with conditions and limitations,
settlement of trusts, articles of partnership or of incorporation,
contractual matrimonial property regimes, and in contracts
generally, men in a sense make law for themselves. This was
much insisted on by metaphysical jurists who sought to deduce
law from liberty and took contract to be the highest manifestation
of liberty. In another way economists have spoken of the " working rules " governing groups of associated individuals in what
Commons calls " going concerns ". As he says, " each going
concern is indeed a government employing its peculiar sanctions ".
But as things are in the society of to-day, the contracts of which
the metaphysical jurists spoke and the peculiar sanctions of the
going concerns or group-governments of which Commons speaks,
operate subject to the scrutiny of the judicial or administrative
process or of both and in subordination to the processes recognized
or established by politically organized society. From the lawyer's
standpoint they are subject to law in the lawyer's sense.

I do not think the thoughtful lawyer believes in " the necessary
and *a priori* pre-eminence of state over other groups ". If he
has given any attention to legal history he cannot. But he cannot
fail to observe that we are, and have been since the sixteenth
century, in an era of paramountcy of political organization of
society and that the social control with which he has to
do is exercised through that organization and presupposes that
organization for its efficacy. For his purposes he assumes that
de facto pre-eminence without needing to postulate it as a necessary
or universal proposition to be accepted by those who look at the

phenomena of social control from other standpoints and for other purposes. The legal order—I purposely use " legal " rather than " jural " in this connection—presupposes its own supremacy and (without denying " that each group has its order, its framework of law, its own jural values ") undertakes to require such orders, such frameworks of law, and such jural values to exist or be carried on or be applied in subordination.

It is not so much that lawyers hold that only the State can make or establish law, in the sense in which the sociology of law employs that term, as it is that they postulate the State or the guinea stamp of the State or the enforcing agency of the State behind law in their more limited use of the term, since the whole development from an undifferentiated social control to the specialized form of social control, which is their concern, has gone on along with and as a result of increasing paramountcy of politically organized society. But this must not blind us to what the historical jurists saw through a glass darkly, and the sociological jurists have been bringing out clearly, with respect to the place of the law of the State in a larger view of the groups and associations and relations, and of their inner order, and the relation of that inner order to social control.

Lawyers will appreciate the discussion of " social guarantees on which are founded the effectiveness of all law ". This should be compared with Jellinek's doctrine of " social psychological guarantee " and the views of the historical jurists in the last century as to sanction. Sociology of law has cleared up this matter. The sanctions of the legal order of a politically organized society are, for the lawyer's purposes, generically distinct in that from his standpoint all the other instrumentalities of guarantee operate in subordination thereto. Indeed, the significant characteristic of the maturity of law (meaning the lawyer's law) is the increased efficacy of its sanctions. The progress in this respect from the want of sanction or feeble sanctions in archaic systems of undifferentiated social control to the organized and thorough-going sanctions of the differentiated and specialized social control through law in the lawyer's sense is a great part of the story in legal history.

Except as there is still in some quarters a certain hold-over from the eighteenth-century opposition of society and the individual, or of the seventeenth-century opposition of government and the individual, with the law of the land standing between them, the thinking lawyer of to-day does not identify the all-inclusive

society with the State.   But beyond this it is true that lawyers
and sociologists are not entirely talking about the same things.

   If lawyers unfortunately tend to ignore what the sociologist
is talking about, it is quite possible for the sociologist, in framing
a theory which will include his idea and the lawyer's idea in
one, to miss a good deal that is significant in the lawyer's law.
The persistence of taught tradition in doctrines and precepts,
the rule as to legacies on impossible or illegal conditions precedent,
the view of partnership which came down from the Roman law,
as against the mercantile view, the jealousy of corporations
extended to the business device of a trading company, the idea
of land as a permanent family acquisition, applied in a pioneer
community where lots were as fungible as corn or potatoes—
these phenomena of the legal order (and their name is legion)
call for the lawyer's study and are very remote from the " living
law " of the sociology of law.   Yet many of them have everyday
application in the courts.   For the study of what lawyers mean
by law we must distinguish it generically for the lawyer's purposes
from the different kinds of law which the sociologist recognizes
as such for his purposes.   What is important is that each should
recognize the legitimacy of the view of the other for the other's
purposes.

   It could be wished that as we have the two words " legal "
and " jural " (the former the lawyer's word) we had also two
words where now we have the one word " law ", used by sociologist
and by lawyer alike but with different meanings.   In the languages of Continental Europe also there is but one word, not wholly
congruent with our word " law ".   The Continental term comes
nearer to the sociologist's meaning.   But historically it has an
ethical connotation on one side and a legal (i.e. a lawyer's) connotation on the other side.   Perhaps it is as well that we haven't
such a word in English.   The word *ius* and its equivalents in the
languages of Continental Europe leads to an unconscious tendency
of juristic thought to lean to one side.   The English word leads
to a like tendency of English and American juristic thought to
lean to the other.

   As to the relation of sociology of law to jurisprudence, we
are told that jurisprudence is a science of social engineering and
that its methods are " different techniques " of such engineering
" suited to the interpretation of particular needs of concrete
systems of law and corresponding types of inclusive societies ".
" These different techniques depend upon their aims and these

aims depend upon a combination of the real life of the law "
(in the sociologist's sense) at a given time and in a given *milieu*,
which is studied by the sociology of law, and the variable jural
(not legal) ideas and values " whose specificity and degree of
objectivity is the particular province of the philosophy of law ".
Thus sociology of law is a foundation subject for jurisprudence
giving us a sociological jurisprudence as philosophy of law is a
foundation subject, giving us a philosophical jurisprudence. If,
however, jurisprudence must build on these foundations, jurists
must insist that the foundations cannot be made the superstructure. Sociology of law is not sociological jurisprudence any
more than the latter can claim to be an adequate sociology of
law. Its great service, from the lawyer's standpoint, is in bringing to light a better foundation for the understanding of lawyer's
law than natural law which had to be given up, and yet left
an empty space requiring to be filled. Indeed, the intimate
relation of jurisprudence, philosophy of law, and sociology of
law is well brought out in Chapter I, in which the author in
reviewing the development of sociology of law at the same time
reviews significant features of juristic thought from Aristotle to
the present day.

It remains to call attention to the contrast between a sociology
of law, which realizes that it cannot replace but must go along
with philosophy of law, and the older sociology, which would
have dispensed with philosophy. Nor does it assume to dispense
with jurisprudence. Perhaps I may be pardoned for repeating
that neither sociology of law nor philosophy of law can replace
jurisprudence, which, if it needs both, as a basis of critique and
to correct its specialized generalizations (if I may so put it), yet
has a field to which neither is wholly adequate, important as
each is to the jurist who would be assured of a wise knowledge
of his subject.

ROSCOE POUND.

SOCIOLOGY OF LAW

INTRODUCTION

THE OBJECT AND PROBLEMS OF THE SOCIOLOGY OF LAW

I. THE PRELIMINARY QUESTION

The sociology of law—a discipline more recent in origin than sociology, of which it constitutes an essential branch—is still in full course of formulation. Despite the constantly increasing attention which it has aroused during the last decades, despite its burning actuality, which we will try to explain, the sociology of law still has no clearly defined boundaries. Its various exponents are not in agreement as to its subject, or the problems requiring solution, or its relations with other branches of the study of law. From where does this lag in the development of the sociology of law come? It derives from the fact that this new science must fight on two fronts for its existence. It has encountered powerful antagonists both in the camp of the jurists and in that of the sociologists who, coming from opposite directions, sometimes unite to deny any place to the sociology of law.

In fact, at first view, it would not appear likely that sociology and law could associate very well, inasmuch as jurists are concerned solely with the question of the *quid juris*, while sociologists are concerned with the description of the *quid facti* in the sense of reducing *social facts* to the relations of forces. Hence, the uneasiness of many jurists and legal philosophers who ask whether the sociology of law does not intend the destruction of all law as a norm, as a principle of the regulation of facts, as a valuation. Hence, likewise, the hostility of certain sociologists, being disturbed by the fear of re-introduction of value judgments into the study of social facts through the mediation of the sociology of law. The function of sociology being to unite that which the traditional social sciences arbitrarily divide, these sociologists, moreover, insist on the impossibility of detaching the reality of law from the whole of social reality, seen as an indestructible totality.

Finally, those who propose to avoid " the conflicts between sociology and law " by sharply defining their fields and methods, have affirmed that the normative point of view proper to the jurist and the explanatory point of view proper to the sociologist,

give social reality and law separate spheres of existence which
bar all possibility of a meeting. But if sociologists and jurists
must mutually ignore each other to pursue consequently the true
object of their studies, we are driven to the conclusion that the
sociology of law is both impossible and futile, and that in order
to do away with all difficulties, it suffices to do away with the
sociology of law.[1]

The alternative between exclusivism, whether sociological or
jural, and the total separation of the spheres into two different
worlds, has, however, been overcome, as it had to be, by the
development both of sociology and jurisprudence.

Nobody has formulated the situation better than the great
French jurist-sociologist, Maurice Hauriou, who declared that
" a little sociology leads away from the law but much sociology
leads back to it ", to which we should add, for the sake of precision, that a little law leads away from sociology but much law
leads back to it. The most important American legal sociologist,
Dean Roscoe Pound, expressed the latter conception with singular
clarity when he wrote that " perhaps the most significant advance
in the modern science of law is the change from the analytical
to the functional standpoint ". The functional attitude requires
that judges, jurists and lawyers keep perpetually in mind the
relation between law and living social reality, a consideration of
" the law in action ". " A fruitful parent of injustice is the
tyranny of concepts," declared Justice Benjamin Cardozo, and
he went on to describe " the limitation of their logic " by sociological considerations taking place in the present-day juridical
process. This, also, was the meaning of an earlier well-known
statement of Justice O. W. Holmes that " the life of the law has
not been logic ; it has been experience ", experience of real
social existence which the juridical process, if it is not to be pure
verbal play, cannot overlook. The revolt against " mechanical
jurisprudence " (Pound) or " legal fetishism " (Geny), is an
indisputable tendency marking all jural thinking of the late
nineteenth and early twentieth centuries. Under the form of a
discussion of " the broadening of the sources of positive law ",
and " free law ", this current has led to the summoning of
sociology to the aid of jurisprudence.[2]

---

[1] Cf. Kelsen, *Der juristische und der soziologische Staatsbegriff* (1921) and his article,
" Eine Grundlegung der Rechtssoziologie " in *Archiv für Sozialwissenschaft* (1915),
No. 39, pp. 830–76.
[2] For a detailed exposition of these discussions, which inspired an enormous literature, see my book, *Le Temps Présent et l'Idée du Droit Social* (Paris, 1932), pp. 213–333.

That is why nobody should be startled to-day, neither socio-logists nor jurists, to discover that, despite so much mutual defiance, " the pick-axes of the two crews, each hollowing out its respective gallery, have finally met " (Bouglé). The meeting place is precisely the sociology of law. Conflicts between socio-logy and law leading to the " impossibility " of legal sociology were only the outcome of narrowness and aberrations in the conception of the object and method of the respective sciences, sociology and law. As Dean Pound pointed out with all good reasons : " These things are as much in the past in jurisprudence as they are in sociology." [1] The sociology of law is incompatible not with the autonomy of the technical study of law, but with the analytical school of John Austin (whose predecessors were Hobbes and Bentham), with continental " legal positivism " and with " normative logicism ". The sociology of law constitutes no menace to sociology proper, but only to " naturalism, positi-vism, behaviourism and formalism " in sociology. Since it is they which have hampered the normal development of our discipline, let us set forth these questionable and often outmoded currents in jurisprudence as well as in sociology. Simultaneously we will demonstrate how the greater maturity both of juris-prudence and of sociology have led each of them separately towards the sociology of law.

II. TRENDS IN JURISPRUDENCE AND THEIR RELATION TO SOCIOLOGY

Analytical jurisprudence has taken two forms, one narrow, related to continental " legal positivism ", the other broader, identifying law with the totality of rules and principles applied by tribunals in making their decisions. That is why we will first of all examine the " analytical " and " positivistic-legal " conceptions in the restricted sense. These conceptions, which dominated the teaching of law in the second half of the nineteenth century, did not consist of an affirmation that all law is positive law, that is to say, established in a given social *milieu*. Their thesis was rather that this positive character came from the com-mand of a superior and dominant will, generally of the State ; this latter had been proclaimed the unique source of law, detached from the spontaneous forces of the social *milieu* as well as from particular groups, and imposing upon them an independent and rigid legal order. Thus, legal positivism and analytical juris-

---

[1] " Sociology and Law " in *The Social Sciences and their Interrelations* (New York, 1927), edited by W. F. Ogburn and A. A. Goldenweiser, pp. 325–6.

prudence, having nothing in common with sociological positivism, projected law into a sphere quite removed from living social reality ; far above this reality soared the State, a metaphysical entity rather than a real fact. For legal positivism, of course, all sociology of law appeared as a crime of lèse-majesté towards the State and its order. The jurist in his ivory tower turned with contempt from all that had to do with the social reality of law. He was proud to argue in the formalistic vacuum of the sanctuary of the State, legislative texts and decisions of official tribunals which barred the road to all contact with the life of society.

The Anglo-Saxon system of law, however, as founded on the idea of the supremacy of the common law, is linked to " judicial empiricism " (Pound) and oriented to the unwritten and flexible law, particularly case law and customary law (Coke and Blackstone). Consequently, the followers of analytical jurisprudence, especially the Americans, inspired by the " pioneers' conception of law " (Pound),[1] insisted on the dependence of all law on court practices and decisions rather than on its dependence upon the State or whatever sovereign agency. Furthermore the formula, " law is the totality of rules applied by tribunals ", may be diversely interpreted. Its sense depends upon whether one views tribunals as organs of the State or as agencies of " the national community ", more precisely of the all-inclusive spontaneous society subjacent to the State, as well as to other groups. This formula also varies in sense, depending upon whether one insists on the binding of tribunals by case law, customary law, and statutory law, or on the preponderant character of the free decision of tribunals (decisionism, forecast by O. W. Holmes and developed by the " legal realists ") or, finally, upon the broad domain of different social codes, springing directly from social reality and imposing themselves on the deliberations of courts (Cardozo and MacIver).[2]

Obviously, the tendency of the analytical school has been to consider tribunals primarily as the organs of the State and to emphasize the subordination of their activity to case and statuory law.[3]

---

[1] Cf. the characteristic brilliance of Pound in *The Spirit of the Common Law* (1921), pp. 112–92 and A. L. Goodhart, " Some American Interpretations of Law ", pp. 1–20, in *Modern Theories of Law* (1933).

[2] Robert M. MacIver, *Society, its Structure and Changes* (1932), pp. 287–302.

[3] Cf. the work of the major American representative of the analytical school, Gray, *Nature and Sources of the Law* (1909, 2nd ed., 1921). It is, moreover, interesting to observe that the very structure of the Anglo-Saxon system of common law, and

Logical normativism, referring back to " Kantian idealism " and basing itself on the irreducible opposition between ought-to-be (*Sollen*) and being (*Sein*), in order to eliminate the possibility of any sociology of law is, in the last analysis, nothing but a recrudescence of " legal positivism " combined with dogmatic rationalism. According to this doctrine, law, being nothing but a pure norm, admits only a normative and formalistic method of study, every other method being destructive of the very object of research. That is why sociology cannot study law and the " science of law " cannot take account of social reality. In the study of law, everything is reducible to the research for a fundamental norm (*Grundnorm*) from which the system of particular norms had to flow, formal logic alone being of any use here. It is not hard to see that " fundamental norm " merely replaces, for this tendency, the metaphysical entity of the State separated from social reality, as found in the thesis of legal positivism. Moreover, the chief representative of this current, Kelsen, finds it perfectly easy to grant that the legal system of norms reduced to a fundamental norm is identical with either a national State or with a world State, and that in this sense all law is State law.

We will insist here neither upon the internal contradictions, nor upon the naïve dogmatism, nor upon the inescapable conflict with facts, of analytical jurisprudence, " legal positivism " and " logical normativism ", when they seek in the name of " the science of law " to eliminate sociology of law. Roscoe Pound and Benjamin Cardozo have made brilliant and exhaustive criticisms of the sterility of analytical jurisprudence. In my earlier works I endeavoured to summarize and synthesize the criticisms of the analogous continental trends. Here it will suffice to indicate the following considerations :

(*a*) Analytical jurisprudence and legal positivism run in a vicious circle, the existence of the State presupposing law, of

particularly its development in the United States, favoured more the broader conceptions of law made independent of and superior to the State—a necessary consequence of the supremacy of the " common law ", if this principle followed. Under the influence of the historical school of jurisprudence, these interpretations took preferably the traditionalistic form of the theory of the primacy of customary law established for centuries. One can, however, see real limitations of this traditionalistic bent and an orientation towards spontaneous and living law of actual society in the latest representative of the American historical school, J. C. Carter (*Law, its Growth and Function*, 1907), as well as in the English theorists of constitutional law of the late nineteenth century, Walter Bagehot (*Physics and Politics*, 1873), and A. W. Dicey (*Introduction to the study of the law of the Constitution*, 8th ed. 1915 ; *Lectures on the relation between law and the Constitution*, 1914).

which it is affirmed to be the only source,[1] and the State being a sector of that social reality above which it is supposed to soar. For even stronger reasons, the tribunals which apply law and which in part create it, presuppose a pre-existing law which organizes them.   Moreover, not all law is sanctioned by tribunals (see below) but only one of its sectors, or rather one of its levels of depth, and even in this limited portion a great part of the rules which are discussed by the tribunals are imposed on the latter directly by the spontaneous jural life of society and of the particular groups which it embraces.

(b) " Logical normativism ", referring to " the pure ought to be ", annihilates itself by replacing the *a priori* content of this " ought to be " by sensible empirical content which cannot be formulated as categorical imperatives.

(c) These two trends accept as the immutable essence of law the technical procedures of systematization employed in certain epochs (epoch of the Roman emperors and of the second half of the nineteenth century on the European continent), and consisting in the reduction of various rules of law to unified sources fixed in advance.

(d) There are well-known facts of the origin and persistence of jural regulation entirely independent of the State : this latter, set up much later, intervenes little if at all in the functioning of law over long centuries.   No less incontestable are conflicts between different frameworks of law affirming themselves as equally valid within a same society.   All these facts show the entirely artificial and dogmatic character of these monistic interpretations of the method and object of jurisprudence.   The tribunals, which obviously often have no relation to the State and which, even when connected with it, sometimes (particularly in Anglo-Saxon law) retain the character of agencies of the all-inclusive society, play themselves a variable rôle in the life of law.   For instance, as the distinguished anthropologist, Bronisław Malinowski, has pointed out, the more important jural regulations in primitive society work without the support of any tribunals (cf. *Crime and Custom in Savage Society*, 1926).

The analytical school, legal positivism, and logical normativism, in proposing to eliminate the sociology of law the better to defend the efficaciousness of jurisprudence, succeed only in

---

[1] This fact was most forcefully and clearly emphasized by H. Krabbe, the Dutch jurist, in *Die Lehre von der Rechtssouveränität* (1906) ; *Die Moderne Staatsidee* (1919, Eng. transl. 1926) ; and by L. Petrazizky, the Russian jurist, in his *Theory of Law and of State* (2 vols. 1908–10).   Concerning these two authors, see my *Le Temps Présent et l'Idée du Droit Social* (1932), pp. 140–9 and 270–95.

compromising it by condemning it to total sterility from the point of view of jurists themselves. In effect, the vocation of the jurist is to resolve concrete cases of litigation according to a coherent system of rules, standards, or principles of law valid in a given *milieu*. But these concrete cases can be in complete rebellion against the application of preconceived patterns. Moreover, the validity of law cannot be established by a simple interpretation and systematization of legislative texts and decisions of tribunals. Legal rules may remain entirely impotent, that is to say, with no application whatsoever, while decisions may contradict each other. If the jurist took no account of the living law, of the spontaneous law in action, of the flexible and dynamic law (which is in perpetual flux and obviously not detachable from the social reality of law), of the behaviour, practices, of the institutions, of the beliefs related to law, he would run the danger of constructing an edifice entirely disconnected from the law really valid, from the law really efficient in a given social *milieu*. How, moreover, to interpret and how to systematize texts without criterion, without penetrating the " spirit of law " which animates it ? A jurist, in order really to concern himself with positive law rather than with formal logic, cannot detach his constructions from sociological research into the efficient law, which can be and, by virtue of its dynamic character, to some extent always is in " revolt against formulated codes ".

Nobody has better described the embarrassing situation of the jurist than did Justice Cardozo in *The Paradoxes of Legal Science* (1928). " The juridical function is dynamic and creative. . . . The reconciliation of the irreconcilable, the merger of antitheses, the synthesis of opposites, these are the great problems of the law. Law defines a relation not always between fixed points but often, indeed oftenest, between points in varying position," that relationship and variation coming from the spontaneity of social life. " Law must be stable and yet it cannot stand still " (Pound). How, under such conditions, can the jurist do anything without sociology of law ?

The sociology of law shows itself indispensable not only to the practical work of the jurist applying law to concrete cases, but also to the jurisprudence or the systematic dogmatization of a peculiar system of law. In effect, this discipline studies the patterns and jural symbols,[1] that is to say, the jural meanings

---

[1] Cf. on the rôle of patterns and symbols in social life and in particular on " spiritual cultural symbols " in the life of law, Sections III , IV and V of this introduction.

valid for the experience of a particular group in a particular
epoch, and works for the establishment of a coherent system of
such symbols.   Thus, it is necessary to know what they symbolize,
that is, it is necessary to recapture what they express and to
unveil what they hide.   But this is precisely the vocation of the
sociology of law.   Furthermore, the criteria whereby are
abstracted normative symbolic meanings detached from the full
reality of law, as well as the principles which inspire the coherence
of any particular system of such meanings constructed by jurisprudence, cannot be established except by recourse to sociology
of law.   It is the latter which brings out the collective beliefs
animating the experience of jural values in a given social *milieu*.
Thus, far from menacing the existence of jurisprudence, the
sociology of law gives that discipline consistency and effectiveness
by serving as an indispensable foundation.

We can achieve the same result by analysing the rather widespread interpretations of jurisprudence as juridical technique.
At first that conception would seem perfectly acceptable, were
it not often and quite erroneously linked to a statement that the
law itself is a mere technique, which seems to us a mistaken and
dangerous point of view.   When, for example, Justice Holmes
wrote that " prophecies of what the courts will do in fact and
nothing more, are what I mean by the law ",[1] or when, much
more recently, Max Radin declared that " the law is a technique
of administrating a complicated social mechanism ",[2] they spoke,
I believe, more of jurisprudence than of the law proper.   In fact,
this characteristic did not prevent Holmes from recognizing that
" the law is the witness and external deposit of our moral life ",[3]
which is surely not a mere technique, nor did it prevent him
from protesting against " cynical " interpretations of his words.
Similarly, Professor Radin finally declares that " humanity is,
after all, the business of law " and recognizes that law is linked,
if not with justice, at any rate with " *humanitas* and *clementia* ".[4]
In so far as it is difficult to regard " morality ", " humanity "
or " clemency " as " techniques ", one must assume that these
authors do not sufficiently distinguish between *law* and *jurisprudence*
which is one among the disciplines in studying law.   We can,
then, without any difficulty recognize that a constituent element

---

[1] " The Path of the Law " in *Collected Legal Papers* (1921), pp. 173, 167–9.
[2] *Law as Logic and Experience* (1940), pp. 163, 195.
[3] Op. cit., p. 170.
[4] Op. cit., pp. 150–1, 164.

of all law is " an ideal element ",[1] Justice or spiritual values (as do Pound, Cardozo, Geny, Hauriou, Radbruch and the present author, see *infra* sections IV and V),[2] and regard jurisprudence as only a technique, especially in the service of tribunals. It would even be very important, in order to avoid all methodological confusion, to agree that jurisprudence or " legal science ", is an art and nothing more,[3] and fitted only to practical ends. Only the sociology of law and the philosophy of law can be true theoretical disciplines. Jurisprudence, on the contrary, is " social engineering " [4] and the various trends within it (analytical and historical jurisprudence, the newer " sociological jurisprudence " as well as " legal realism ") are only different techniques of such engineering suited to the interpretation of particular needs of concrete systems of law and corresponding types of inclusive societies.

But—and this is the decisive point—all technique is based on theoretical disciplines which serve as a foundation,[5] as well as on practical ends which it is designed to serve. Medicine's technique rests on physiology and anatomy, as well as on the aim of restoring health. The art of the bridge engineer rests on mechanics, as well as on the aim of supporting heavy loads. Thus, one might say, the sociology of law, on the one hand, and philosophy of law, on the other, are the two theoretical disciplines which must constitute the bases of any jurisprudence conceived as an art, i.e., as a judicial technique. For the work of systematized prediction of what tribunals will do, the sociology of law gives the jurist an objective description of the social reality of the law valid in a given social *milieu*. The philosophy of law gives him a criterion of jural values, aiding him in their particularized manifestations to reach concrete goals.

In fact, the juridical techniques employed in different epochs

---

[1] Pound, *The History and System of the Common Law* (1939), pp. 15–16, and " The Ideal Element in American Judicial Decision ", in *Harvard Law Review*, vol. 45.

[2] See also Morris R. Cohen, *Law and Social Order* (1933), pp. 165 et seq. ; and 219 et seq.

[3] Albert Kocourek in his very stimulating *Introduction to the Science of Law* (1930), has tried to oppose a purely theoretical-formal jurisprudence or " science of law " to the " constructive or functional jurisprudence " which is an art (pp. 32–5). He regards such an " abstract-logical theory of jural relations " (pp. 235 et. seq.) as distinct not only from technique but also from both the sociology and the philosophy of law. I must, however, confess that I believe Kocourek's logical jurisprudence to be a heritage of the analytical school and akin to Kelsen's " pure theory of law ". It, too, represents an absolutization of the logical elements working in a certain technique, elements which in fact change with the technique itself.

[4] Pound, *Interpretations of Legal History* (1923), pp. 141–57.

[5] See, in the same sense, Karl N. Llewellyn, " Legal Tradition and Social Science Method ", in *Essays on Research in Social Sciences* (1936), pp. 89–120.

and cultural spheres (e.g., on the continent of Europe or in Anglo-Saxon countries, in England or the United States ; in the Roman Republic or the Roman Empire, in the eighteenth or nineteenth or the present century) are not at all identical. Justification of the diverse and highly variable juridical techniques depends on their aims. The aims depend on the combination of the concrete situation of the real life of law at a given moment and in a given *milieu* (studied by the sociology of law) and on the variable jural ideas and values (whose specificity and degree of objectivity is the particular province of the philosophy of law).[1] For example, even the reduction of all sources of law to State law, or at least to abstract propositions fixed in advance and dogmatized into immutable "logic of law" by the analytical school, legal positivism and normativism can be justified only by the sociology of law which acknowledges the adaptation of this technique to a particular type of juridical life. The opposite techniques, too, insisting on the social functions, or on anti-conceptualistic decisionism or on the plurality of equivalent sources and on the preponderance of living and flexible law, find themselves no justification except in the sociological acknowledgment of entirely different situations in the reality of law corresponding to other types of society, and so on.

Juridical technique, or jurisprudence, can be more or less adapted to the type of the real life of the law, for the transformations of technique often lag behind variations in real jural life. Jurists have an inveterate tendency to dogmatism and conservatism, the identification of entirely relative techniques with the eternal idea, the "Logos" of the law. The intense constructive element, the particularly thick conceptual crust characterizing all juridical technique, leads to a "mummification" of categories and formulas with consequent slowness and serious difficulty in adapting jurisprudence, with its "ceremonial mysteries" (Thurman Arnold), to the new living reality of law, a perpetual dynamism, always in motion, always in flux.

Where an ever-widening gulf yawns between traditional jural categories and the reality of law, the sociology of law becomes a burning actuality. This is the case in our epoch ; for here is a situation in which abstract jural formulas prove themselves to be totally incapable of capturing the turbulent flood of the law's real life, with its novel and unforeseen institutions arising with elementary spontaneity. The jurist can no longer make a

[1] See *infra*, Section V and Conclusion.

single step without doing the work of a sociologist, without calling in the sociology of law. And since this last, as a methodical science, is often absent from legal education and never occupies the place to which it is entitled, we see here and there the birth of spontaneous sociology of law in the work both of legal theorists and judges.

Obviously, this is not the first time in our epoch that conflicts have arisen between a laggard juridical technique and a particularly turbulent life of law. But in earlier epochs—e.g., in the seventeenth and eighteenth centuries—the efforts to allay these conflicts and adapt juridical technique to the reality of law, had recourse to " natural law ", allegedly deduced from pure reason but in all truth only living law in revolt against rigid law which was imprisoned in abstract formulas. To-day, owing to the great complexity of the reality of law ; owing to the new philosophical atmosphere which grants reason neither stability, nor unity, nor a capacity to produce concrete contents ; finally, owing to the development of sociological knowledge, this subterfuge of natural law,[1] to which some jurists still resort, cannot solve the problem. Under present circumstances the sociology of law alone is able to give jurists themselves a satisfactory solution to the problems of jurisprudence.

Our analysis of the relations between the sociology of law and jurisprudence has been an effort to eliminate a series of objections to the possibility of the former, advanced by the exponents of the latter. We must now treat in the same way objections raised by sociologists. We have noted that the sociology of law comes into conflict not with sociology, of which it constitutes an essential part, but with " sociological positivism, naturalism, behaviourism and formalism ". Let us now elucidate these doctrines and show how they have been destructive to the development of sociology itself, as well as of sociology of law, and how they have been superseded.

III. TRENDS IN SOCIOLOGY AND THEIR RELATION TO LAW

Sociological positivism, introduced by Auguste Comte, has taken different forms, often contrary to the inspiration of the founder of sociology. For Comte, " sociology " has a double sense. On the one hand, it was a positive science of social facts. On the other, it was " the total science ", the science of sciences,

---

[1] See my article " Natural Law " in *The Encyclopedia of Social Sciences* and my *Expérience Juridique et Philosophie Pluraliste du Droit* (1935), pp. 103–37.

a sort of " prime philosophy " replacing ancient metaphysics. This second conception of sociology led Comte to identify sociology with a philosophy of history, with a theory of progress, to graft on to it ethics and a Religion of Humanity, and to confuse, here as elsewhere, judgments of reality and of value. Hence, too, the foisting into sociology of what might be called an " imperialist " tendency, denying the possibility of any other study of social reality and claiming to absorb and to dissolve every previously established social science and every philosophic reflection on morality, law, religion, or history. Hence, Comte was led to reject any division within sociology except that between static and dynamic sociology. The unity of society was destined to serve as a basis for " total spiritual unification "—the aim of his " positive politics ".

Comte's position excluded the possibility of the sociology of law not only because of his concentration on the study of general rules of the development of society and his exclusion of special branches of sociology, but even more because of his hostility to law, to which he denied any reality. Law for him was but a " metaphysical vestige . . . absurd as well as immoral ". Positivism " causes the idea of law to disappear irretrievably ". Comte's " social point of view " could not admit anything but " duties flowing from functions " and resting directly on morality and love. Society, according to Comte, is based upon a pre-established harmony which excludes all antinomies, all conflicts, which in order to be resolved would demand the formal guarantees characteristic of jural regulation. The only concession made by Comte—and it is to this that, so to speak, his reflections on law boil down—is the admission that law plays a rôle in epochs of " revolutionary transition ", the illusion of the " equality of rights " reinforcing the disintegrating and anarchical character of the epoch.

After Comte, sociological positivism gradually renounced its identification of sociology with a prime philosophy, with a theory of progress, and likewise renounced its exclusive unitarianism. It restricted its conception of sociology to that of a positive science of social facts. But at the same time it eliminated the spiritual element which Comte found at the bottom of social reality. It interpreted the latter increasingly in analogy with natural reality, preferably physical or biological. While thus renouncing the Comtian maxim of the irreducibility of the spheres of the real, and limiting the object of sociology to that which is tangible, perceptible to the senses, sociological positivism did not renounce sociology's claim to absorb all social sciences and philosophic reflection on social facts. It persisted, likewise, in denying the possibility of special branches of sociology and in seeking universal syntheses giving a monistic explanation of the phenomena of social life. This led post-Comtian sociological positivism to reduce all social reality to those externalizations perceptible to the senses. It saw in society only a combination of " social forces ", ignoring all other elements which penetrate and guide these forces. Obviously, sociological positivism thus impoverished social reality to a considerable extent. By its love of poorly understood reality, it was led to exclude from the field of its studies sectors of social reality as fundamental as the reality of law, morality, religion, etc. Sociological positivism thereby became social naturalism, reducing the problems of sociology to those of mechanics, theory of energy, geography, demography, finally biology, under the triple form of anthropo-racism, social Darwinism, and organicism.

Among these currents, perhaps organicism alone took some account of the problem of societal regulation, including the law. This appears in the works of Herbert Spencer and Schaeffle, a fact explicable by the implication in biological organicism of more ancient elements of " spiritual organicism " having a metaphysical basis (Krause, Ahrens). It is biological organicism which first inspired ethnographic research in the legal field. But its arbitrary premises excluded any objective study of the specificity of social reality, as well as of the rôle which law plays therein.

Social psychologism, which overcame the prejudice of naturalism and mechanism thanks to the work of Lester Ward (*Dynamic Sociology*, 1883 ; *The Psychic Factors of Civilization*, 1897 ; *Pure Sociology*, 2 vols., 1908), Gabriel Tarde (cf. *infra*) and I. M. Baldwin (*Social and Ethical Interpretation*, 1897), however, understood neither how to distinguish the psychological aspect of social life (collective psychology) from individual psychology, nor how to avoid narrow subjectivism in the interpretation of psychic life, nor how to show the specific rôle of law in the structure of society. It is true that Tarde (see farther on), a jurist himself, through his works in the field of criminology became one of the closest forerunners of the sociology of law. It is true, too, Baldwin assigned a rôle to legal and ethical regulation, while Ward attributed no importance to law, seeing therein only arbitrary inventions. But this is not decisive testimony on behalf of psychological sociology. In fact, as Roscoe Pound emphasized in his important programmatic study, " The Scope and Purpose of Sociological Jurisprudence ",[1] jurists by their effort to construct " legal sociologies ", or at least theories of law on a sociological basis, came even to utilize sociological theories denying the reality of law. As examples, we might cite the application of mechanical sociology by L. Gumplowitz, *Die soziologische Staatsidee* (1902), and *Grundriss der Soziologie* (1886, posthumous edition 1926), and the utilization of social Darwinism by Vaccaro (*Les Bases Sociologiques du Droit et de l'État*, 1893). To us there seems no doubt that these authors—and even Tarde (to be discussed further)—did not find social reality of law, thanks to their sociologies, but imported law from their independent legal studies.

To conclude this brief account of the trends in sociology which have been unfavourable to the development of the sociology of law, we should mention two other more recent tendencies, German sociological formalism and American behaviourism. Sociological formalism, whose principal representatives are George Simmel (*Soziologie*, 1908) and L. von Wiese (*System der allgemeinen Soziologie*, 2 vols., 1926–33, English translation by Howard Becker, 1932), limits the entire study of sociology to " pure forms of interhuman relations ", exclusively. It bars all the cultural and spiritual content of such forms, e.g., law, morality, religion, knowledge, and æsthetics as well as the material basis of society, whether demographic, geographic, instrumental, economic or whatever. According to partisans of this conception, to begin to study not simply abstract forms of " sociation " but also the totality of concrete social manifestations, is to dissolve sociology in other social sciences or in history. Sociology thus loses its special object ; there can, therefore, be no interrelation between sociology and particular social sciences ! If this trend has had the merit of renouncing sociology's initial claim to dissolve all particular social sciences, and if it has favoured the study of types of sociations and groupings, it has, by rendering sociology perfectly sterile, paid far too high a price for its gains. This conception is nothing but an abstract and anti-historical rationalism combined with a nominalistic prejudice concerning social reality.[2] In their methodological considerations the formalists

---

[1] *Harvard Law Review* (1912), vol. 12.
[2] Cf., for a criticism of sociological formalism, my *Essais de Sociologie* (1938) and P. Sorokin, *Contemporary Sociological Theories* (1928), pp. 488–513.

forget that the object and method of a science are different matters and that a single object—social reality—may be studied by diverse methods : typological (sociology), individualizing (history), normative and technical (jurisprudence, etc.). Furthermore, formalist sociology, barring all sociology of culture and spiritual life (sociology of knowledge, religion, law, etc.), which is actually in full development, is rightly rejected by the crushing majority of contemporary sociologists.

Behaviourism was at first merely a very disputable application to psychology of the purely bio-genetic theory of conditioned reflexes of the Russian physiologist, Pavlov. The aim was to eliminate the specificity of human conduct as distinguished from animal behaviour (John B. Watson, *Psychology from the Standpoint of a Behaviourist*, 1914). Subsequently it was introduced by a series of American authors to the solution of problems of social psychology and sociology. Social behaviourism, in the strict sense of the term, undertakes to reduce all social life to physico-physiological reflexes as responses to external stimuli. To be consistent, it cannot escape the narrow circle of external stimuli and reflex-responses. But since, on such a base, no communications and connections, let alone profounder unions, are possible between human conducts, even the most radical behaviourists (e.g., Floyd Allport, Read Bain, and George Lundberg) have been forced to introduce, on the one hand, the concept of " social stimuli " and, on the other, " reflective responses " (internal environment), resulting in " reflective behaviour ".[1] Now, the conception of reflective responses and reflective behaviour re-introduces the problem of consciousness and of the communication of consciousnesses. Here reappear all the problems which behaviourism sought to eliminate. As for " social stimuli ", the term is veritably a vicious circle in itself, because it assumes as known that which the behaviourists proposed to explain physio-logically and naturalistically, the extremely complex structure of social and mental reality.[2] This is confirmed startlingly by the fact that the works of the most radical behaviourists are replete

[1] See F. Allport, *Social Psychology* (1924), pp. 148 et seq. ; Read Bain, " Trends in American Sociological Theory ", pp. 107 et seq. in *Trends in American Sociology* (1929), ed. by R. Bain *et al*. ; J. E. Marney, " Trends in Social Psychology ", pp. 134 et seq. in R. Bain *et al*. ; G. Lundberg, *Foundations of Sociology* (1939), pp. 221 et seq.

[2] It should be noted that the behaviourists' principle of " social stimulation " is contradictory in still another sense. Their premises drive them towards the most thoroughgoing individualist nominalism, if not towards physiological solipsism. In this sense, the complete negation of the reality of groups and collective conduct of groups is, in F. Allport (*Institutional Behaviour* (1933), p. 238 et seq.), much more consistent than the recognition of their reality in G. Lundberg (op. cit., p. 163 et seq.).

with considerations of " societal patterns and symbols ".[1]   As
though the symbols, even if quite erroneously reduced to simple
signs or expressions, were possible and could have an effect without an understanding of their inner significance and without
" insight " !   In the light of all those internal contradictions and
all this inability to follow consistently from the point of departure,
it is not astonishing that among the most moderate behaviourists
(and still more among a rather large number of sociologists and
psychologists who have adopted some behaviouristic terminology
because it is fashionable), everything comes down to a rather
trite conclusion long accepted by the majority of students.   It
consists, as Florian Znaniecky emphasizes with reason, solely in
the demand " that human actions and their changes, as empirical
data, must be studied in the spirit of scientific objectivity ".[2]
This excludes the method of subjective introspection which replaces the mentality of the observed by that of the observer.   But
it in no way excludes the method of interpretive comprehension,
of insight into the internal significance of the individual and
collective human conducts observed.[3]   While the behaviourist
conception was a pure and simple return to social naturalism
based on physiology, while it offers nothing new, it has, at the
same time, produced total confusion concerning the rôle in social
life of regulation, rules, values, ideas, in short of the spiritual
element.   It has transformed all those constituent elements of
social reality into " stimuli " acting in more or less mechanical
fashion.   Thus it has been an obstacle to the development of
the sociology of law, as well as to all precise theories of " social
control ", more broadly to all sociological study of " the non-
material aspects of culture, of higher social values ".[4]

W. G. Sumner's conception of " folkways and mores " as one
of the most fundamental fields of sociological study may be con-

---

[1] The works of Lundberg (op. cit., pp. 9 et seq., 45 et seq., 106 et seq., 195 et seq.,
253 et seq., 311 et seq., 399 et seq. ; also *Social Research* (1929), pp. 14 et seq.) are
particularly characteristic.   He uses and abuses the term " symbol " to hide the
contradictions of his thought.

[2] *Social Actions* (1938), pp. 17 et seq., 52–3.

[3] It should be noted that in France the sociologists most inclined towards objective
methods, Émile Durkheim and Lucien Levy-Bruhl, finally recognized the necessity
of studying the internal significances of human conduct.   Durkheim, in his last works,
insisted on the rôle of values and ideals in social reality, and Levy-Bruhl devoted
himself to research into the primitive mentality (cf. my *Essais de Sociologie*, 1938,
and my *Morale théorique et Science des Mœurs*, 1937).

[4] See C. A. Ellwood, *Methods in Sociology* (1933), pp. 54 et seq.   For a general
criticism of behaviourism, see pp. 46–56, as well as the preface, pp. vii et seq., and
pp. 43 et seq., and 519 et seq. ; in R. M. McIver, *Society, its Structure and Changes*
(1931), and MacIver, *Is Sociology a Natural Science ?* in American Sociological Society
Publications (1931).

sidered as Anglo-American sociology's first step towards problems of sociology of law and morals. In his two works, *Folkways, A Study of the Sociological Importance of Usages, Manners, Customs and Morals* (1906), and *The Science of Society* (in collaboration with A. G. Keller, 4 vols., 1927), Sumner established that the irreducible character of social reality in regard to individuals and their interrelations shows itself most palpably in the regulation of conduct by "folkways". The latter, at first, impose themselves unconsciously and anonymously. "Folkways are habits and customs of the society . . . ; then they become regulative and imperative for succeeding generations. While they are in vigour they very largely control individual and social undertaking. The folkways therefore are not creations of human purpose and will." The regulative and imperative character of folkways is concentrated in the "mores", "including a judgment that they are conducive to societal welfare and exercising a coercion on the individual to conform to them, although they are not co-ordinated by any authority". "Institutions and laws are produced out of mores. An institution consists of a concept (idea) and a structure." To "crescive institutions" (for instance, property, marriage, religion) must be contrasted "enacted institutions"—law. "Rights are in the mores before they are in law and go with a regulative system, whether that is well organized or not." "It is impossible to draw a sharp line of distinction between mores and laws. The difference is in the form of sanctions which, in the law, is more rationalized and organized."

Sumner insists strongly on the rôle of "societal regulation" which is one "of the life necessities" of society, "indispensable for societal maintenance". But his premises and methods do not permit him to achieve any exact differentiation among simple social pressure, technical regulation or, finally, cultural regulation proper, nor to reach any precise distinction within the latter among regulation by law, by morality, by religion or by æsthetics. Sumner sets out from premises which are on the one hand utilitarian, on the other evolutionistic. These make it impossible for him, despite constant efforts, to distinguish between cultural values and patterns, on the one hand, and technical habits and patterns on the other. He is even incapacitated from seeing in technical, moral, and jural usages anything more than stages in a continuous evolution, artificially constructed by him. The only distinction is found in the growing force of sanction, due to increased habitual routine. He does not see that different folkways conflict as irreducible principles, excluding mutual continuity, or that the character of sanctions is not sufficient for understanding the internal structure of the regulation they support. We must add that Sumner's conception artificially reduces all moral and jural life exclusively to tradition and custom, "inertia and rigidity", barring the element of spontaneous innovation, of collective creation, of revolt or amendments. Moreover, Sumner eliminates from the ethos every element of "telos", of spiritual values, of the ideal, declaring that "the mores having the authority of fact are the only criteria of right and wrong". Thus we must conclude that the effort of Sumner and his school to enable sociology to encompass the study of the social reality of law and morality failed.

Sumner's conceptions were fruitfully criticized by F. H. Giddings. This sociologist showed that the author of *Folkways* did not succeed in distinguishing "the non-appreciative and the appreciative esteeming patterns" connected with "societal telesis" (*The Scientific Study of Human Society*, 1924, pp. 74 et seq., 143 et seq., 69 et seq.). According to Giddings, among "mores" in the latter sense it is necessary to distinguish between mores penetrated by moral values, and "themistes", mores connected with justice (pp. 264 et seq.). Finally, this author emphasized that "folkways", with their diverse significances, must be contrasted with "stateways", the perpetual tension between the two cutting across the foregoing distinctions (pp. 190 et seq.). In this way Giddings' criticism broke the evolutionistic and utilitarian harmony of Sumner's constructions and showed the impossibility of achieving, on the given basis, a sociology of law and morality. The same must be said of the writings of E. Westermarck on *The Origin and Growth of Moral Ideas* (2 vols., 1907) and *Ethical Relativity* (1932). His work must be distinguished from that of Sumner and Keller favourably, however, because of his abandonment of utilitarian prejudices and his description of the emotive basis of mores. But thoroughgoing psychological subjectivism prevents Westermarck from finding an exact place for the sociology of law and morality in sociology, which he does not distinguish from ethnography and social psychology.

Much more important for the broadening of sociology, in the sense which concerns us, was the introduction into American sociology of the theory of "social control". After its author, E. A. Ross, had formulated its foundations in a series of articles published in the *American Journal of Sociology* (1896–8), and in his book, *Social Control, A Survey of the Foundation of Order* (1901), this problem became one of the main centres of American sociological interest and inspired a very considerable literature. The point of departure of Ross's conceptions were two main theses. First was the distinction between " social influences " (" direct psychological pressure, stimulation or suggestion of the society on the individual as a manifestation of social forces ") and " social control as regulative institutions ", " imposing adjustments " and " designed to repress undesired conduct and to encourage desired conduct ". Second was the idea that " order " in social life is not instinctive and spontaneous, but rests on and is the product of social control. Since society is impossible without order, social control is the indispensable constituent element of social reality. This second thesis is reinforced in Ross by two arguments of unequal value. Quite justified is his insistence on the multiplicity of irreducible conflicts in social life which can be only provisionally stabilized by constantly renewed applications of social control. Quite controversial, however, is his interpretation of the " social " in a radically nominalistic sense, as an assemblage of isolated individuals and even as a sort of fiction, the sole connection between the individuals stemming from social control. The basis and sources of social control itself are consequently left without consideration. Among the various types of social control, law is for Ross " the cornerstone of the edifice of order, the most specialized and highly finished engine of control employed by society ". The integration of law in the general body of social control permits its study in its functional relation to concrete societal situations, and favours the development of a sociology of law. For the latter, " law and imperatives would be, as in fact we find them, neither uniform nor immutable, but adapted to the situation in which society happens to find itself ". Even the importance of law, as compared to other types of social control (morality, religion, art, education, etc.), can vary with the type of society. These ideas of Ross gave rich results in the studies of the greatest American sociologist of law, Roscoe Pound, to whom Ross dedicated his *Principles of Sociology* (1902), and who, in turn, emphasizes constantly his acceptance of Ross's general principle of social control (see further).

Despite all these promises of Ross's theory of social control, however, it has not shown itself a sufficient basis for an effective reformation of sociology which would permit the development

of a sociology of law. First, the sharp opposition between
" influences or social forces " and social control, implying regulation, has been very much weakened, if not abolished, by confusion
in the author's analysis of (*a*) " kinds of control ", (*b*) " means
(or methods) of control " and (*c*) " agencies of control ". If we
take account of the fact that differences among kinds of control
(law, morals, religion, etc.) are differences among values served
as well as among their structural significances, and that for the
achievement of its specific regulation every kind of control can
employ the most variable methods (or means such as influences,
stimulations, etc.), we realize that to identify kinds of control
with means of control is to destroy the basis of the whole conception. Thus, Ross is led to include in social control the things
which he first opposed to it (pressure, suggestion, illusion, public
opinion, habit, prestige, etc.), as a consequence of failing to
observe that every kind of social control can utilize the enumerated
means in its operations in a different direction or in different
combinations. As a consequence, he unintentionally wipes out
all lines of sharp demarcation between the problems of social
control and those of collective psychology, which led in later
discussions to such a broadening of the notion of social control
as to deprive it of all precise meaning. Thereafter it was, by
many authors, assimilated to a general psychological description
of " social stimuli ".[1] The identification of kinds of control with
agencies of control has been no less fatal. In fact, agencies of
control are the various social structures (e.g., various forms of
sociation, of groups, of blocs of groups or inclusive societies),
each of which can serve as a support for several kinds of control
simultaneously, and each of which exercises a control on its own
members. The problem of the relation between social control
and the different types of groupings within an inclusive society
entirely escaped Ross. This was probably because his radically
nominalist conception did not let him grasp the reality of collective
units and of their specific orders. He connected the various kinds
of social control only with the inclusive society. He considered
order created by social control as a unique order ; as though
order were an absolute and not a relative principle, and as though
there were not in every society an inextricable pluralism of orders
and agencies of social control for achieving them ! For Ross,

---

[1] The most elaborate doctrine in this direction is that of L. L. Bernard, *Introduction
to Social Psychology* (1926), Chapters XXXV–XXXVI ; *Fields and Methods of Sociology*
(1934), pp. 47 et seq. ; and *Social Control in its Sociological Aspects* (1939).

there was but one way to give his theory of social control more precise contours. Having clearly distinguished among kinds, means and agencies of control, this was to connect the kinds of control to collective spiritual values which inspire them and which make of them authentic bodies of normative regulations. In fact, for certain types of social control (morals, religion, etc.), Ross envisaged this road alluding to their link with " social ideals and valuations ". Not only did he not insist on this link, however, but he flatly excluded it from other types of social control, particularly from law (*Social Control*, pp. 411 et seq., and *Principles of Sociology*, pp. 423–30) transforming law, too, into a pure technique.

Among continuators of Ross's social control theory, C. A. Ellwood unquestionably showed the strongest tendency to define and limit the notion of social control by demonstrating its indispensable link with the ideal and spiritual elements which are the constituent principles of social reality itself. Inspired by the spiritualistic rationalism which was the basis of the social evolutionism of the English sociologist, L. T. Hobhouse,[1] Ellwood insists on the idea that social control leans on " the social idealism" in realizing " the spiritual side of social life ", which is represented " by higher cultural values, ideas and ideals ", through the regulation of conduct. With Ellwood, the kinds of social control, moreover, are reduced to those which contribute to create social order in the strict sense of the term, i.e., social morals, law, religion, and education. At the same time Ellwood believes in the continuous progress of social life towards an ever-augmented spiritualization and rationalization, aided by an ever more conscious, more elevated, and more effective social control.[2] Despite Ellwood's merits in having brought out the link between the problem of social control and that of the intervention of spiritual values in the constitution and action of social reality, his way of developing and formulating this idea gives rise to grave objections. It is not a question simply of the implications of the altogether questionable idea of social progress, based on a confusion of judgments of reality and judgments of value, or of his belief in a continuous evolution, which is more and more rejected by

---

[1] *Morals in Evolution* (1906), *Mind in Evolution* (1918), *The Rational Good* (1921), *The Elements of Social Justice* (1922).

[2] *The Social Problem* (1915, 2nd ed., 1924) pp. 21–48, 92, 115, 191–9, 207 ; *The Psychology of Human Society* (1925), pp. 390–468 ; *Methods in Sociology* (1933), pp. 21 et seq., 129–214. See also his stimulating article " The Sociological Foundation of Law ", in *Green Bag*, vol. 22 (1910).

sociologists. What is more important is the fact that Ellwood, instead of studying the functional relations between spiritual life (which, moreover, do not at all necessarily have to be rational, that is to say intellectual), and the various manifestations of social reality, treats of the " spiritual " as of a disembodied and immutable realm in the manner of an abstract and dogmatic idealism. Thus, he subjects sociology to a precise philosophy of his own, harking back into a purely ideological method excluding all relativity and all the infinite plurality of the symbolic aspects, significances, and spiritual values in their bilateral relations with social reality. By his idealistic dogmatism he thus involuntarily compromises the indispensable idea of the sociology of the spirit, which with him takes the form of a return to an ancient sort of social philosophy which confuses the social ideal and " the nature of society ".

A very important contribution to the problem of social control and sociology of human spirit was made in the well-known works of C. H. Cooley. It is only in his last book, *Social Progress* (1918), that Cooley employed the term social control explicitly, but the problem, in connection with that of the structure of social reality, occupied him from the outset, i.e., in *Human Nature and Social Order* (1902), and especially in *Social Organization* (1909). Contrary to the " nominalism " of Ross, and to the attitude of Ellwood which had a compromise character, Cooley takes a sharply " realistic " position in regard to social entities. He insists on the irreducibility of the " social whole " to its parts, and on the essential specificity of social reality. This specificity consists in the fact that " self " and " social unity " are only the abstract aspects of the " organic and living whole of mind " in perpetual creation. This " creativeness of the living mind ", in which self-consciousness and social consciousness are " twin-born ", gives rise to social ideals and valuations, to symbols and standards, which are, at the same time, products and producers of social reality. The spiritual life, which through significant meanings, as immanent element of the social reality, manifests itself equally in the " we " and in the " self ", constantly transcends itself. According to Cooley this process leads to an identity " between moral and social whole ", as opposed to the " sensual ", the ideal of goodness and rightness being the " creative social whole " itself. Social control, whose regulation is directed by social valuations and ideals, is thus a process immanent in the self-creation of society. It is a " self-control " by society, imposed not on individuals, who cannot be isolated " from the social mind ", but on and by the living whole itself. This control manifests itself in inclusive societies as well as in particular groups, and thus reveals the plurality of agencies coexisting in each domain of control. This conception, so different from and even opposed to that of Ross, introduces into the ideal of social control the principle of dynamic spontaneity. It enables Cooley to bring out the fact that not all social control is achieved by rules and standards, and to underline the difference between unconscious (or implicit) social control, and rational social control (institutionalized) based on crystallized standards. These important distinctions being accepted by many sociologists, some of whom added others (such as between organized and unorganized, formal and informal control, etc.), certainly have great value. For, without threatening in any way the differentiation of types of control according to their structures, related to differentiation in spiritual values, they permit a description of the regulative function of religion, morality, law, etc., *on several levels of depth*, a point of view which plays a very important rôle in present-day sociology of law. If, however, Cooley's conceptions succeeded in deepening the problem of social control and in opening the way to the study of the functional relationships between the spiritual meanings and the different manifestations of social life, their general sociological basis remained very much up in the air. The total absence of clarity in Cooley's analyses has often been pointed out : his basic hesitation between considering spiritual values as simple, unilateral products of social life, and the dogmatic idealization of that life itself as an ideal,[1] a weakness covered by lack of precision and a floating conception of creativeness, semi-vitalist, semi-mystical,[2] prevented Cooley from solving the problem of the sociology of human spirit, which he sensed. The majority of sociologists who tackled the question of social control after Cooley, instead of deepening his analyses, arrived at eclectic theories combining the influences of Ross, Cooley, and Sumner,[3] and contributing to this important problem nothing but additional confusion.

Cooley's general conceptions recall in several respects those

---

[1] See T. V. Smith, *Beyond Conscience* (1934), pp. 110–32.

[2] See S. M. Levin, " C. H. Cooley and the Concept of Creativeness ", in *Journal of Social Philosophy* (1941), pp. 216–29.

[3] See, for example, R. E. Park and E. W. Burgess, *Introduction to the Science of Sociology* (1921), pp. 785–864 ; " Social Control " in American Sociological Society, *Proceedings*, vol. XII (1917) ; F. E. Lumley, *Means of Social Control* (1926), and *Principles of Sociology* (1928), pp. 48–505 ; and P. H. Landis, *Social Control* (1939).

of the great master of French sociology, Durkheim, who worked
on the same questions in a very detailed fashion, albeit employing
a totally different terminology. On the other hand, the great
German sociologist, Max Weber, by his reform of sociological
method, posed with particularly logical precision the central
problem of the sociology of the spiritual meanings. Since these
two continental sociologists simultaneously contributed especially
to the founding of the sociology of law as a sector of sociology,
and since their doctrines both oppose and complement each
other, we will pause for a more detailed consideration of their
views than for those of any others.

Émile Durkheim (1858–1917), by profoundly transforming
the conceptions of Comte and simultaneously rejecting with great
vigour every tendency of the new science towards naturalism,
formalism, or dogmatic metaphysics, contributed mightily to
giving the sociology of law an important place within the field
of sociology. He deepened the thesis of the *specificity of the
" social "* by refusing to admit any explanation of social phenomena appearing in " the whole " except in terms of the specific
character of " the whole ", and by relegating to a far-distant
future any study of the general laws of the development of society.
The criteria of this specificity are, on the one hand, " pre-
established institutions " (collective conduct expressed in organizations and practices) which exercise constraints and pressures, and,
on the other hand, collective symbols, values, ideas, and ideals
which penetrate social reality (and which enabled Durkheim to
define " the principal social phenomena as value systems "), and,
finally, states of collective consciousness, collective representations
and aspirations, which are irreducible to individual consciousnesses and serve as a basis for every manifestation of social life.[1]

1. On the surface of social reality is found the geographic and
demographic basis of society, as well as buildings, channels of
communication, tools, food products, etc. This entire material
basis is, however, social only in so far as it is profoundly
transformed by collective action and penetrated by the symbols,
ideas and values which the collective mind attributes to it.

[1] *De la Division du Travail Social* (1893, Engl. transl., 1915 and 1933) ; *Règles de
la Méthode Sociologique* (1894, Engl. transl., 1938) ; *Le Suicide* (1897) ; *Les Formes
Elémentaires de la Vie Religieuse* (1912, Engl. transl., 1926) ; *Philosophie et Sociologie*
(1924) ; *Éducation Morale* (1930). Of articles by Durkheim the most important are :
Détermination du fait moral (1907) (" Bulletin de la Société Française de philosophie ")
and *Jugements de réalité et Jugements de valeur* (1911) (" Revue de Métaphysique et de
Morale "). For a critical analysis of Durkheim's ideas see my *Essais de Sociologie*
(1938), pp. 69, 115, 279–306.

2. Under this material or, as Durkheim called it, " morpho-logical surface ", are found the *institutions* (pre-established " ways of doing ") and collective behaviours, crystallized either in habitual practices or in organizations, the former exercising pressures, the latter constraints properly so called.

3. Next come the *symbols*, corresponding to institutions and serving as rallying signs and means, e.g., emblems, flags ; holy objects, rites, dogmas, for religious practices ; sanctions, pro-cedures, statutes, customs, etc., for jural practices.

4. Underneath the symbolic level are found the collective values, ideas and ideals which are symbolized by the symbols, and whereby collective conduct is inspired. These values and ideas—simultaneously products and producers of social life—lead us towards the " free and least crystallized currents " of collective mind, of which they are the aspirational terms.

5. Finally, we penetrate to the deepest level of social reality, to the states of collective mind themselves—collective representa-tions, collective memory, collective feeling, collective tendencies and aspirations, collective volitions and effervescences, partly transcendent, partly immanent in individual consciousnesses.[1]

It is the analysis of these dimensions of social reality, con-stituted by several levels of depth, that led Durkheim to a recogni-tion of the necessity of differentiating within sociology particular, specialized branches :

I. " *Social morphology* ", which studies the material surface of society, calculable and mensurable.

II. " *Social physiology* ", which studies institutions, collective symbols, values, and ideas, and which embraces sociology of religion, of morals, of knowledge, of law, of economics, of lingui-stics, and of æsthetics.   This part of sociology which Durkheim, rather unhappily, designated social physiology can better be called the *sociology of the human spirit*, because all the " manners of doing " with which it is concerned are guided by significant symbols and oriented towards values and ideas.

III. *Collective Psychology*.

IV. *General Sociology* studies the integration of all levels and aspects of social reality in what Mauss, chief continuator of Durk-heim, has called " total social phenomena ", and describes their types of groups and of inclusive societies.

American sociology has during recent decades achieved a

---

[1] For a criticism of Durkheim's conception of the transcendence of the " collective consciousness " see my *Essais de Sociologie* (1938), pp. 141–69.

more detailed specialization of the various sociological disciplines, sometimes reckoned to total thirty.[1] Some distinctions are very useful, others rather artificial, but what is most striking is the fact that there is no criterion of subdivision and that the divers fields have been established rather haphazardly. Durkheim made the first attempt of rational subdivision of sociology into special disciplines, an attempt obviously not definitive (see below, Section IV of this Introduction). In assigning, alongside the sociology of ethics, religion, etc., a precise place to the sociology of law within the sociology of the human spirit, distinguished from social morphology, collective psychology, and general sociology, Durkheim gave a new orientation to Continental sociology. He eliminated to a considerable extent, and more profoundly and systematically than did the American theory of social control, the obstacles placed in the way of legal sociology by sociological positivism, naturalism and formalism.

One might even say that, from a certain viewpoint, Durkheim's entire sociology, especially in its beginnings, has a certain "juralizing" tendency. In fact, he saw the essential criterion of the social in "compulsion", sanctioned imperativeness, it is the essential trait of law, emphasizing discipline and regularity above all else, even in ethics. At the same time, he considered law a "visible symbol" of all "social solidarity", the unique point of departure for its study, and he proclaimed that "the number of social relations is necessarily proportional to the number of legal rules determining them", and that "the general life of society cannot extend itself without jural life simultaneously extending to the same boundaries and relations, all the essential varieties of social solidarity being necessarily reflected in law".

Despite this rather exaggerated importance for the study of social reality attributed by Durkheim to jural symbols, which made it possible for his sociology to inscribe upon the edifice it constructed that "none may enter here who is no jurist", he did not succeed, I believe, in eliminating all obstacles to good understanding between jurists and sociologists. There are several reasons for this. Firstly, Durkheim did not renounce the aggressive tendency of sociology which denied all right to existence to social sciences founded previous to sociology and remained autonomous. Particular sociological branches, according to him,

[1] See, for example, L. L. Bernard, "The Fields of Sociology", in *The Fields and Methods of Sociology* (1934), pp. 12 et seq.

were to replace such social sciences as law, economics, philology, etc. Even problems of epistemology could be solved only by a " sociology of knowledge ". In other words, Durkheim recognized no method for the study of social phenomena other than the sociological. In particular, sociology of law would replace the instruction given by law schools. Durkheim forgot that the various patterns, symbols, and, even more, ideas and values, can be studied by a systematic method which works out their coherent frames and verifies their intrinsic veracities on the basis of capacity for integration in a whole having autonomous validity. He forgot also that philosophy of law, on the one hand, and jurisprudence, on the other, with their systematical and technical methods could render considerable services to the sociology of law as points of departure for its studies.

The second and decisive reason for Durkheim's partial failure in his effort to constitute the sociology of law lay in his conception of the symbolic sphere and the domain of values, ideas and ideals, in short, of the " spiritual ", as a unilateral product and projection of " collective consciousness ". From the indisputable fact that certain patterns, symbols, ideas, ideals, values, cannot be established or grasped except collectively, Durkheim concluded that they are epiphenomena of " collective consciousness ", or at the best identical with it. Thus he was faced by the alternatives of collective subjectivism (at the outset of his career), or of elevating collective consciousness to heights of supra-temporal spirit (at the close of his career), forgetting that collective mind can equally well dwell in the spiritual world of ideas and values or turn from it, being in this respect no whit different from the individual consciousness. Hence Durkheim's tendency to resolve philosophical problems by means of sociological analyses, sociology replacing not only the autonomous social sciences, but also epistemology, ethics, and philosophy of law, with the " collective consciousness " thus becoming a metaphysical entity, Spirit. Obviously, a sociology of law based on such premises goes beyond the limits of positive science and, by replacing the philosophy of law, conflicts with every conception distinguishing between existence and value, fact and norm. At the same time, it is proper to ask whether, on this basis, it is possible to differentiate jural from ethical or religious institutions, since such differentiation presupposes differentiation among the symbols guiding these various conducts and among the values inspiring the symbols, a differentiation made impossible once one considers them only as the unilateral products or manifestations of collective mentality rather than specific contents- resisting it.

The third and last reason for Durkheim's failure to eliminate all obstacles which had hampered the development of the sociology of law lay in his tendency to reduce all problems of this discipline to those of the genesis of legal institutions. By identifying the " archaic " and the " elementary ", and by admitting an evolutionary continuity in the transition among social types, Durkheim came to believe that the study of the origin of legal, religious, and ethical institutions in archaic society could serve as a decisive point of departure for the understanding of the same institutions in contemporary society. Thus, all the achievements of the Durkheim school connected with legal sociology have been in the field of the genetic sociology of law, and this within a single type of society : backward society. Now, the domain of legal sociological investigations is infinitely vaster. *Systematic sociology of law*, which studies relations between " forms of sociality " and " kinds of law ", combining and balancing within every group, and *differential sociology of law*, which studies the jural typology of particular groups and inclusive societies, must precede genetic sociology, applicable only inside a single type of inclusive society.

The final obstacles to the consequent development of the sociology of law originating within sociology itself, were razed by the reform of sociological method effected by the most important German sociologist Max Weber (d. 1927).[1] All sociology, according to Weber, must be a sociology of the interpretative comprehension of the internal meanings of social conducts (*verstehende Soziologie*). The method of sociology can be only typological, and consists in the study of " ideal qualitative types ", e.g., the construction of mental images according to particularized and specific significant meanings serving as points of departure for this construction. It is these strictly particularized meanings which give a qualitative character to social types and oppose them rigorously to the middle sums established by simple inductive generalization, whose quantitative character has no application to social reality, penetrated as it is by significant meanings : purposes, aims (*Wertrational*), emotive-volitional values, etc. The work of the sociologist stops with the investigation of *subjective meanings* and with the study of *probability, the*

---

[1] Cf. among Weber's works particularly *Wirtschaft und Gesellschaft* (1922) ; *Gesammelte Aufsätze zur Wissenschaftslehre* (1922), and *Gesammelte Aufsätze zur Religionssoziologie* (1921), vols. I–III

chances of social behaviour, according to these meanings. The verification of the objectivity of these meanings belongs to philosophy, their coherent systematization to the dogmatic-normative sciences, such as, e.g., jurisprudence or theology. Thus, while taking meanings and above all values, as points of support, sociology is liberated not only from value judgments but also from every preconceived hierarchy of values and discussion of their objective validity. That is the meaning of the *Wertfreiheit* of sociology proclaimed by Weber. But, at the same time, in order to study the chances of effective social behaviours according to their significant meanings, it is of capital importance for sociology to utilize the results of the coherent systematization of these meanings, whose validity does not at all depend on the chances of their being realized. On the other hand, subjective meanings, serving as a point of support for sociological research, do not at all exclude the existence of objective meanings, but rather assume them, and in fact reflect them and are inspired by them. Since, at the same time, all causal explanation in sociology can, according to Weber, be achieved only on the basis of an antecedent interpretative understanding of meanings, which alone gives the means of constructing frameworks of ideal types within which causal explanation is uniquely possible, Weber renounces any study of the origin of meanings, any effort to establish a link between symbols, values or collective ideals themselves and social reality. That is why the ambition of his sociology is infinitely more modest than that of his predecessors. It does not claim that the sociological aspect of law, ethics, religion etc., exhausts the phenomenon. On the contrary, it tends to make the sociology of the human spirit dependent unilaterally on the disciplines which systematize ideal meanings, sociology limiting itself to a study of the repercussions on the effective behaviours of the systems of dogmas or norms which they work out.

Let us consider as an example the procedure of Max Weber in the field of the sociology of religion, wherein his researches were especially fruitful.[1] He begins with a penetrating study of the dogmas of Calvinist, Jewish, Buddhist, and other theologies, in order to inquire how they are expressed in real social conduct and how they affect, above all, economic behaviour. In the same way, in the sociology of law, he first studies the various " legitimate systems " constructed by jurists, in Roman, feudal,

[1] *Gesammelte Aufsätze zur Religionssoziologie* (3 vols. 1921).

capitalistic, and other societies, going on to the question of how
these systems of norms are reflected in corresponding social
behaviour. It is unnecessary to stress the fact that sociology of
law thus conceived, far from menacing the jurisprudence and the
philosophy of law, presumes them and even bows before them,
as the sociology of religion presumes and bows before theology
and the philosophy of religion.

Modesty is surely reasonable for any science, and especially
for one which, like sociology, began by making unjustifiably
great claims. In this sense, we can only praise Weber for having
eliminated aggressiveness from sociology and for having recognized the legitimacy of the particular social sciences which had
been established previously and which continued to maintain
their autonomy. Thus he made a special contribution to good
understanding between sociologists and jurists, between sociology
of law and jurisprudence. One must, however, ask whether,
reacting to his predecessors, Weber did not go too far in making
concessions to dogmatic-normative sciences. Above all, we must
ask whether his legal sociology has not suffered overmuch from
his way of accepting the elaboration of coherent systems of legal
norms which are, so to speak, suspended in the air and which
lack any connection with the living reality of law, of which
they are but more or less rigid symbols.

In fact, we have seen that, to escape sterility, jurisprudence
requires the sociology of law even more intensely than legal
sociology requires jurisprudence. In inquiring into the chances
of effective social behaviours realizing rigid legal rules fixed in
advance and elaborated in a coherent system, Weber does not
notice that under these rigid rules there are flexible and *ad hoc*
principles, that beneath these there are living collective beliefs
which give law its real effectiveness and which reveal themselves
in " *normative facts* ",[1] spontaneous sources of the positivity of
law, of its validity, " source of sources " and basis of a perpetual
dynamism constituting the real life of law. In so far as it im-
poverishes artificially the reality of a law reduced exclusively to
behaviours guided by rigid and systematized rules, and artificially
enslaves legal sociological research to a particular jural technique,
Weber's sociology of law gives only relative enlightenment and
is not a great aid to jurisprudence. It limits itself, moreover,
to a legal typology of inclusive societies, and never touches

---

[1] On the subject of the " normative fact ", see my works, *L'Idée du Droit Social*
(1932) and *L'Expérience Juridique* (1935) and *infra*, Section V of this Introduction.

problems of systematic sociology of law or of the jural typology of particular groups.

The shortcomings of this legal sociology do not, however, derive from its very fruitful method of interpretative understanding of inner meanings, the basis of constructing ideal types. Nor do these shortcomings derive from Weber's will to understanding and collaboration between sociologists and jurists. Their true root is an over-narrow conception of the *social fact*, which certainly constitutes a regression from the gains of Durkheim's thought. Weber reduced the social fact exclusively to meanings and behaviour, giving no consideration to other elements of social reality : the morphological basis and the collective psyche, without distinguishing between organizations, practices, and innovating behaviours in the conducts themselves. Moreover, guided by a very marked nominalistic tendency, reminiscent of that of E. A. Ross, Weber reduced social to individual conducts oriented towards social meanings (related to the conducts of others) ; he does not even raise the question of how, in view of his affirmation of the exclusive existence of the individual psyche (self-contained consciousness), such meanings are possible. Having elaborated an admirable sociological method, Weber did not know how to apply it to a social object grasped in its full depth. He impoverished social reality to the point of annihilating it. Hence his overweening confidence in rigid systems of meanings worked out by dogmatic-normative disciplines which, for him, replaced all effective social patterns, symbols and values profoundly linked to the spontaneous life of the collective mind experiencing, comprehending, and in some measure formulating and creating them.

For, if one may state that ideas and values which are collectively experienced are not consequently products of the collective mind, this thesis cannot be defended with reference to symbols which express and conceal the ideas and values and which have, in this sense, the character of social products. Moreover, if the tested values and ideas resist the collective mentality, the sector of their infinite world which is grasped by a particular collective experience depends upon the characters of that experience which brings about the selection. Thus is posed the problem of social perspective, conditioning the grasping of particular aspects of the spiritual world of ideas and values. In this sense, meanings may be as little detached from social reality as may social reality be detached from meanings : the relationship here is not unilateral but reciprocal and bilateral. The problem of functional relationship between concrete forms of social structures and meanings which inspire them (and in the constitution of which they participate), this central problem of the sociology of the noetic mind is not solved even by Weber.

We have seen how contemporary sociology was increasingly transformed so as to enable it to embrace the sociology of law as well as the sociological study of spiritual values more generally. Thus we have seen arising the problem of the sociology of the human spirit devoted to the sociology of knowledge and of ethics which have been making progress. The problem of the sociology of knowledge was raised by thinkers as far apart as Durkhèim in France and the pro-Hegelian philosopher, Wilhelm Dilthey, in Germany.[1] It was simultaneously favoured by the intellectual atmosphere of the pragmatic philosophy of James and Dewey. It took a more distinct form in the works of Max Scheler (*Versuch einer Soziologie des Wissens*, 1924) and Karl Mannheim (*Ideologie und Utopie*, 1929, English modified and considerably enlarged edition, 1936), the latter combining Marxist influences with those of Weber and Scheler. The general development of present-day value theories has had great importance for the sociology of morals. Combined with the idea of an immediate moral experience of collective character, this orientation enabled Max Scheler in Germany and Frederic Rauh as well as the present writer in France,[2] to develop a sociology of morals which places the spiritual element of moral life with its infinite particularizations, into functional relation with the types and forms of social structures.

The very important discussions of social symbols and their rôle in social life and in noetic collective mentality, such as the works of Ernst Cassirer (*Philosophie der symbolischen Formen*, 3 vols., 1925), Lucien Lévy-Bruhl (*L'Expérience mystique et les Symboles chez les Primitifs*, 1938), G. H. Mead (*Self, Mind and Society*, 1935), emphasize and resolve in their respective ways one of the most fundamental problems of the sociology of spiritual functions, i.e.,

---

[1] See *Gesammelte Schriften*, 7 vols. (1923–33). The works of Heinrich Rickert, beginning with *Die Grenzen der naturwissenschaftlichen Begriffsbildung* (4th ed., 1921), which influenced Weber, are devoted to a purely formalistic methodology and have not great importance for our subject. See my article, " La Philosophie des Valeurs de M. Rickert ", in *Revue Philosophique* (1938).

[2] Cf. my *Morale Théorique et Science des Mœurs* (1937), *Expérience Juridique et Philosophie Pluraliste du Droit* (1935), *Les Tendances Actuelles de la Philosophie Allemande* (1930), in which the contributions of Scheler and Rauh are analysed in detail and my own conceptions set forth.

the mediational rôle played by symbols between types of social mentality and the noetic realm. A very different tendency is expressed by the works of such authors as Sorel, Pareto and, more recently, Thurman Arnold, who see in symbols only illusions, myths and idols but, however, admit their playing an important rôle in social life.

Finally, authors so different as the sociologists, R. M. MacIver on the one hand and P. Sorokin on the other, as well as the philosopher, E. Jordan, setting out from quite different quarters and different problems, show in their various ways a considerable interest in the general problem of the relation between social reality and spiritual meanings.[1]

An entire book would be needed to analyse all these trends and efforts. We must limit ourselves to stating that the sociology of the human spirit is increasingly winning the attention of present-day sociologists and philosophers, and that the methodical study of the problems of the sociology of law seems to us to be possible only on the basis of that sociology of the noetic mind. Let us then, in a number of brief theses of purely programmatic character, formulate what we understand by this branch of sociology, inasmuch as no complete agreement has even been reached on this point.

IV. THE SOCIOLOGY OF HUMAN SPIRIT AND THE STRUCTURE OF SOCIAL REALITY

The best approach to problems of the sociology of the noetic mind (or of human spirit) and to the determination of its exact place among the various sociological disciplines, would seem to be via the levels—or depth—analysis of social reality.[2] This type of analysis is inspired by the " method of inversion " (Bergson) or " phenomenological reduction " (Husserl), i.e., an immanent downward reduction through successive stages towards whatever is most directly experienced in social reality. Obviously, all the strata or levels of depth which we shall distinguish are in real

[1] See MacIver, *Society, Its Structure and Changes* (1931), especially the chapter on civilization and culture ; Sorokin, *Social and Cultural Dynamics* (vol. II, 1937), especially the chapter on fluctuations of truth, ethics and law ; Jordan, *Forms of Individuality* (1927) and *Theory of Legislation* (1937). Interesting discussions of problems of the sociology of spiritual functions or of the noetic mind may also be found in Talcott Parsons, *The Structure of Social Action* (1937), R. K. Merton, " Civilization and Culture " in *Sociology and Social Research*, vol. xxi (1936), pp. 103–13, " The Sociology of Knowledge " in *Isis*, vol. xxvii (1937), pp. 493–503, and " Karl Mannheim and the Sociology of Knowledge " in the *Journal of Liberal Religion*, vol. II (1941).

[2] Cf. for a more detailed treatment my *Essais de Sociologie* (1938), pp. 22 et seq.

life indissolubly connected, interpenetrating one another and constituting a whole.

(1) On the surface of social reality we find externally perceptible things and individuals : the geographic and demographic basis of society, as well as buildings, means of communication, tools, food products, etc. All this material surface of society, however, is social only in so far as it is profoundly transfigured by collective human action and penetrated by symbols, ideas, and values attributed to them by the collective mind.

(2) If we dig more deeply into social reality, we encounter next organizations or rather organized superstructures, i.e., collective conducts, hierarchized, centralized, according to rigid and reflected patterns fixed in advance. It is these organized superstructures which exercise compulsions, which can be more or less remote or distant, which are separated from spontaneous social life by a more or less wide abyss. Obviously the organizations themselves are but partial and always inadequate expressions of levels which, lying deeper, represent more immediate steps of social reality.

(3) Thus we arrive at a level of patterns of different kinds, of standardized images of collective conducts. These patterns need not be rigid or fixed in advance. They may be elastic, flexible, subject to modification in various degrees, proceeding from rites and traditions, passing through daily practices and extending to incessantly changing fashions. On the other hand, a sharp distinction must be drawn between non-symbolic patterns, simple standardized technical models such as economic patterns, and symbolic-cultural patterns linked to spiritual values and ideas, that is to the noetic, spiritual realm.

(4) Underneath the universe of various sorts of patterns, we find unorganized collective conducts. If they are guided by patterns, they take on the characters of the latter. Then their spontaneity, even where fashions are concerned, is greatly limited by standardization. These habitual conducts, tending to become practices, often go beyond patterns, however, and even modify or clash with patterns. This occurs particularly when symbolic cultural patterns cease to express sufficiently whatever it is they are called to symbolize.

(5) This leads us to a still deeper layer of social reality, that of social symbols. Without these, neither organizations nor cultural patterns, nor collective conducts guided by such patterns, are possible. The symbols are not simple expressions or signs

of something, as they are occasionally altogether mistakenly defined. Still less are such symbols illusions. The symbols are the inadequate sensitive expressions of spiritual meanings, taking the place between appearances and things in themselves (*an sich*). They are the intermediaries between these two and depend on both. They simultaneously reveal and conceal, or rather they reveal by concealing and conceal by revealing. What they express and what they hide is on the one hand the spiritual, on the other reality (physical, biological, psychological, sociological), in which the spirit partly embodies itself, partly reveals itself. As George Santayana so well put it, " symbols are presences and they are those particularly congenial presences which we have inwardly invoked ".[1]   Social symbols are inadequate expressions of the spiritual realm, adapted to concrete social situations, to typical social structures, and to definite collective mentalities, in which different aspects of the spirit realize themselves and by which it is grasped. Social symbols are thus simultaneously conditioned by social reality and by the spirit which realizes itself therein ; they vary in function to this reality, as well as in function to the spirit. That is why symbols are at one and the same time products and producers of social reality and why they are the principal object of the sociology of the human spirit.

Social symbols can take the most varied forms. Is not language composed of symbols (symbolizing ideas) by means of which we communicate ? Are not banners symbols of values attributed to a group ? Is not the policeman on the corner a symbol of the incarnate values which some established order has for us ? Are not the rules of law and judicial procedures symbols of the jural values and ideas embodied in certain institutions ? And so on for other types of symbols.

Social symbols are not necessarily connected with patterns, not necessarily standardized and generalized. They may be images valid for a unique behaviour, they may rise and vanish with unique situations. Nor need they any more necessarily be directed towards conduct. Inversely, social patterns may, as we have already seen, be merely technical and non-symbolic. But all cultural patterns, especially those having regulative and control functions, that is to say, bearing in them a normative element, are pervaded by symbolic meanings, expressing spiritual values embodied in social facts. While they are intermediaries, social

[1] *Reason in Society* (1932), p. 196, vol. 28 of " *The Life of Reason* ".

symbols pose the problem of the deeper levels of social reality which they symbolize.

(6) Penetrating even more deeply, we find below the level of symbols first of all those collective behaviours which innovate, smash patterns, create new patterns. These innovating and unforeseeable social behaviours are particularly observable in situations of social effervescence : revolutions, great epochs of reform, religious disturbances, wars, etc. But creative collective behaviours are constantly proceeding more or less palpably, social life being, from a certain point of view, a permanent struggle between tradition and revolution. Innovating and creative collective conducts are the collective behaviours least dependent on symbols. They cancel some symbols, weaken or change others, create new ones and sometimes do not need them at all. In the last case such conducts become direct manifestations of social bonds resting on collective intuitions of varying degrees of intensity (mass, community, communion ; cf. below). These links must be sharply distinguished from others resting on communication through signs (varying sorts of interaction), to which sociologists often mistakenly reduce all social life.

(7) Below the creative and unforeseeable social conducts, as well as below conducts guided by symbols and cultural patterns, we find a realm of values and of collective ideas which, as motor-motives, inspire them and serve as a spiritual basis for symbols. Let us consider, as an example, particular behaviours of a savage tribe and particular cultural patterns and symbols of it : emblems, dances, chants, etc. How shall we decide whether we are observing magical or religious or jural conduct, military or gymnastic exercises, an act of courtesy and so on, if we do not interpret the inner sense of the behaviours and of the symbols, if we do not scrutinize the values and ideas which the actors are thereby striving to realize. On this level of social reality, we encounter the intervention of the spiritual realm proper, of the realm of values and ideas which are heterogeneous and irreducible to acts which realize them and to states of collective mind which grasp them. If this is the case, and if this be the proper domain of the spirit, how shall we continue speaking of collective or social values and ideas ? Because there are aspects or, more accurately, sectors of the infinite whole of the spirit, which cannot be grasped except collectively. Moreover, spirituality, which is supra-temporal, does not at all imply that every aspect and sector of its totality is simultaneously visible and accessible to a deter-

mined collective mind (as well as to the individual consciousness). At different epochs, in different cultural spheres and in different groups, there appear constantly new sectors, new aspects, and other aspects vanish.[1] *Thus the field of vision of the spiritual realm may be and ought to be sociologically limited and thus vary from social epoch to social epoch, from social structure to social structure, without any effect on its objectivity and supra-temporality.* The study of the particularization of spiritual values and ideas according to the social structures capable of grasping and embodying them, clearly defines the framework of the sociology of the noetic mind for which the study of cultural patterns and symbols is but a step on the road to this ultimate task.

(8) Spiritual values and ideas, particularized with reference to social epochs and structure, must be grasped, tested, and experienced. This assumes the existence of collective mentalities aspiring towards such values and ideas, enlightening itself through them and resisted by them. Here we strike the deepest of all levels of social reality, the level of the collective mind itself. This collective psyche which displays itself on every level of social reality, may be studied in a state of greater or lesser detachment from its content, its " data ", as is the aim of collective or social psychology. The latter is all the more indispensable as the stream of collective mentality distinguishes itself sharply from the spiritual realm of values and ideas, which it can grasp, but from which it can also deviate. It is in exactly the same situation as the individual mind. The two also find themselves in a " reciprocity of perspectives " and represent merely two abstract aspects of the same concrete stream of mental life.[2]

Our description of the levels of depth of social reality enables us, I believe, to define clearly the aim of the sociology of the human spirit or of the noetic mind : *It is the study of cultural patterns, social symbols, and collective spiritual values and ideas in their functional relations with social structures and concrete historical situations of society.* The elements mentioned participate in the constitution of social reality at the same time as they are produced by it, or become accessible solely through it. It is the presence of these elements within social reality, which is thoroughly permeated by

---

[1] Cf. my *Morale Théorique et Science des Mœurs* (1937), pp. 130–97, and *Les Tendances actuelles de la philosophie allemande* (1930), passim.

[2] See my *Essais de Sociologie* (1938), pp. 11–169. The term " reciprocity of perspectives " belongs to Theodor Litt, *Individuum und Gemeinschaft* (3rd ed., 1926). In the United States, C. A. Cooley, J. Dewey and specially G. H. Mead have developed a similar conception. For examples of the reciprocity of perspectives see my article : " Mass Community and Communion ", in *Th Journal of Philosophy* (1941, August).

them, that demands the application in sociology of the interpretative method of inner meanings, " *Verstehen* ", insight. This leads to the fact that essential sociological method is that of the investigation of qualitative ideal-types (Weber) excluding the quantitative generalization of the natural sciences.

The proper domain of the sociology of the human spirit, however, is sharply marked off from other branches of sociology, particularly those which study the material basis of society (geographical, demographical, ecological, instrumental, etc.), collective psychology, the study of purely technical patterns and behaviours (particularly sociology of economics) and, finally, general sociology, which deals with types of social structures (groups and forms of sociality). The sociology of spiritual functions uses all these studies, but always for its proper ends, i.e., the study of particularized embodiments of spirituality. This branch of sociology, consequently, considers other elements of social reality solely as points of departure and support, or as extrinsic factors of social change studied from the genetic viewpoint.

The specific character of the sociology of human spirit, as contrasted with all other sociological disciplines, manifests itself most clearly in its mutual interdependence with philosophy. In fact, the realm of spiritual meanings, of values and ideas, as well as of their expressions through symbols, is the object of the study of philosophy as well as of the sociology of the noetic mind. Here philosophy and sociology meet. Do they meet as enemies or as friends, are they mutually exclusive, or do they compete, or do they collaborate ? That obviously depends upon the tendencies within philosophy and sociology. Dogmatic rationalism, sensualist empiricism, and even criticism [1] are philosophies as hostile to any sociology of spiritual functions as are sociological naturalism, positivism, behaviourism, and formalism. Philosophy and the sociology of human spirit can admit each other and collaborate only if all these tendencies are eliminated. It is my belief that one of the great virtues of the sociology of the noetic mind is the fact that it insists upon eliminating these currents. Philosophy studies the spiritual realm in itself, verifying the objective validity of spiritual values and ideas by integrating them into the spiritual whole. But to achieve this it needs all the facts concerning the infinitely particularized aspects and sectors of the spirit which embody themselves in real life and which are put at philosophy's

---

[1] Cf. with respect to the dogmatic prejudices of criticism my *Expérience Juridique et la Philosophie Pluraliste du Droit* (1935), pp. 19 et seq.

disposal through the broad investigations of the sociology of human spirit. The latter, studying values and ideas as functions of social structures within which they appear, and raising no question of objective validity or veracity, certainly has need of philosophy. It is philosophy which teaches sociology how to distinguish symbols from the spiritual content which is symbolized. Philosophy, too, can alone give sociology the criteria of specificity, opposing values and logical ideas as well as differentiating moral, jural, æsthetic, and religious values. In fact, it is impossible to study the social reality of law, morality, religion or æsthetics without using a criterion which is furnished by philosophical reflection and which makes it possible to isolate in the reality of collective conduct and external patterns the working of law, of morality, of religion or æsthetics. Thus the sociology of human spirit and philosophy have a reciprocal need of each other. There is no sociology of knowledge without a theory of knowledge and vice versa. There is no theory of morals without a sociology of morality and vice versa. There is no sociology of religion without a philosophy of religion and vice versa. There is no sociology of law without a philosophy of law and vice versa.

But how can we escape an apparent vicious circle? Solely by admitting a *collective immediate experience*, whether logical, jural, moral, æsthetic or religious, an integral experience involving spiritual as well as sense data. In his last works, William James in the United States, Bergson, Rauh and the phenomenologists, Husserl and Scheler, in Europe, have shown the road.[1] The various branches of the sociology of spiritual functions and the various philosophical disciplines are merely different ways of utilizing the data of infinitely variable, immediate, integral collective experience. Philosophical reflection leads from symbols to such experience, and establishes the criteria of specificity of differentiated immediate experience. The sociology of the human spirit reveals the importance for philosophy of the collective aspect of this experience, and describes for each of its differentiated fields the infinite variations of its data, in their particularization and functional relation to the social structures in which they are embodied.

We will have occasion to return to this complex problem, particularly at the conclusion of this book, where we shall discuss

---

[1] Cf. with respect to these philosophers, my *Expérience Juridique et la Philosophie Pluraliste du Droit* (1935), pp. 25–51, and my *Tendances de la Philosophie Allemande* (1930), passim. My own views of immediate experience are summarized in my *Morale Théorique et Science des Mœurs* (1937), pp. 125 et seq., 159–96.

with more detail the relations between the sociology and the philosophy of law. For the moment it is enough to conclude that the sociology of law, in search of its object—the social fact of law —cannot avoid borrowing from philosophy a criterion linked to the specificity of jural values. It is with the definition of law that we must now concern ourselves in order to prepare to fix accurately the field and problems of the sociology of law.

V. The Definition of Law

Definitions of law are innumerable. Those current among jurists describe the systems applied in their respective countries and consequently are merely generalizations of particular juridical technics adapted to concrete social situations. Often, as Dean Pound has correctly pointed out, these definitions are equally influenced by the special point of view of the citizen-subject, of the lawyer, of the judge, of the jurisprudent. Moreover, the jural phenomenon is extremely complex, its structure being anti-nomic. Within it there come together autonomy and hetero-nomy, ideal elements and real elements, stability and mobility, order and creation, power and conviction, social needs and social ideals, experience and construction and, finally, logical ideas and moral values (see, among older authors, Proudhon, among more recent, Justice Cardozo, Radbruch, Hauriou, and the present writer).[1] This complexity has given rise to numerous attempts artificially to isolate one element in order to establish simplified definitions of law which shut the eyes upon all other elements. Hence, in particular, the various metaphysical, transcendental, normative, psychological, utilitarian, materialistic, and socio-logical definitions of law, all of which, despite flagrant opposition to each other, are equally arbitrary and dogmatic constructs, without interest except from the point of view of their dependence upon a particular type of thought. We must add the fact that law may be acknowledged by numerous different technical pro-cedures, playing a totally unequal rôle in the various systems of law and at various moments of their existence (custom, statute, flexible standards and usages, judicial and extra-juridical pre-cedents, collective bargains, and collective declarations, etc., wind-ing up to the direct intuition of interested parties). Confusion among particular procedures of acknowledgment and law itself has provoked a third series of unacceptable definitions of law.

---

[1] See my *Expérience Juridique et la Philosophie Pluraliste du Droit* (1935), pp. 52–80, 200–31.

None of these innumerable definitions can be accepted as a point of departure for the work of the sociology of law, nor for that of the philosophy of law. As far as the former is concerned, all these definitions serve merely to bar the road to the study of the full social reality of law, in all its levels of depth and in the quasi-infinite variety of its types. As far as the philosophy of law is concerned, they serve only to compromise it, linking its fate to a rationalistic dogmatism which works with fixed and mummified categories and which instead of grasping merely dissolves the specificity of the complex reality of law. From its first step, however, the sociology of law could not avoid raising the question of the determination of the "jural fact". The social reality of law is neither an immediate datum of intuition nor a content of sense perception, but is rather a construct of reason, moreover, detached from social reality as a total phenomenon. Hence our discipline must begin by delimiting the jural facts from those social facts which, being equally related to spiritual values, are most closely akin to the facts of law, i.e., moral, religious, æsthetic and similar facts. And it is here, as we have already remarked, that the various branches of the sociology of spiritual functions require the aid of philosophy, a help which does not narrow their field of research but illuminates it. This is why the help of philosophy, by defining the criteria of the jural as distinguished from those of the moral, the æsthetic, and the religious, can be solely an inversive reduction to the various specific immediate experiences and their infinitely variable data of spiritual values. If, with philosophy's help, we can fix precisely what constitutes the formal structure of the immediate jural experience and what is the universal characteristic of jural values, we have found the criterion for the definition of law. In fact, this point of departure does not exclude any other aspect of law, for jural values inspire and penetrate all levels of depth and all manifestations of the jural. Since we cannot here develop a detailed philosophical analysis,[1] which would lead us beyond the confines of our present subject, let us simply formulate as theses a few of the results of such analyses.

(1) Immediate jural experience consists in collective acts of recognizing spiritual values as incarnated, embodied in social facts in which they are realized. It is that incarnation and realization of values in facts which is the most profound datum of jural

---

[1] I have made such an analysis in my *Idée du Droit Social* (1932), pp. 95–153 and *L'Expérience Juridique et la Philosophie Pluraliste du Droit* (1937), pp. 13–152.

experience. The act of recognizing facts which realize values is quite different from direct participation in these values. One may, for example, be insufficiently endowed to grasp the æsthetic values of a symphony, but this does not in the least prevent one from feeling indignation against whoever may disturb the quiet of listeners. The disturber will be regarded as acting against "justice", that is against jural values. In fact, the act of recognition has only indirectly to do with other values as values of justice,[1] specific jural values in which acts of cool recognition participate directly. Moreover, the most immediate data of jural experience are "normative facts"[2] and the "justice" which governs them. These two data are closely interlinked, and represent two abstract aspects of the same datum. Jural immediate experience as an act of recognition is essentially intermediate between an emotional-volitional experience of values and an intellectual experience of logical ideas. It diminishes the direct warmth of the experience of values by interposing the coolness of intelligence in order to reconcile them. For it is impossible to recognize a normative fact which would realize equivalent values in inextricable conflict. A normative fact can be recognized only in so far as it represents a reconciliation of values, at least preliminary, and unstable, and this reconciliation is achieved by justice as a more logicized, quantified and generalized shelter, permitting other values to be equilibrized and realized. On the other hand, immediate jural experience and jural values are essentially intermediate between spiritual and sense data because here the tangible realization of values embodied in facts is decisive. The effective importance of logical ideas and of emotive-volitional values, as well as that of the spiritual and sense elements in jural experience is altogether different in different places, circumstances, and social structures. This leads not only to a particularly antinomic and dramatic character of jural experience, but also to a *particularly intense variability* in jural values and in justice itself.

(2) Justice or jural values are the most variable elements among all manifestations of the spirit, because they vary simultaneously in function : (a) variations in the experience of

---

[1] Cf. my article " Justice " in *Encyclopedia of the Social Sciences*, vol. II, pp. 509–19.

[2] Cf., on the question of normative facts, my exposition in *L'Idée du Droit Social*, pp. 113 et seq. ; *L'Expérience Juridique*, pp. 38 et seq., 138 et seq. In the United States Professor E. Jordan, in two suggestive works, *Forms of Individuality* (1927) and *Theory of Legislation* (1937), through his conception of " realized or embodied values " or " objective corporate social structure " as a basis of law, arrived at an idea quite close to my " normative facts ".

values, (b) variations in the experience of logical ideas and in intellectual representations, (c) variations in reciprocal relations between emotional-volitional experience and intellectual experience, (d) variations in the relation between the experience of the spiritual and the experience of the sense-data.[1] That is why to define law as an attempt to realize justice in a given social *milieu* presents no danger, if one takes account of the variability of the aspects of justice itself. But this definition is only an indication of the general direction in which we must seek a non-dogmatic definition of law. For to make it acceptable we must insist on the fact that justice is neither an *ideal*, nor an immutable element. Justice cannot serve as a criterion of evaluation because it is a constitutive element of all law, even that which from the moral point of view is worst. Only a confusion of justice with a moral ideal has led some to oppose justice and " order " or " security ", and others to exclude the idea of justice from the definition of law. The principles of order and security are only immanent elements of the idea of justice, manifestations of that amalgam of values and logical ideas which is its salient trait. But there are as many degrees of order and security as there are aspects of justice, these principles being as relative as the aspects of justice (i.e., of the preliminary reconciliations of conflicting values embodied in a social fact) are infinite. We may express the same point by saying that " order " and the " normative fact " are only two words for the same datum, and that there are as many kinds and degrees of order as there are different normative facts, without which justice is a term emptied of all meaning.

Among the conflicting values which arise in a social *milieu*, it is the moral which have a tendency to claim primacy and to rule antinomies among all other values. This claim is justified in part. But in the domain of moral values, harmonized in the ideal, irreducible conflicts among equal values, such as those of the self, the *alter ego*, the whole and, on the other hand, of action, work, etc., arise in the reality of life. Thus moral values themselves require for their always partial realization a preliminary reconciliation through justice. It is this reconciliation which is the most important task of justice. The specific traits of justice consequently emerge most clearly when we confront it with the moral ideal. The moral ideal, i.e., the infinite whole of moral

---

[1] I have given many examples of these variations in my *Expérience Juridique*, pp. 75 et seq.; 120 et seq. Cf. also my articles, " Justice " and " Natural Law " in *Encyclopedia of Social Sciences*.

values, is marked by its trend towards creative liberty. This latter constitutes the profoundest and most immediate datum of moral experience (which represents a gradual drive towards participation in creative liberty). Moral values are the most dynamic, the most creative, driving most powerfully towards constant surpassing. They are least bound, then, to what is already established. At the same time, they represent the character of uniqueness and individualization, as well as of qualitativeness.[1] Now, justice or the totality of jural values are, on the contrary, directed towards the maintenance of normative facts, of the already established and realized. Jural values are the least creative, the most schematized, the most generalized and quantified. Thus, in them there is substituted for strict individualization of moral requirements, a generalization of commandments ; for subjects not comparable to each other, types ; for creative movement, a certain schematic stability of normative facts ; for pure quality, an intensified quantitative element. But it is precisely within the boundaries of generality, some logical schematism and quantification placed by justice at the service of emotional-volitional values, that the moral ideal can display its creative force, its richly individualized and complex tissues, its pre-eminence over all other values. In this sense, justice is an indispensable medium, a necessary ambiance for the realization of the moral ideal, while essentially distinct from it.

(3) The specific marks of law, of the " jural " or " legal ", flow from the characteristics of the immediate jural experience and of justice as we have shown it. Law or jural regulation or legal social control is distinguished from all other kinds of social regulation or control (moral, religious, æsthetic, or educational) by the following characteristics :

(a) *The determined and limited character of jural commandments* versus the unlimited and infinite character of other commandments, especially of strictly individualized moral exigencies. For instance, the commandment, " thou shalt not kill ", has different senses in law and in morals. In law, there are set cases in which one can, others in which one must kill (self-defence, war, executions, etc.). In morals, the prohibition may include not only all these cases, but also all acts which might become indirect causes of death, from a refusal of aid in dangerous circumstances to hurtful words which might shorten somebody's life. Hence,

---

[1] Cf. my description of the moral experience and moral values in *Morale théorique et Science des Mœurs* (1937), pp. 159-91.

too, rules, although far from absorbing all the domain of the jural, play here a rôle incomparably more important than in all other domains of social control.

(*b*) *Bilateral or more precisely, multilateral character of jural regulation, constituting its imperative-attributive structure*, as opposed to the exclusively unilateral *imperative* character of all other types of regulation. The imperative-attributive structure of all manifestations of law consists in an indissoluble link between the duties of some and the claims of others. This link is possible only in jural regulation in connection with the determined and limited character of its commandments which permit the application of a common measure to related claims and duties.

The imperative-attributive trait of all jural regulation implies that all law rests on collective experience and presupposes an authority not identical with the rules themselves. Only by a collective recognition of social facts which realize values, is it possible to establish a close interconnection between claims and duties. Only if the rules of law are not entirely autonomous is it possible to have a guarantee that this interconnection will be effective. Thus, jural experience alone is necessarily *collective experience*, while moral, æsthetic, and religious experiences can be individual or collective. The great Russian-Polish scholar, Leon Petrazizky (1864–1931), who had the great merit of discovering the imperative-attributive structure of law,[1] limited himself to a purely psychological analysis and hence overlooked these necessary consequences of his conception, as well as the link between imperative-attributive regulation and the idea of justice. That is why he envisaged only the distinction between law and morals, overlooking other kinds of regulation and control.

(*c*) *The indispensability of a " social guarantee " of effectiveness of law giving assurance for a real correspondence of claims and duties and showing itself in the necessity for all law to be " positive ", that is, to derive its validity from normative facts.* It is normative facts which unite the characters of authority, not identical with rules, and the efficient social guarantee, excluding both the autonomous character (specific to morals and æsthetics) and the heteronomous character (specific to religion and education). To play this rôle, normative facts, social structures embodying realized values, need

---

[1] *Theory of Law and of the State* (2 vols., 1908–10, in Russian). Concerning Petrazizky, see my *Le Temps Présent et l'Idée du Droit Social* (1932), pp. 279–95 ; *Expérience Juridique* (1935), pp. 153–69, and my article " Petrazizky " in the *Encyclopedia of the Social Sciences*. See also H. Babb, " Petrazizky " in *Boston University Law Review*, 1937–8 (Nos. 17–18) and A. Meyendorf, *Modern Theories of Law* (1933), pp. 20–37.

not necessarily be organized, need not possess fixed means of external constraint, still less the unconditional constraint characteristic of the State. The confusion of all normative facts with some of their special types—a confusion which the analyses of sociology of law are competent to eliminate definitively—is one of the reasons for some of the unacceptable definitions of law, those which link its fate to external constraint, power, organizations, and even the State. These definitions all forget that these elements, as Petrazizky and Krabbe showed so well, so far as they play a rôle in the jural life, already presuppose the validity of law and are based upon it. To achieve their rôle of efficient authorities socially guaranteeing the strict interconnection of claims and duties, normative facts need meet but one condition. They must *really exist* and incarnate spiritual values. Normative facts take the most different and varied forms, which we shall study in this book, e.g., forms of sociality, types of groups, types of inclusive societies.

(*d*) *Not necessarily requiring its execution by precise exterior constraint, law admits the possibility of being accompanied by this constraint,* while moral and æsthetic requirements exclude the possibility of execution by this constraint, and religious and educational commandments exclude the possibility of its having any precise or fixed character. This is a consequence of the fixed, limited, and multilateral imperative-attributive trait of law. To avoid any misunderstanding let us clearly distinguish *external and precise constraint* from the more general phenomenon of sanction, and sanction from social guarantee. All law accompanied by constraint presupposes law not accompanied by such constraint but which is fit to justify the former. Moreover, it is well known that even the most important parts of constitutional law are not accompanied by constraints, let alone international law, etc. *Sanctions*, i.e., varied and sometimes quite spontaneous reactions to infringements of regulations, are observable in the domain of morals and æsthetics, not less than in other domains, although there they have not always a character of social reprobation as is the case in law. In any case, all law is sanctioned by the reprobations of the social *milieu* in which it is violated, but not all law is accompanied by constraints. Finally, the *social guarantee* of efficiency, characteristic for all law deriving its validity from normative facts, only here manifests itself in sanction, while in other domains (morals, æsthetics, religion, education) the sanctions are not necessarily the expression of the social guarantee.

(*e*) Thus we reach a definition of law : " *Law represents an attempt to realize in a given social environment the idea of justice (that is, a preliminary and essentially variable reconciliation of conflicting spiritual values embodied in a social structure), through multilateral imperative-attributive regulation based on a determined link between claims and duties ; this regulation derives its validity from the normative facts which give a social guarantee of its effectiveness and can in certain cases execute its requirements by precise and external constraint, but does not necessarily presuppose it.*"

(*f*) Perhaps the question will arise as to what we do with other social regulations aside from law, morals, religion, æsthetics, and education, such as mores, usages, social ceremonies, conventions, rules of courtesy, politeness or fashion, and finally, custom. The answer is that this category of regulations as an independent field is only the result of confusion in the scholars who insist upon it.[1] *Customs and usages* are not special regulations, but exclusively particular methods of acknowledgment of the different regulations we mentioned. They are to be differentiated according to the latter. For instance, there are jural customs and usages, moral, religious, æsthetic, and educational customs and usages. Customs and usages can, moreover, relate not to cultural-spiritual regulation, but to technical regulations (economics, etc.). *Mores* is a term having meaning exclusively for archaic societies in which differentiation of values and corresponding regulations has not yet come about or not sufficiently.[2] " *Conventional rules* " (Stammler) are a contradiction in terms, for all regulation and all rules demand obedience contrary to the arbitrary will of the party involved. As for rules of *courtesy, politeness, and fashion* and certain *social ceremonies*, we have here either æsthetic social regulation, or a combination thereof with jural regulation. These combinations appear when an imperative-attributive regulation is oriented more towards æsthetic than towards jural values. But these are extreme cases.

Having achieved a definition of law which seems to us simultaneously broad enough and precise enough to permit us to

---

[1] From this viewpoint the discussion at the second congress of the " International Institute of the Philosophy of Law and Sociology of Law " are quite typical. Cf., *IIme Annuaire : Droit, Moral, Mœurs* (Paris, 1936, ed. by G. Gurvitch). The partisans of the existence of a special category of customs, usages, mores, despite numerous expositions of this doctrine, did not succeed in arriving at any precise conclusion. Sometimes they confused this category with unorganized law, sometimes with social morality. Their opponents and critics, such as Messrs. G. Radbruch, G. Del Vecchio, and the present author, had no trouble in showing their contradictions.

[2] Cf. my discussion at the above-mentioned congress, pp. 248–9.

envisage all levels and manifestations of the social reality of law, we may now proceed to describe exactly the object and problems of the sociology of law.

VI. The Definition of the Sociology of Law

We are now in a position to define the precise framework of this new discipline, that is to say, its object and its method as well as the fundamental problems which it is called upon to solve.

The Sociology of Law is that part of the sociology of the human spirit which studies the full social reality of law, beginning with its tangible and externally observable expressions, in effective collective behaviours (crystallized organizations, customary practices and traditions or behavioural innovations) *and in the material basis* (the spatial structure and demographic density of jural institutions). *Sociology of law interprets these behaviours and material manifestations of law according to the internal meanings which, while inspiring and penetrating them, are at the same time in part transformed by them. It proceeds specially from jural symbolic patterns fixed in advance, such as organized law, procedures, and sanctions, to jural symbols proper, such as flexible rules and spontaneous law. From the latter it proceeds to jural values and ideas which they express, and finally to the collective beliefs and intuitions which aspire to these values and grasp these ideas,* and which manifest themselves in *spontaneous " normative facts ", sources of the validity, that is to say, of the positivity of all law.*

A jurisprudence, or the " dogma of positive law ", can only establish a coherent system of normative patterns and symbols (more or less rigid or flexible), valid for the experience of a particular group at a particular period and having as its aim facilitating the work of tribunals. *But legal sociology envisages the quasi-infinite variety of the experiences of all societies and all groups, describing the concrete contents of each type of experience* (to the extent that they are expressed in phenomena externally observable), *and revealing the full reality of law which patterns and symbols veil more than they express.*

We must distinguish and clearly separate—and this is often neglected—*three problems of the sociology of law* which are distinctly different from each other : (1) *Problems of systematic sociology of law :* the study of the manifestation of law as a function of the forms of sociality and of the levels of social reality. These problems can be solved only by means of what we propose to call the *microsociology* [1] *of law.* (2) *Problems of the differential sociology of law :*

[1] Cf. *infra*, Chap. II and my *Essais de Sociologie* (1938), passim.

studying the manifestations of law as a function of real collective units whose solution is found in the *jural typology of particular groups and inclusive societies*. (3) *Problems of the genetic sociology of law*, analysed by means of the *dynamic macrosociology of law* : studying the regularities as tendencies and factors of the change, development, and decay of the law within a particular type of society.[1]

To understand this subdivision of the sociology of law into three parts, it is necessary to take account of the fact that every society is composed of a multiplicity of particular groupings, and that each particular group—each real collective unit—is composed of a multiplicity of " forms of sociality "—*of ways of being linked to the whole and by the whole*. That is why, when one speaks of a social. type, it is essential to know whether what is meant is a type of *sociality*, a type of *group*, or a type of *inclusive society*. For example, contemporary inclusive societies are quite different from each other when it comes to the types of divers particular groups composing : the State, municipalities, public services, trade unions, co-operatives, political parties, churches, clubs, philanthropic societies, families, etc. The types of these various groups are clearly distinct from the forms of sociality which constitute them. For example, within such a group as the State, the trade union or the club, may be observed varying degrees of intensity and actuality of the inter-individual relations of *rapprochement* and separation, and of fusion into mass, community, and communion, etc. That is to say, there is a plurality of forms of sociality.

Obviously in the framework of law, which corresponds to the types of groupings (e.g., trade union law, State law, co-operative law, canon law), and, even more so, in the " systems of law " which correspond to the types of inclusive society (e.g., feudal law, bourgeois law, European law, Oriental law, American law, primitive law, and civilized law), there are always merging a multiplicity of " kinds of law ", linked to a plurality of forms of sociality. If one did not distinguish between the *microphysical* and the *macrophysical sociology of law* one would miss the moving maze of *perpetual tensions* and sharp *conflicts* which agitate the effective life of all law and one would close one's eyes to the depths of the inextricable pluralism which penetrates this life and which is in itself a factor of the perpetual transformations of jural reality, of its spontaneous dynamism.

These considerations show that genetic sociology of law, which

[1] Cf. my article " Major Problems of the Sociology of Law " in *Journal of Social Philosophy* (1941), vol. 6, No. 3.

alone attracted attention in the nineteenth century, cannot proceed without the support of the microsociology of law and the
differential sociology of law, the first providing points of support
for the study of changes, and the second fixing the discontinuous
types within which it is alone possible to find regularities of
development.   In fact, it is no longer possible to speak of a
unilinear direction in the development of legal institutions.   For
example, the limitation of statute by contract, which a Spencer
or a Henry Maine regarded as a general principle of the development of law, is valid only for the primitive type of society.   In
civilized societies the direction of the movement was reversed
repeatedly.   In our present-day type of society one could observe
rather an inverted tendency, that towards the limitation of contract by statute, the development of trade unionism being sufficient
illustration (cf. *infra*, Chapter IV).

   The distinction between systematic sociology of law or microsociology, differential or typological sociology of law and genetic
legal sociology makes it possible to avoid a whole series of confusions and to eliminate from this field conflicts of schools which
often arise solely from misunderstandings.   These conflicts find
their basis in the fact that scholars take their point of departure
from a single one of the three divisions of sociology of law which
we have distinguished and, by bringing this one to the fore, give
it predominance over the two others by confusing quite distinct
problems.   Thus, in the nineteenth century, there was interest
solely in genetic legal sociology, to which specialists looked for a
solution of all problems.   This tendency persists in Sumner-
Keller and Durkheim.   After having had the extremely happy
idea of starting research in sociology of law with the problem of
relations among forms of solidarity (sociality) and kinds of law,
that is to say, after having had a presentiment of the problems of
the systematic microsociology of law, Durkheim transposed the
distinction between mechanical and organic solidarity (and the
corresponding distinction between repressive and restitutive law)
into historical phases of the development of inclusive society.
Genetic legal sociology, without any limitation on the qualitative
types of inclusive societies—where alone it is valid—thus
triumphed over every kind of study in Durkheim.   If, among his
disciples, it produced very precious gains, that was because they
limited their studies to the archaic type of society alone.

   On the other hand, the most recent representatives of the
sociology of law—Pound, Cardozo, Commons, Llewellyn, and

Arnold in the United States ; Kantorowicz, Eugene Ehrlich and Hugo Sinzheimer in Germany ; Duguit, Hauriou, Leroy, and Morin in France—were occupied mainly with sociological description of the actual state of law and the conflicts surging within its bosom between rigid law and spontaneous, living law. Their efforts have been concentrated above all (despite the wide divergence among their various conceptions) either on the description of modifications of juridical technique and the activity of tribunals with reference to major changes intervening in the social reality of law, or on a general description of the transformation of the actual system of law under various aspects, particularly under that of the growth of the jural framework of the economic society expressed in the growing rôle of the autonomous law of labour unions and trusts. Thus, except for some precious indications by Ehrlich, Pound, Hauriou, and Llewellyn, the distinction between systematic sociology of law and genetic legal sociology, as well as between differential jural typology of inclusive societies and that of particular groups, and moreover that between microsociology of law and the jural typology has not been clearly worked out. This has led frequently to a much too dogmatic tendency in analyses. Some legal sociologists have attributed to juridical techniques of a certain kind a too important rôle and have verged on identifying the technique of modern " sociological jurisprudence " or of its opponents, the " legal realists ", with the fate of the sociology of law itself. Others attribute to a framework of law corresponding to a particular type of group (labour law, trade union law, State law, church law, international law) characteristics too precise and uniform, as though there raged no struggle within each typical group among a multiplicity of forms of sociality and corresponding kinds of law. Finally, the current of modern sociology of law, represented by Max Weber, reduced all sociology of law to the typology of legal systems with reference to the " ideal types " of inclusive society. In this last field it achieved very appreciable results. But it overlooked not only the problems of the microsociology of law and of the genetic legal sociology, but also the problem of the typology of particular groups and corresponding frameworks of law. This artificial limitation of the sociology of law to a single problem, accompanied by the impoverishment of social reality, and consequently of the reality of law, envisaged in but one of its levels of depth, greatly diminished the value of this branch of Weber's sociology, despite all its merits.

According to our conviction, the sociology of law cannot work fruitfully except by considering at one and the same time the three strictly delimited domains, microsociology of law, differential jural typology of groups and all inclusive societies, and genetic legal sociology.   It must simultaneously take account of the necessity of autonomy and close collaboration among the three disciplines, as well as of their hierarchical relationship, microsociology of law being presupposed by the two other branches, and genetic legal sociology leaning upon differential or typological sociology of law.

To conclude our definition of the aim and problems of the sociology of law, let us warn against a current dangerous misunderstanding which confuses this discipline with a " sociological theory of law ".   Numerous examples of this confusion might be cited, especially during the second half of the nineteenth century (Ihering, Post, Kornfeld in Germany ; Duguit in France ; Ferri and Vaccaro in Italy ; Sergevitch, Muromzev and Korkunov in Russia ; more recently N. Timashev in the United States ; not even E. Ehrlich or K. Llewellyn have been entirely free from this error).   In discussing the problems of the sociology of the human spirit and its relations with philosophy, and in borrowing from a non-dogmatic philosophy of law our criteria for a definition of law, we have already pointed out the impossibility for the sociology of law to take the place of a theory of law.   Here we must emphasize once more that the " sociological theory of law " is for us a contradiction in terms.   The task of the sociology of law is not at all to define law or to work out a system of jural categories or jural values.   The so-called " sociological theory of law " is merely the positivistic interpretation of the philosophy of law. Seeking, finally, like all positivistic doctrines, to derive values and norms from facts, closing its eyes to spiritual (noetic) elements embodied in social reality, and particularly in the reality of law, and substituting sociology for philosophy, it succeeds only in compromising the scientific sociology of law by assigning it tasks which it is incapable of undertaking and fulfilling.

Before beginning a systematic exposition of the main problems of sociology of law, of which we have now given an inventory, it should be useful to halt a long while for a critical exposition of the conceptions of the principal forerunners and founders of present-day legal sociology.   Thus, by means of examples, we should be able to give a more lively and concrete picture of the work thus far done and the difficulties encountered in this field.

CHAPTER I

THE FORERUNNERS AND FOUNDERS OF THE SOCIOLOGY OF LAW

SECTION I : THE FORERUNNERS

The forerunners of the sociology of law are extremely numerous, for this branch of knowledge arose spontaneously in the course of historical or ethnographic studies relating to law and in the course of researches on law pursuing other aims ; such as the establishment of a social ideal, or a mechanist, realist, or relativist philosophy of law or a technical discussion about " sources of law ". Of course, this " spontaneous sociology of law ", as opposed to methodical sociology of law, did not ordinarily touch on more than one of the problems we have designated (owing to the character of the works in which it appeared) : we find the authors dealing exclusively either with problems concerning the origin of law, or concerning the relation between the social reality of law and the other social phenomena, or concerning the jural typology of groups often wrongly limited to State forms. The interdependence of the different parts of this discipline has in any case never been envisaged in this discussion.

I. *Aristotle, Hobbes, Spinoza, Montesquieu*

Aristotle in antiquity (385-322 B.C.) and Montesquieu in modern times (1689-1755) have most closely approached methodical sociology of law. Aristotle anticipated the body of problems it is called upon to solve ; Montesquieu, influenced by the " social physics " of Hobbes (1588-1679) and by Spinoza (1632-77) purified the study from judgments of value and based it on systematic empirical observation.

Aristotle's sociology of law is found in his *Ethics* (see in part *Nicomachean Ethics*, 1, V, VIII and IX) and in his *Politics* ; it is integrated in his practical philosophy which studies the ultimate aims of individual and collective conduct, and the means of attaining them. In this sense, Aristotle's formulation of the problem has nothing in common with sociology as a positive science. His naturalistic finalism, seeking *entelechies* in the real being where they are operative, leads him, however, to proceed in ethics and politics less by dialectical construction than by a description of actual types and existing social groups in the hope of subsequently finding their special entelechies in the rôle of aims (or rather of final causes), which would be integrated in the ultimate and perfect aim of human conduct.   Thus Aristotle, to establish the meaning of justice, first describes the different sorts of positive law, in their relation to the *Nomos* (the really efficient social order), the *Philia* (sociality or social solidarity), and the particular groups (*Koinoniai*), of which the State is but the crown. And to find the best form of government, Aristotle begins by studying all the really existing types of government in their relations to the effective structure of the different types of society (he even undertook a purely comparative description of the principal constitutions of Greece, of which only the fragment concerning the constitution of Athens has come down to us).

All law, whether established by human will or independent of human will (and in this sense " natural ") is, according to Aristotle, only the rational formulation of the requirements of the *Nomos* (*Nic. Ethics*, 1129 et seq.).   The *Nomos* is not the body of laws decreed by the State but the living and spontaneous body of rules governing social conduct, the effective societal regulation in a given *milieu* (*Pol.*, 1287 a, 1326 a), this dynamic order going beyond the distinction between law, even flexible and unorganized, and social morality.   Law in the Aristotelian sense, that is, jural requirements fixed in formulas, is more abstract, more static than the concrete and dynamic *Nomos*, which law tends to lag behind and to which it must always adapt itself anew, a fact which sharply suggests the problem of the social reality of law.

The types of law themselves can be established only as functions of the different types of *philia* and of *koinonia*, for the living reality of law can affirm itself only in a social *milieu* ; the social *milieu* is constituted by the forms of sociality and by the particular groups.

The usual translation of the term *philia* by " friendship " has greatly obstructed a true understanding of Aristotle's sociological ideas.   There can be no *koinonia*—or real group—says Aristotle, unless the *philia* and law are realized within them (*Nic. Ethics*, 1159 b).   In each group there are as many kinds of law as there are kinds of *philia*, for law develops with the development of the *philiai*, both applying to the same persons and the same objects and running a parallel course (1160 a).   *Philia* means social bond or sociality, whether it be based on love, pleasure or interest, whether it apply to kinship, civism, participation in a brotherhood or any other voluntary association, or, finally, to simple friendship of a transitory or durable kind (1156–1162). To the extent that the *philia* is based on disinterested love, and realizes the good, it possesses a kind of virtue, an "ideal solidarity" ("perfect *philia*", 1156–1157 a), opposed to "*de facto* solidarity"; but to establish the former, Aristotle describes a multiplicity of types of the latter. And he discovers the important fact that if the *philia*, though imperfect, can under certain conditions dispense with law, law is impossible without the *philia*, which serves at once as its foundation and its complement. For the sociality is a more profound, more elementary, and more vital bond than abstract law and even the *Nomos*, whose source it is (1155 a). Unfortunately Aristotle limits himself to describing concrete cases of *philia*, instead of classifying them according to precise criteria, and he does not examine the fundamental question, i.e., which types of *philia* are productive from the point of view of law and which types are sterile. And, although he anticipates the important opposition between "microsociology" and "macrosociology" by distinguishing between *philia* and *koinonia*, he hesitates to recognize clearly that each group (*koinonia*) contains multiple forms of sociality (*philia*). He does recognize it in dealing with the conjugal family, within which he distinguishes the *philia* in the relations between husband and wife, in the relations between parents and children (1558 b), and a corresponding number of parallel types of law (1161 b); but he declares that only a single form of *philia* corresponds to each form of government in the *koinonia politike*—the State—(1161 a); and sometimes he seems to say that each form of *philia* is determined exclusively by the *koinonia* to which it entirely corresponds (1160 a, 1161 b). Thus he mixes the microsociological and macrosociological points of view—an error which we shall meet again in a number of systematic sociologies of law.

When it comes to studying the kinds of law as functions of social types, however, Aristotle distinguishes with perfect clarity between jural microsociology and jural typology of groups, for in opposing (*Nic. Ethics*, Book V) the law governing the distribution of property and honours, contract law, and penal law (1130–1131 a), he relates them (Book VIII) to the different sorts of *philia* (1162 b, 1160 a). Penal law is based on the "*philia* bound by mores", contractual law on the "*philia* bound by rules" acting among equals (a more rigid and determinate sociality); finally, distributive law is based on the same regulatory *philia* among unequals.

These three kinds of law based on microsociological considerations, lead Aristotle to his famous theory of commutative and
distributive justice (or, more precisely, of inequality) (1301 a
et seq.).   To them he opposes frameworks of law established in
regard to group types (*koinoniai*) : the law of the conjugal and
domestic family (this last being an economic production group
implying the right of domination over slaves), the law of villages
constituted by the association of families, the law of cities, the law
of various fraternal associations, and finally the law of the political
group, the State.   The last is breaking down into as many types
as there are forms of government : monarchic law, aristocratic
law, and a law corresponding to the *politeia* (a perfect form of
government) ; tyrannical law (very ineffectual) ; oligarchic and
democratic law—these being degenerate forms of the first three
and further divisible into several sub-types (*Pol.*, II, 1. III,
1280 et seq. ; IV, VI ; *Nic. Ethics*, VIII, 1. Chap. XI–XIII).

This jural typology of groups is greatly reduced in Aristotle,
however, by the thesis that the State, being a perfect *koinonia*,
enjoys metaphysical " priority " to all the particular groups,
which can exist only as its subordinate parts (I, 1252 b, 1255 a ;
Nic. Ethics, VIII, 1160 a).   State law alone makes possible the
autonomous law of the particular groups and takes precedence
over the group law to such an extent that Aristotle hesitates to
characterize the latter as true law, designating it as something
" analogous to law " ; only the *dikaion politikon* is law in the
strict sense of the term (*Pol.*, 1153 a ; *Nic. Ethics*, V., 1143 a–
1135 a).   This dogmatic reasoning, based on statism *a priori*,
relates also to the types of law engendered by the different *philiai*,
and clearly marks the limits of Aristotle's sociology of law : since
all social bonds are absorbed in the political bond, the eternal
hierarchy of groups and the primacy of political law—the only
law in the strict sense—remain impervious to any sociological
observation.   Aristotle's successors retained his dogmatic conclusions, but failed to comprehend the far more profound questions which he raised and was unable to answer.   It required the
genius of a Grotius and of a Leibniz (see below) to free Aristotle's
sociology of law from servitude to his political metaphysics.

Under these conditions it is not surprising that Aristotle's
sociology obtained concrete results only in its applications to
political law and, in particular, to the genesis and decadence of
the different types of constitution.

In the State he distinguished the political community in itself (*koinonia politike*) from its organized superstructure, the form of government (*Pol.*, 1276 e). All constitutions are relatively good to the extent that they are adapted to the variable substructure of the political community, and here the elements to be considered are density of population, the various industries, and economic activities, the relation between the social classes, the number of classes (1289 b, 1294–1326 a et seq.). Since the equilibria between these factors are extremely mobile, the relativity of the forms of government is very great ; and Aristotle seeks countless nuances of constitutional sub-types to correspond to the variety of social sub-structures (1290 a–1293 b). The means by which each government maintains itself and the causes of its dissolution are also found to be very numerous (1301–1316 b). What Aristotle calls the " perfect constitution " is merely a mixed form of government, adapted to an artificially equilibrated sub-structure, a *koinonia* neither too large nor too small, with a population neither too dense nor too sparse, in which the " middle classes " dominate economic life and are favoured in every way—all of which factors guarantee maximum stability (1294–1297 a). Of course, this notion of a perfect form is a dogmatic and artificial conception, based on a combination of final causes and effective causes, but at the same time it is penetrated through and through by the social relativism which Aristotle so forcefully introduced into the study of political law—a relativism which seems to triumph over his quest for the ideal state.

To sum up, Aristotle, despite his integration of sociology of law with his dogmatic metaphysics, achieved a bird's-eye view of the fundamental problems of this discipline : the microsociology of law, differential sociology of law, and genetic sociology of law. But it is only in this last field, further limited to the State law of the Greece of his time, that he achieved precise results.

Between Aristotle and Montesquieu lies the development in modern times of the experimental sciences, the mechanism of Descartes, and the attempt at establishing a " social physics of law ", associated particularly with the names of Hobbes and Spinoza. We can be very brief in discussing these thinkers, for they were concerned not with sociology of law but with a *societal-naturalistic philosophy of law*, based on the application of mechanics to the study of social phenomena ; moreover, this application led them to an extreme individualism, destroying precisely the reality which they wished to study, that is, the social reality. Just as the physicists of their time decomposed things into atoms,

Hobbes and Spinoza broke down society, which they identified
with the State, into its irreducible elements, which were, according
to them, isolated individuals placed in a hypothetical " natural
state ".   To the mechanical movement of atoms corresponded
the *conatus sui tuendi et conservandi* of identical individuals, coinciding with their " natural law ", which is not distinguished from
the force at their disposal.   The resultant " clash " of the atom-
individuals and of their mechanical forces (*bellum omnium contra
omnes*), however, stands in contradiction to their tendency of self-
preservation and leads them to follow the commands of *reason* :
that is, to agree to combine their individual forces into a predominant force, that of the public power, the State, thereby
creating an equilibrium of forces and guaranteeing order and
peace, which are identical with positive law.   The theoreticians
of social physics avoided the dissolution of their object—law—into
brute force, by combining their naturalistic mechanism with a
vigorous rationalism, and it was this rationalism which glossed
over the glaring contradiction between the idea of a social physics
and contractualism based on the principle of *obligation*—a contradiction which undermined the entire doctrine.

Moreover, it is precisely the divergent interpretations of the
rôle of reason which led to a profound gap between the conclusions which Hobbes and those which Spinoza drew from their
social physics of law.   Whereas Hobbes introduced the demands
of reason only to put an end to the *bellum omnium contra omnes* and
to arrive at the mechanical force of the State, which he
endowed with a total absolutism ;   Spinoza, regarding reason as
a force in itself and one incomparably greater than mechanical
force, concluded in favour of individual liberty and democracy.
He stated that the mechanical force of the State would be unable
to penetrate the interior of the human conscience, for it would be
stopped by the invincible force of individual reason, related to
the infinite reason of God.   On this basis, Spinoza in his *Theo-
logico-Political* and *Political Treatises* built up a far more subtle
analysis of the variable social equilibria—qualitatively different
forces which would reciprocally check one another by constituting different types of State—than the political and simplistic
mechanics of Hobbes.

To sum up, all we can retain of the social physics of law is
the methodological principle admirably formulated by Spinoza,
" neither to laugh nor weep, but solely to understand " when
studying human conduct from the sociological point of view, and

to start out by contemplating these patterns of conduct as external objects ; that is, objects unknown to the observer by introspection.

In his celebrated *Esprit des Lois* (1748), Montesquieu tried to synthesize the rich heritage of Aristotle (of which he retained only the portion applying to the political group) with the method of social physics particularly in the form given it by Spinoza. The title of his work has a twofold sense, meaning that he proposes, (*a*) to look behind the formal scurf of juridical rules for their inspiration and their connection with the form of government, hence with the variable social sub-structure of the underlying political group ; (*b*) to establish the laws as natural regularities (" the necessary relations deriving from the nature of things ") which would explain the genesis of the different politico-juridical types by their dependence on other social phenomena. From this latter point of view, Montesquieu broadens the base of Aristotle's investigations ; he poses the problem of the relation between the sociology of law and the other branches of sociology (particularly with social ecology which studies the volume of a society, the configuration of the soil, geographical characteristics, etc., in their bearing on the density of population).

This broadening, through which he expects to recover the natural regularities of the life of law, is emphasized by the title of the first edition of the work : " *The spirit of law, or on the relation which must exist between the laws and the constitution of every government, mores, climate, population, religion, commerce, etc.*" For " several things govern man : climate, religion, laws, the maxims of government, the example of things past, mores, manners ; whence is formed a general spirit, resulting from all these things ". Among these heterogeneous factors no hierarchy can be established, since all are equivalent, the result depending on the measure of quantitative effectiveness of each qualitative component regardless of its intrinsic character. Thus, since the rules of law are " relative to the physical configuration of the country, whether the climate is glacial, torrid or temperate ; to the quality of the terrain, its situation and size ; to the type of life led by its peoples, whether they are tillers of the soil, hunters or herdsmen ; to the degree of liberty which the constitution may allow ; to the religion of the inhabitants, their inclinations, their wealth, their number, their commerce, their mores, their manners ", each of these factors takes on a different importance depending on the concrete situation of the inclusive society in question. Montesquieu's relativism is, in this sense, infinitely more consistent and more profound than that of Aristotle ; it embraces an incomparably vaster field, and at the same time precludes over-hasty statements in regard to general laws of social evolution.

Montesquieu's sociology of law by virtue of the complex multiplicity of interwoven factors of variable effectiveness, which it advances, introduces into the study the *historical spirit* with its tendency towards individualization of facts. It orients the naturalistic requirement to study collective conduct as physical things—towards real and consequent empiricist observation ; it substitutes radical empiricism for the rationalism so pronounced even among such successors of Montesquieu as Condorcet and Comte. Thus for the first time it liberates sociology of law from all metaphysic and dogmatic tendencies, and brings it closer— perhaps too close—to the study of comparative law. In any case, Montesquieu, by describing the concrete content of jural experience in the most different types of civilization, was able, with more reason than any of his predecessors, to say of law that " it speaks of what is and not of what ought to be " and that it " does not justify usages but explains them ". At the same time his thesis that every institution and every power tend to be per- verted by their abuses, which can be limited only by a reciprocal counterbalancing of institutions and powers, anticipated the idea of the inextricable antinomic structure of social and jural life, bound up with their pluralism.

Yet, important as it was, Montesquieu's renunciation of the rationalism of " social physics " and the finalist metaphysics of Aristotle in favour of a radical empiricism brought him face to face with the delicate problem of the specificity of the social reality of law in relation to brute force, both social and extra- social. Numerous texts show that he was perfectly aware that *spiritual meanings* enter into the social reality of law, inspiring and guiding jural institutions and practices. " Before there were any completed laws, there were possible jural relations. To say that there is nothing just or unjust except those things ordained or prohibited by positive laws, is the same as saying that before a circle was described, all the radii were not equal." Moreover, conscience, intelligence, and will intervene in human conduct, offering the possibility of violating laws and of changing those which have been established. " Those legislators who have favoured the vices induced by the climate are bad, and those who have opposed them were good." " Physical causes lead man to repose, and, to the same extent, ethical forces must lead him from it." Hence there is no doubt that Montesquieu's sociology of law repudiates a purely naturalistic basis by maintaining contact between the social reality of law and the spirit (this is manifested in the title itself : *Esprit des Lois*).

But since the spiritual meanings inspiring jural institutions and practices are itemized and localized, admitting of no hierarchy, they cannot be rationally deduced ; hence Montesquieu can seek them only in the mobiles of motivation, in the psychological moving power guiding actual conduct. Hence Montesquieu's famous distinction between the " nature " of a government, " that which makes it what it is "—or its external structure—and " the principle of a government ", " that which makes it act "—or the meanings which animate it.

In reducing all the jural typology of groups to the study of forms of government (that is, in relapsing into statism) ; in discerning, despite the wealth of material he assembled, only three principal forms of government (republican, monarchic, and despotic) ; finally, in failing even to envisage the possibility of conflicts between the form and principle of a government, Montesquieu restricted the field of his investigations in a manner that is notably unacceptable. But at the same time, his considerations on the principles of virtue (probity, spirit of sacrifice) as the moving power behind republican institutions, on honour (" the prejudice of each individual and each condition ") as the moving power behind monarchic institutions, and on fear as the inspiration of despotic institutions, do point to the necessity of studying the spiritual meanings of effective jural conduct and of itemizing them according to the circles in which they occur.

Since these summary indications lead to no distinction between jural meanings and moral meanings, however, Montesquieu, to delimit the object of sociology of law, is forced to rely on another criterion : in his work, law appears as " established by a legislator ", fixed in advance from above in rigid formula—in brief, as reduced to legal commands, i.e., to what is decreed by the State. Also, Montesquieu draws a total distinction between law and mores : " Laws are established, mores are inspired." " Laws are particular institutions fixed by the legislator, mores and manners are the institutions of the nation in general." Montesquieu's sociology of law limits itself to studying the conditions by which legal commands are adapted to the special type of society which they are intended to govern.

It gives practical advice to legislators, pointing out the obstacles arising from the social *milieu*. Such a conception is obviously " anti-sociological ", for it places the legislator, and more generally the State, beyond real society, and also sets jural regulation outside spontaneous and living social reality. This " legalism " (or juridical positivism), so contrary to the sociological spirit, penetrating Montesquieu's work, strikes us as a glaring contradiction.

Thus it is unquestionable that Montesquieu, committed to a statist tendency, reinforced by his interpretation of the State not as a specific group or an objective order (*koinonia*) but as a commanding subject ; handicapped also by the necessity of finding the criterion of the jural which evaded him, failed to take into account one of the most important problems of the sociology of law : that of the living reality of law, of spontaneous law and flexible law, behind which organized and fixed law always lags. In this he is far inferior to Aristotle : ignorance of the problems of microsociology, concentration on the genetic sociology of law applied exclusively to the political field and, moreover, solely to the organized superstructures of the State, have an unfortunate effect on the results of his researches. If to this we add the fact that, despite the intensity of his sociological empiricism, Montesquieu does not avoid pursuing a practical aim, that is, the justification of individualist liberalism, we will realize that despite all the methodological progress he has made, the publication of the *Esprit des Lois* was far from constituting a sociology of law.

II *The Doctrines dealing with the Jural Order of " Society " opposed to the State*

The long series of these doctrines beginning with Grotius and Leibniz and extending to Proudhon in France and Gierke in Germany, does not raise the problem of a methodical sociology of law, but does in a spontaneous way considerably advance the study of the jural typology of groups. These doctrines insist on the fact that each particular group and each combination of groups generates a particular framework of law, quite independent of its relations with the State, and distinguish as many types of " social law " as of groups ; thus social reality has been liberated from all identification, submission or dogmatic tie with the State, thanks to the negation of the *a priori* hierarchy of groups—a prejudice which dominated the thinking of Aristotle and Montesquieu, not to speak of Hobbes and Spinoza. Persisting in the search for an ideal social order (however, in this case, of an anti-statist, federalist tendency) ; basing their analyses on a dogmatic spiritualism either rationalist or romantic ; taking little or no account of the problems of the genesis of law and of the microsociology of law ; finally, confusing the jural framework of " society " opposed to the State with a system of positive values —the representatives of these currents tended towards a speculative dogmatism even farther removed from the descriptive and positive study of the social reality of law than the conceptions of Aristotle and Montesquieu.

Hugo Grotius (1583–1645), having detached the *appetitus societatis* and the *communitates* based on it from all necessary bond with the State, on the one hand, and with the *corpus mysticum* on the other, opposed to the statist or religious monism of his predecessors a pluralist conception of equivalent social orders : international society, churches, States, particular groups within the State, engender their own autonomous law, whose structure varies with the type of group. The *custodia societatis* is the foundation of all law, and the " autonomous society of beings gifted with limited reason " and bound together by the *appetitus societatis* is a generic notion, of which the State is only a particular species possessing no privileged position. Hence, says Grotius, there are as many frameworks of law (whether positive or natural) as there are types of groups, and he distinguishes in particular between the *jus latius patens* engendered by international society, the *jus civile* engendered by the State, and the *jus arctius* engendered by smaller groups. Thus State law is surrounded without and within by autonomous frameworks of law. The *jus arctius* is further differentiated into *jus rectorium*, governing the relations between parents and children, between masters and servants (domestic family, economic groups), between administrators and the administered (communes, villages, cities), and *jus equatorium* (conjugal family and fraternal and voluntary associations).

Even before Grotius, Johannes Althusius, in his *Politics* (1603) distinguished a multiplicity of *species consociationis* and the corresponding species of autonomous frameworks of law. He was, however, unable to free himself completely from Aristotle's domination, and remained faithful to a pre-established hierarchy of groups, which Grotius succeeded in destroying through his theory of international society.

The great philosopher, Leibniz (1647–1716), who, along with his mathematics, busied himself all his life with law, took up the jural typology of groups where Grotius left off. According to Leibniz, law consisted in " the perfecting of the society of beings gifted with reason " and was in this sense connected with morality, whose charity he relaxed and limited by logical calculation ; it was, however, always engendered by a real group, with which it varied. Not only positive, but even natural law is essentially contingent ; both arise from " truths in fact " and not from " eternal truths ". An empirical study of the variations of law thus becomes necessary, and Leibniz began vast historical researches on the sources of international law as well as on the specificity of Germanic customary law in relation to Roman law. It is this latent empiricism, combined with a reluctance to reduce law to a command of a superior, which permitted Leibniz to insist with special vigour on the very limited rôle of the State in the life of law, on the complete independence of positive law from the State, on the pluralism of equivalent groups engendering their autonomous frameworks of law, and, finally, on the preponderant rôle of custom as against law. This anti-statism, both empirical and constructive, leads Leibniz, after having vigorously combated the prejudices of the individualists, Hobbes and Puffendorf, as well as of Aristotle, to draw all the consequences of the fact that society and the State cannot be identified, since *omnem civitatem esse societatem sed non contra.*

In an exceedingly important little work, *Divisio societatum*, Leibniz distinguished the following groups existing alongside international society, the State and the Church : households, domestic societies, guilds, insurance societies, congregations, convents, villages, cities, regions, etc. ; no group can satisfy all needs at once ; a number of equivalent groups and federations are indispensable ; only a functional and territorial federalism can express the whole of a society in organized fashion. Every group engenders and possesses its own *jus societatis sive congruentium*—an autonomous law of integration into the whole, a law of peace and harmony (*De tribus juris gradibus*, Mollat edition, pp. 12 et seq.) ; this autonomous social law is differentiated into as many types as there are types of groups, the social law of the guilds, for example, differing from that of the State, which, in turn, differs greatly from that of the Church.

All power derives from the *jus societatis*, and all *jus societatis* presupposes a harmony between equivalents ; hence the associations for domination (*societas herilis inequalis*) and the law they engender do not issue from the common life of the group but from its abnormal enslavements to the law of individual property. Here Leibniz touches on the problem of microsociology of law and to the *social law* acting within each group opposes as inter-individual law in the form of *jus proprietatis*, a limitative law *par excellence*, rather a law of war than a law of peace, for *inter personam et rem . . . perpetuum est jus belli*. The law of domination, which in principle should be applied only to the relations between men and beasts, arises among men only in so far as the social power emanating from the group is submitted to the law of property, which by the intermediary of things and beasts, succeeds in dominating men themselves. These subtle analyses, opening large perspectives, were almost outweighed in Leibniz by his metaphysical theory of pre-established harmony, eliminating in advance all irreducible and dramatic conflicts in the entire world as well as in the social and jural field. This theory prevented Leibniz from pursuing to their conclusion the antinomies between the jural framework of " society " and the jural framework of the State, on the one hand, and between the *jus societatis* and the *jus proprietatis* on the other.

The disciples of Leibniz—Wolf, Ickstadt, Daries, and especially Nettelbladt—despite their infinitely greater dogmatic rationalism, despite their elimination of their master's most profound visions, continued to concern themselves with the jural typology of groups, and their classifications of corresponding types of autonomous framework of law were more systematic and more precise than those of Leibniz. Daries and Ickstadt, for example, distinguished five types of frameworks of social law, corresponding to the types of groups in which they are engendered : (1) *Jus sociale oeconomicum specialis*, corresponding to domestic society ; (2) *Jus sociale oeconomicum generalis*, corresponding to broader economic groups (guilds, industries, etc. ; in this category they also include cities and villages) ; (3) *Jus sociale politicum* ; (4) *Jus sociale ecclesiasticum* ; (5) *Jus sociale gentium.*

Nettelbladt insisted on the distinction between *jura socialia societatis*—the frameworks of autonomous law governing the internal life of each group and the external law of groups governing their relations—an inter-groupal law of the same type as inter-individual law. Hence, while the organized group constitutes a complex jural person in its internal life (*nexus juridicus socialis*), it is a simple unit in its contractual relations with other groups. The *jus sociale societatis* is the foundation of the *potestas socialis* of which the State power (*imperium*) is only a single type among a multiplicity of others. On the basis of these considerations, Nettelbladt opposes the *regimen societatis*—a bloc of economic groups and their frameworks of law—to the *regimen civitatis*— the framework of law governing the State and the *collegia publica* dependent on it, and he envisages possible conflicts and unstable equilibria between the two blocs. " Thus ", he writes, " there arises a double government, the civil or public government and the private government, the latter consisting in the social power belonging to the autonomous groups quite independently of the State power."

A. L. Schözer, historian, statistician, and jurist, deduced from this an opposition between *bürgerliche Gesellschaft* (civil and economic society) and the State, as two independent frameworks of law, one corresponding to the totality of groups based on activity, and the other corresponding to the totality of groups based on locality. This opposition has become fundamental for differential sociology of law and was taken up for a more profound analysis by a number of French and German thinkers in the first half of the nineteenth century.

Parallel to the Leibniz-Wolf school in Germany, the physiocrats in France, whose philosophical inspiration derives from Malebranche and Leibniz, juxtaposed the spontaneous jural order of society conceived as a whole to the State order. Quesnay, Le Trosne, Dupont de Nemours, Mercier de la Rivière—by their reflections on the " fundamental and essential order of (economic) society " which the State is incapable of modifying, by their realization that the law decreed by the State always gives way before that of economic society—became simultaneously founders of political economy and promoters of sociology of law. Considering this autonomous economic society not as a complex of particular groups but as a unified whole, no less capable than the State of representing the general interest, they arrived at the idea of a framework of common social law corresponding to economic life ; this economic law, far from lagging behind political law, outstrips it and is superior to it. In case of conflict, they held, the framework of economic law annuls the law formulated by the State. " The laws of the State ", writes Dupont de Nemours, " should be no more than acts acknowledging the essential laws of the social order. If the statutes of the sovereign were contradictory to these laws, they would be obligatory on no one." " The positive legislation of the State is therefore essentially subordinated to the law of society ", Quesnay concludes. It is easy to anticipate more profound ideas in these formulations which establish a hierarchy of groups contrary to that of Aristotle and manifest an absence of historical spirit ; they point to the general opposition between the organized level and the spontaneous level in social and jural life, and also to the dynamic antagonism between the political and the economic aspect of society.

Research on the jural typology of groups, in the form of opposition between the framework of law of society and the State order, was resumed in the nineteenth century by the French socialists Saint-Simon and Proudhon, and by the circle of the German philosophers, Fichte and Krause and their followers, as well as by the " historical school of jurists " and the " germanists ".

Fichte (1762–1814) merely noted the fact that the jural order of " society " is infinitely richer than the jural order of the State, both in spiritual content and in the force of its spontaneous life. He thought himself justified in concluding that moral progress would render the State useless and " make it disappear in society " ; his disciple Krause (1781–1832), however, after sharply limiting his master's idealization of " society ", established one of the most complete classifications of the types of groups and the corresponding types of frameworks of law. In his *Urbild der Menschheit* (1811), Krause affirms that the " State represents but a single sector of the total life of society, and that the other associations are not subordinate to the State but co-ordinated with it ". He distinguishes three fundamental types of group. First, inclusive societies such as the Nation and International Society ; then the " basic groups " which exercise universal sway over the lives of members, such as the family or the union of friends, the village or the municipality, and their various federations ; finally, the groups serving special aims, such as economic associations, churches, States, pedagogical associations, and several others. To each inclusive society correspond a number of basic groups, and to each basic group correspond a multiplicity of groups with limited aims. Law does not issue from will, but from each of these multiple groups, which thus become the primary and objective sources of a plurality of frameworks of law. The conflicts and equilibria between these frameworks constitute the life of law. Each group engenders its own framework of law, which is possible only in so far as each real collective unit realizes an ideal end, through penetration by an individualized spiritual vocation. Guided by his dogmatic " panentheism ", Krause, who was exceedingly rationalistic in his tendencies, does not seem to admit that a group might realize negative rather than positive values. By mixing judgments of reality with judgments of value, he thinks he can establish, on the basis of a jural typology of groups, a federalist social ideal, valid in all times and all places and based on a stable and immutable equilibrium between the different frameworks of law. This confusion, even more pronounced in his disciples (Ahrens and others), and tempered by no sense of historical relativity, as well as accompanied by the total identification between the forms of sociality (*Geselligkeit*) and the types of group (*Verein, Verband, Bund*), greatly compromised Krause's sociological visions, so valuable in themselves.

Savigny and Puchta, the founders of " the historical school of jurists " which exercised a profound influence on the study of law in the nineteenth century, derived from the same philosophical source as Krause the ideas of Fichte. But they particularly underlined Fichte's irrationalist and romantic tendencies, deriving from them a profound respect for the living historical reality of law. According to them, effective law had only an unconscious, anonymous, and spontaneous development. This necessarily is a slow silent process, analogous to the evolution of a language and excluding all abrupt disturbances, whether through the State legislation or revolutions. This traditionalist conception of the genesis of law " built solely by inheritance, transmitted by the continuous and imperceptible succession of generations ", is combined in the historical school of jurists with a sociological idea which is much more profound : the idea of a spontaneous framework of law of unorganized society, of the mobile and variable *Volksrecht* against which State law is without power but can only acknowledge it. Unfortunately, Savigny and Puchta reduced the conflict between State law and the spontaneous and living social law to that between statute and custom, which in itself is only a procedure of formal acknowledgment fixed in advance of the social reality of law, a traditionalist procedure *par excellence*, excluding all innovation. At the same time, they proved false to their historical and sociological tendency by considering Roman law as a sort of *ratio scripta* and ignoring another jural tradition close to them : that of

Germanic law in its specificity.—The Germanist jurists (Beseler, Maurer, Wilda, Bähr) have in this sense been more faithful to the principle of historical relativity. At the same time, they narrowly limited the traditionalism of their predecessors. They emphasized the fact that the spontaneity of the *Volksrecht*, the law of unorganized society, can be manifested in innovation as well as in tradition, and they brought out the importance of the autonomous jural frameworks of particular groups in addition to custom. They did not, however, avoid a new and very dangerous type of idealization : that of the specificity of Germanic law, and this in turn obstructed their tendency towards sociology of law. We shall not stop to examine the Hegelian theory of the " objective spirit " and of " civil society ", which is no more than a dialectical step in the constitution of the omnipotent State, for, in comparison with the above-mentioned doctrines, this theory brings nothing new to the sociological point of view and, in fact, represents a considerable retrogression, owing to Hegel's statism, combined with his fidelity to the individualism of Roman law.

The junction between research in the jural typology of groups and genetic sociology of law, anticipated in certain German doctrines, found a particularly clear expression in the French socialist doctrines of Saint-Simon and, more particularly, of Proudhon.

In Saint-Simon, the opposition between the State and Economic Society—the two great blocs of local and professional groupings—constitutes the very centre of all these considerations. If, like Fichte, he ends by predicting the dissolution of the State in society " ushering in the final establishment of the industrial regime ", this is due to his technocratic conception, combined with his belief in the exclusive efficacy of love in socia'ist society. Yet he emphasizes throughout that economic society possesses its own autonomous framework of law and, for him, the " industrial constitution ", by which " tribunals of commerce and industry " will replace State tribunals, is the first step towards the future organization. His attacks on law narrow down to a critique of the principles of Roman law, which reflect the absolutism and the individualism of the imperial epoch, and are inapplicable to present-day society. The relations between the jural order of the State and the framework of law of economic society vary with the stages of development of the inclusive society. State law predominates in the military and theological epoch ; it is greatly limited in the legist and metaphysical period (inaugurated

in the Middle Ages by setting free autonomous cities and communes) ; it plays a subordinate rôle and tends to vanish in the
industrial epoch.   On the other hand, law generally plays a more
important rôle in the " critical periods " of social life than at
" organic periods ", one of whose manifestations will be the
" industrial regime ".   The sociological spirit permeating these
considerations of Saint-Simon is clear.   But genetic analyses
predominate in all his thinking and threaten to engulf the true
problem of the jural typology of groups.

Proudhon (1805–65), on the contrary, attaches, with special
clarity, importance to the law as a principle regulating the
unstable equilibrium between the irreducible antinomies constituting all social reality.   He distinguishes between general
sociology and sociology of law, which he places between the study
of material forces and that of collective reason.   In this sociology
of law the problem of the jural typology of groups is dominant,
although the genetic question is not neglected.   Opposition
between the State and " society " implies, according to Proudhon,
opposition between political law and economic law ; the former
seemed to him closer to the law of war than to the law of peace
and collaboration, and he foresaw in his earlier works the dissolution of the State into society as a triumph of law over force.
But in his mature phase, beginning with *La Justice dans la Révo-
lution et dans l'Église*, Proudhon became aware of the utopianism
of his earlier conception and began freeing the framework of
society as opposed to the State from false idealization ; in so
doing, he brought to light the multiplicity of groupings making
up social life, reciprocally limiting and complementing each other.
He distinguished the groups of producers, consumers, mutualities,
co-properties, the State (group of citizens), autonomous public
services.   He went on to demonstrate that each of these groups
is a source of an autonomous and specific framework of law.   The
order of law engendered by non-statist society as a bloc, and by
special associations other than the State, is larger than the framework of economic law, a term which Proudhon retains, however,
side by side with mutualist law, probably in order to make it clear
that the tensions, conflicts and unstable equilibria between the
different frameworks of law normally gravitate around the
antinomy of groups based on locality (State and public services—
" political federation ") and economic groups (" agricultural-
industrial federation "), an antinomy reinforced by the fact that
the economic federation must rest on mutualized property in

order to resist unconditional State constraint. In utilizing these analyses to elaborate his projects for reform towards an autonomous " social constitution " of economy, based on " industrial democracy ", Proudhon takes into account concrete historical situations (industrial democracy replaces " industrial feudalism " and combats the menacing spectre of " industrial empire "— fascism). This is made particularly clear in his manner of treating the problem of property ; the relativity of types of property is most felicitously emphasized (Roman property, feudal property, capitalist property, mutualist property). Yet Proudhon, despite this increasing relativism, was never able to rid himself of his tendency to idealize non-statist society and its economic law ; Proudhon's dogmatic rationalism did not permit him to perceive the variability of the rules which resolve the conflicts between the different orders of law. This limited his sociology of law, so that, despite his profound idea of the antinomic pluralism in the reality of law, we must call his doctrine a pre-sociology.

In Germany in the second half of the nineteenth century, after R. von Mohl, under the double influence of Krause-Beseler and of French socialists, had formulated the problem of the opposition between society and the State, two thinkers in particular continued investigating the jural typology of groups : L. von Stein and O. von Gierke. Stein, some of whose conceptions were not without influence on Marxism, gleaned his doctrine from a profound study of the social movement in France and from the combined theories of Fichte, Krause and Hegel. Stein recognized the irreducibility of economic society and of the State, as well as the possibility of their univocal dependence. Despite the fact that he manifested a realist tendency, he concentrated, under Hegel's influence, all positive values in the State : for him the State was an incarnation of spiritual activity and of the principles of equality and liberty. Economic society, left to itself, would always lead to the enslavement of the weak, to associations of domination. The social law issuing from this society is a class law, consecrating the power of owners over the dispossessed (master and slaves, lords and serfs, capitalist and workers). This social law enthralls public law if economic society dominates the State. The State in this case becomes inequalitarian and betrays its mission, which is to limit the domination of classes and to combat the harmful effects of such a domination. The dissolution of the State into economic society would lead to a caste regime, of which history offers many examples. But the State

succeeds again and again in raising itself above economic society
and in opposing to the inequalitarian social law of the society its
public law and, in particular, its administrative law, which
redresses social inequalities. Furthermore, this State intervention in the order of law of economic society often takes the
form of decentralized public services, which realize an economic
self-government under the patronage and control of the State
(the autonomous law of these public services constitutes a synthesis
between the framework of law of society and the preponderant
law of the State). Thus the State and economic society, engaged
in a perpetual struggle and exchanging thrust and counter-
thrust (*Stoss und Gegenstoss*), sometimes dominate one another
unilaterally, sometimes balance and interpenetrate one another
in varying degrees. Stein no doubt had a profound vision of the
social reality of law and of its antinomic dynamism ; by it he
furthered both typological and genetic sociology of law. Unfortunately, having escaped from the idealization of society as
opposed to the State, he relapsed into idealization of the State,
that is, into a sort of jural statism. According to him, law corresponding to the idea of justice is to be sought solely according to
the Roman tradition, the very concept of law should have only an
individualist basis sustained by the State. On the other hand,
Stein failed to envisage the fact that every form of sociality
engenders its own kind of law and that every framework of law
corresponds to a group, which represents a microcosm of kinds
of law, and can become sometimes an association of domination,
and sometimes an equalitarian association.

Gierke—the great historian of the Germanic law of fraternal
associations (*Genossenschaftsrecht*)—started out in the opposite
direction from Stein ; his differential sociology of law again
inclines towards the idealization of the autonomous law of groups
opposed to the State. Gierke characterized all organized groups
as the subject of their own autonomous order of law (which
regulate their internal life) as a complex collective person (*Gesamt-
person*)—synthesis of unity and of multiplicity in a concrete system.
He proclaimed law's independence of the State and went on to
develop a methodical classification of the types of these collective
persons and of their frameworks of law. Thus, on the one hand,
he opposes collective persons on a territorial basis, among them
the State, to collective persons on a family basis, as well as to
collective persons having an extra-territorial basis (economic,
professional, religious), and, on the other hand, collective persons

based on collaboration (*Genossenschaften*) to collective persons based on domination (*Herrschaften*). The two classifications do not entirely cross each other, for the groups based on locality, according to him, always have a mixed character, into which there enters an element of domination and an element of collaboration, while in the kinship groups, domination and collaboration are distributed among the parent-children group and the master-servant group on the one hand, and the fraternal group on the other. Only the groups based on activity can be either solely *Genossenschaften* or solely *Herrschaften*, for example trade unions and co-operatives for the former, factories and capitalist enterprises for the latter. Each of these different types of complex collective person engenders a special type of framework of social law (a social law of domination and a social law of collaboration, a social law of a territorial, family, professional or canonic type). But the framework of law of that special type of local group which is the State prevails over all the others.

The system of law of inclusive society and the historical genesis of its reality were viewed by Gierke as a perpetual and dramatic struggle between associations of domination and associations of collaboration, a struggle sometimes leading to the predominance of one over the other, sometimes to an equilibrium and inter-penetration of the two. Modern legal history begins with the pre-eminence of the *Genossenschaft* over the *Herrschaft*. Under feudalism this gives place to the triumph of the associations of domination based on landed property. But from the beginning of the thirteenth century down to the fifteenth, feudalism is opposed by the rise of free, equalitarian associations, represented by the cities (which originally were only confederations of trade associations), by the guilds and fellowships. These, however, easily degenerated into closed and obligatory bodies and were annexed by the State which, in the sixteenth century, assumed a definitive territorial form and at first was everywhere autocratic and absolutist in character. For in the State, although like all local groups it is a mixed collective person standing between the *Genossenschaft* and the *Herrschaft*, sometimes one, sometimes the other of these two organizational principles may predominate. The *Genossenschaft* principle begins to prevail in the State from the end of the eighteenth century to the beginning of the nineteenth, under the double form of democratization of central organs and the development of local self-government. But the limitation of the *Herrschaft* within the organization of the State necessarily causes the State to favour the development of free associations, autonomous *Genossenschaften* outside its own organization. Thus at this epoch, it tends more and more to be balanced by an autonomous economic society made up of independent collaboration associations.

Unfortunately, Gierke, despite his reference to mixed cases, does not distinguish between " forms of sociality " and " real collective units ", and consequently his jural typology of groups is far too simplistic and summary. His tendencies towards sociology of law are, moreover, obstructed by this triple error : attribution to the *Genossenschaft* of all sorts of positive values, which it does not necessarily embody ; limitation to Germanic law of this form of organization, transformed in the same time into an ideal ; finally the dogmatic *a priori* affirmation of the jural pre-eminence of the State (at all times and under all circumstances) over the other groups. Gierke's attempt at sociology of law could not surpass the narrow limits set by Krause and Proudhon, although in the circle of doctrines which we have examined, he went furthest in clearing a path for this discipline.[1]

III. *Universal history of law. Comparative law. Jural ethnology. Criminology.*

The third series of forerunners of sociology of law occupied themselves principally with the problems of the genesis of law, which they proposed to study by going back to the most ancient societies and seeking a continuous and uninterrupted line of development. In this task they failed because of the impossibility of establishing a unilinear direction of movement (by juxtaposing and comparing institutions of law arising from different qualitative types of society and from different civilizations). To tell the truth, this type of research, instead of resolving the problem of the genesis of law, i.e., of the factors governing its transformations, contributed rather to a specific inclusive society : the *archaic society*. Thus it is the jural typology of inclusive societies which profited from this kind of study and not genetic sociology of law which can establish regularities as tendencies and study their factors only within the framework of a single qualitative type.

Henry Sumner Maine in his *Ancient Law : its Connection with the Early History of Society and its Relation to Modern Ideas* (1861)

---

[1] Cf. the detailed account of the doctrines mentioned in paragraph 2 and their bibliography in my *Idée de Droit Social* (1932), pp. 171–567.

initiated this type of research by insisting on certain analogies between Hindu and Irish law. He called attention to the " village communities " (localized forms of clan) in different spheres of civilization. These communities were based on collective landed property and diffused sovereignty, which he regarded as the " germs " of all jural development (*Lectures on the Early History of Institutions*, 1876 ; *Dissertations on Early Law and Custom*, 1884). Maine believed that, through his studies in comparative history, he could establish a general law of jural evolution : " Up to the present the movement of progressive societies has consisted in passing from the statute to the contract " ; this " law of evolution " which Herbert Spencer also discovered, is connected with the search for the " germ " of development, a search based on the conviction " that our mental constitution is stable and that the legal institutions in which it manifests itself are less variable and relative than Montesquieu had claimed ". To " dogmatic comparative jurisprudence", Maine opposed this comparatist method, taking into account the historical phases and juxtaposing only legal institutions occurring at the same historical level. The scholars in legal history of the succeeding generation, such as Maitland and Vinogradoff, justly criticized Maine's method, showing that it was arbitrary to establish a parallelism in historical development, that true historical method dealt only with unrepeatable and strictly individualized facts (Rickert), that the discontinuity and complexity of the evolution of law in the different types of society were such as to exclude consideration of archaic law as a basis for the universal genesis of law. It was recognized that, held within its proper limits, the historico-comparative method could not lead beyond a single legal type of a particular inclusive society (Vinogradoff, *Outlines of Historical Jurisprudence*, 1920–2, vol. I).

From this point of view the classic work of Fustel de Coulanges, *La Cité Antique* (1864), revealing the effect of beliefs in supernatural forces, and particularly of religion, on the type of Law corresponding to the primitive form of the Græco-Roman *polis*, is more satisfactory. In demonstrating the tie, in the Græco-Roman sphere, between the home, royalty, landed property, the law of inheritance and marriage, and religion, Fustel does not pretend to establish general laws governing the development of law, but limits himself to comparing two cultural circles standing in a particularly close relationship to one another. Gustave Glotz, recently (in his remarkable work, *La solidarité de la famille dans le droit criminel en Grèce*, 1904, and his *Cité Grecque*, 1928) has again attacked the problems which concerned Fustel. He rightly reproaches the latter with over-simplification and over-generalization, and with a failure to envisage the complexity of the evolution of the ancient city, which cannot develop in con-centric circles at whose centre is the family—clan (*genos*)—but only by conflicts and interactions between the law of the city and the jural order of families.

Maxime Kovalewski, who has continued in the tradition of Maine, handles the historico-comparative method with more prudence than his predecessor, in his *Tableau des origines et de l'évolution de la famille et de la propriété* (1890), and particularly, in his *Coutume Contemporaine et lu Loi Ancienne* (1893). Kovalewski still finds in " the comparative history of law the realization of sociological empiricism in this field " ; he believes that the func-tion of this discipline is " to seek analogies rather than differ-ences ". At the same time, however, he applies his effort not to the study of the continuous filiation of legal institutions, but to " reconstitute the obscure process which gave birth to the earlier legal institutions ", that is, to establish the type of archaic law. For, he recognizes, " the intermediate links are missing ". Even more circumspect is Dareste in his *Études d'Histoire de Droit* (1889) and his *Nouvelles Études d'Histoire de Droit* (1902) ; he limits himself to describing ancient law, people by people, and comes out against a sociological generalization of the evolution of law, and even against the "juridical ethnology " which estab-lishes a common type of archaic law.

The Austrian jurist, R. v. Ihering, well-known historian of Roman Law (cf. *Geist des Römischen Rechts*, vols. I-III, 1865-9), proceeded differently. He treated Roman law in a broadly sociological spirit, integrating its transformations with the evo-lution of Roman society as a whole and rightly attempting " to break the charm which holds us captive and makes us turn the science of law into mathematics ". Then, on the basis of con-crete observations, he attempted to build up a " sociological theory of law " valid for all times and places. At first he limited himself to stating, in opposition to the historical school of jurists, that the development of law is always based on combat, the conscious struggle for claims. He excluded the possibility of an unconscious development, slow and peaceful like that of language (*Der Kampf ums Recht*, 1873). This thesis is, of course, exaggerated and not valid for all types of law or for all groups of society ; its sole merit lay in its opposition to the theses of his predecessors. In his *Zweck im Recht* (2 vols., 1884–6), Ihering adventured further, transforming the beginnings of a sociology of law into a purely dogmatic theory of law. According to this theory, all law is bound up with the conscious aim of defending social interests, and this defence is effected by the State. Consequently, all law is connected with State constraint. Thus Ihering's sociology of law starts out with disproportionate pretensions only to end by succumbing to the prejudices of the dogmatic jurists of his time in favour of a statist theory of law. In this he runs counter to the spirit of sociological relativity, " closes his eyes to the entire history of law " (H. S. Maine) and, more generally, to the living reality of law.

More interesting in this sense were the efforts of the German historian, B. W. Leist, who amended the doctrine of the historical school of jurists in a spirit quite different from Ihering's. In his *Über die dogmatische Analyse römischer Rechtsinstitute* (1854), *Über die Natur des Eigentums* (1860), and *Die realen Grundlagen und die Stoffe des Rechts* (1877), Leist generalized his historical observations, not in order to establish regularities governing the genesis of law or to establish a new theory of law, but to raise one of the fundamental problems of systematic legal sociology : the problem of the relation between jural rules fixed in advance in statute and custom, and the living reality of law. The *Lebensverhältnisse*, the living social relations, engender their own jural regulation which underlies all rigid and formal rules of law. The first is the objective element, the " physis of law ", the *naturalis ratio* of the Romans, which has nothing in common with natural law, and which constitutes the more profound level of law : " real legal institutions ". These institutions must be studied by a special discipline, as distinct from the dogmatico-systematic study of rigid rules as well as from the philosophy of law. This physics of the living and institutional reality of law, which the systematizations drawn up by the State and the jurists can modify but which they are forced to take into account, is the subject of sociology of law. Leist does not employ this term, but his analyses imply it. As Hugo Sinzheimer (*The Task of the Sociology of Law*, 1935, in Dutch, pp. 50–3) has said, Leist anticipates many of the ideas of such representative founders of modern sociology of law as Hauriou and Ehrlich. Yet Leist did not succeed in realizing his point of view, for he placed the living reality of law outside the positive law which he attached to the State, and

limited legal sociology to the study of a single level of the social
reality of law : spontaneous law.

*   *   *   *   *

In addition to the contributions of the historians of law and
the students of comparative law, we must reserve a special place
in the formation of the sociology of law to the ethnographers and
ethnologists.   The influence of this branch of research can be felt
strongly in Maine, Kovalewski, and Dareste.   But Letourneau
(*Évolution Juridique*, 1891) in France, Post in Germany, Steinmetz
in Holland, attempted to make radical use of the works of Lub-
bock, Tylor, Morgan, and other ethnologists, in order to build,
on the basis of their generalizations, *a genetic sociology of law.*
Particularly the German scholar, A. H. Post, in a long series of
works : *Einführung in die Naturwissenschaft des Rechts* (1872) ;
Allgemeine Rechtslehre auf vergleichend-ethnologischer Grundlage (1880–
2), vols. I and II ; *Die Grundlagen des Rechts und die Grundzüge
seiner Entwicklung* ; *Leitgedanken für den Aufbau einer allgemeinen
Rechtswissenschaft auf soziologischer Grundlage* (1884) ; *Die Aufgaben
der Rechtslehre* (1891) ; *Grundriss der ethnologischen Jurisprudenz*,
I and II (1894–5), states his belief that the ethnology of the
different legal institutions was likely to throw light on the causes
of the genesis of all jural life and to establish the laws governing
its evolution in all societies.   He believed this ethnological
sociology to be the sole possible source of a theory of law, which
it replaces, " succeeding in the definition of the notion of law by
comparative induction ".   Post's enormous effort, however, produced a mere " catalogue of legal institutions confusedly borrowed
from the most diverse societies and catalogued in an arbitrary
fashion " (Fauconnet).   No explanation of these institutions, no
law governing their evolution, no concept of law distinguishing it
from Morals and Religion issued or could have issued from such
research.   Moreover, Post himself sensed that his original programme had not been entirely realized.   In his last works he
recognized " that the comparative ethnography of law is only a
part of legal sociology and that this last is only one of the foundations of the theory of law ".   S. R. Steinmetz, Post's successor,
produced three important works, *Ethnologische Studien zur ersten
Entwicklung der Strafe* (Leiden, 1894) ; *Rechtsverhältnisse von
eingeborenen Völkern in Afrika und Ozeanien* (1905), and " Classification des types sociaux " in *Annuaire Sociologique*, vol. III (1900).
Although he believed that sociology of law combined with

psychology could replace the theory of law, he was much more circumspect than his predecessor. In his opinion, comparative ethnology of law arising from the " science of culture " and not from the " science of nature " cannot seek general laws of evolution but only particular types of jural life corresponding to given inclusive societies, e.g., to archaic society, itself divided into types. Finally, sociology of law, like any sociology, " cannot be reduced to ethnology ". Steinmetz's description of the various backward societies is more scientific and more prudent, for before making any comparison, it integrates each concrete phenomenon of law with the whole social life of the society in question. Thus Steinmetz moved in the direction taken by modern ethnographers, such as Boas, Goldenweiser, Lowie, Malinowski, and Thurnwald (cf. below).

The ethnological anthropology of Frazer, who analyses relations between magic and religion in archaic society and their repercussions on primitive law (see *The Golden Bough*, 1890 ; 3rd edition, 7 volumes, 1911–15, and his conclusion concerning archaic juridical institutions in *The Magical Origin of Kings*, 1905, and *Psyche's Task*, 1909) raise a series of truly fundamental questions concerning archaic law. Despite over-hasty generalizations and a highly questionable evolutionism, it apparently does not, however, pretend to replace the whole of legal sociology or to set itself up as a substitute for a theory of law.

To sum up, the ethnology of law has, in developing, gradually renounced its initial claim to establish general laws of legal evolution and resolve the problems of genetic sociology. This " downfall of evolutionism ", as A. Goldenweiser pointed out, is a general trait of modern ethnology.[1] At the same time, we find that in contributing to the jural typology of a particular society—archaic society—the earlier ethnologists failed to arrive at a satisfactory sociological explanation of the phenomena they discovered, for they were not able to integrate them with the general picture, the " total social phenomena " among which these institutions arose. Only those ethnological works which have followed a severe method (such as Franz Boas' school of historical ethnology in America, the functional school of B. Malinowski and A. Radcliffe-Brown in England, and the French school of Durkheim and his disciples, Mauss, Fauconnet, Davy, as well as L. Lévy-Bruhl's path-breaking work on the " mentalité

---

[1] A. Goldenweiser, " Cultural Anthropology ", pp. 221 et seq. (in H. E. Barnes, *Prospects of the Social Sciences*, 1925).

primitive ") have cast definite light on the type of jural life corresponding to backward society and on the evolutionary factors at work within this type.

* * * * *

To complete our survey of the forerunners of sociology of law, we must say a few words on the development of this discipline in the field of penal law. The Italian scholars Lombroso (*Criminal Man*, 1876) and Garofolo (*Positive Criterion of Criminality*, 1878), reacted against the abstract classical conceptions which detached crime from the criminal and made it a metaphysical entity. They introduced anthropo-psychological and biological consider-ations into the discussion, insisting on the physiological pre-disposition of criminals. Since then, a number of criminologists have developed a *sociology of criminality* in opposition to this point of view. Here I shall mention only two representatives of this theory, Enrico Ferri in Italy and Gabriel Tarde in France ; the conclusions of the two men, it must be said, are clearly divergent.

Enrico Ferri, author of *Criminal Sociology*, 1899 (Engl. transl. 1917) seeks to solve all problems of criminality by " the positive study of the social fact of crime ". In this he includes every act which threatens " the collective utility of the group " and pro-vokes " the defensive reaction of society bent on self-preserva-tion ". Thus the systematic study of the rules of criminal law is rendered useless by criminal sociology, and practical reforms (" criminal policy ") would result directly from a descriptive knowledge of criminality. Despite this naïve naturalistic positi-vism which eliminates from criminality its essential meaning as a violation of a jural regulation and, finally, of collective spiritual values, Ferri is perfectly aware that criminal sociology does not dissolve in general sociology but is a part of sociology of law. He does not, however, say exactly in what its specific nature consists. He is obviously unaware of its character as a sort of " sociology of the spirit ", and this damages all his analyses, causing him to hesitate between a pure technique of preventive social hygiene, which would lead to the punishment of dangerous subjects who had thus far committed no crime, and the principle of *nullum crimen sine lege, nulla poena sine lege*, a principle which he finds himself incapable of explaining sociologically. Yet the insistence with which Ferri, utilizing statistical data, revealed the " social factors of crime " (" varying density of population, the state of public opinion and religion, the composition of the family and the system of education, industrial production, alcoholism, economic and political organization, public administration, etc."), the clarity with which he indicated " the part played in crime by professional and civil status ", and age ; finally, his thesis that the forms of crime vary with the types of society (" in feudal society the predominant form of crime was violence and in bourgeois society fraud and swindling ")—all these theses of Ferri represent valuable contributions to the genetic sociology of penal law. It is easy to see that these contributions, which helped to prepare the way for sociology of law, were made in a field which, far from giving a basis for a theory of crime, punishment, and responsibility, presupposes that these ideas are already clarified and formulated, and assumes a systematic jural typology of groups and of inclusive societies.

Before the well-known French sociologist Gabriel Tarde (1843–1904) elaborated his theory of social imitation, consisting in the repetition of individual inventions, he had busied himself intensively with the problem of criminality. His position as magistrate and chief of criminal statistics in the Ministry of Justice particularly qualified him for this kind of research, which beyond a doubt became one of the sources of his sociology. In his *Criminalité Comparée* (1888), *La Philosophie Pénale* (1890), *Études Pénales et sociales* (1892), *Les foules et les sectes criminelles* (1893), reproduced in *L'Opinion et la foule* (1901), he devoted his effort to a study of crime as a function of what he conceived to be social reality. Tarde did not share the naturalistic and utilitarian prejudices of Ferri. He oriented his study of the " social causes of crime " towards " intermental psychology " and was well aware that the sociology of crime could not dispense with jural symbols, ideas, and values, what he later, in *La Logique Sociale* (1893), called the " categories of the social mind ". Thus this discipline, far from replacing the juridical analysis of crime, stood, according to him, in a relation of interdependence with this study, merely liberating it " from its scholastic character ". The modesty of Tarde's aims in his criminal sociology did not prevent, but rather helped him to bring out the fact that " criminality is determined by the organization of society ", and to demonstrate that " it is society which chooses and consecrates its candidates for crime ". By utilizing criminal statistics, Tarde brought out the rôle played by " the professional group of criminals " ; he studied the activity of crowds and sects in criminality, correcting the exaggerations and confusions of Le

D

Bon (*Psychologie des Foules*) and of Sieghele (*La Foule Criminelle*, 1892). He compared " the crowd " and " opinion " and demonstrated that " assemblage " must not necessarily be regarded as a " microbe of evil ". Unfortunately, Tarde thought fit to explain crime exclusively by the imitation of individual initiative and attempted to base the principle of responsibility itself on " the imitability of the act ", combined with " the personal identity of the agent ". These arbitrary constructions, contrary to the sociological method, removed Tarde from factual reality and seriously compromised his researches, otherwise so important, in the criminological field.[1]

Tarde supplemented his criminal sociology by general investigations concerning sociology of law. In his two works, *Les Transformations du Droit* (1893), and *Les Transformations du Pouvoir* (1899), he forcefully combated the evolutionist thesis that juridical institutions develop with homogeneous continuity, and that the germ of these institutions is to be found in archaic society. His polemic on this subject would be very valuable had he not combined it with his general thesis on individual invention—collective repetition by imitation, opposition, adaptation—thus eliminating from the life of the law its most fundamental element, the collective nature of its working out and recognition. On the other hand, by applying his general scheme throughout, he arrived himself at a theory of unilinear and continuous development of law which, in his view, tended towards a broadening of the circle of persons bound by the same law. This, then, he held, constituted " legal progress ". Despite his fallacies, Tarde arrived at instructive conclusions on certain questions of detail : the rôle he attributed in the life of the law to initial precedents on the one hand, to usage and the decision of the tribunals on the other ; his description of the development from customary law (a sort of custom imitation) to legislative law (a sort of fashion imitation), which in turn retreats before a more recent customary law (in which fashion and custom are combined), constitute an interesting contribution to systematic and genetic sociology of the sources of law. Thus the name of Tarde deserves to be cited among the closest forerunners of modern sociology of law, whose methodical elaboration we shall now study.

---

[1] After Ferri and Tarde, the sociology of criminality is developed in a more precise and limited study, as one of the special sections of the sociology of law. See the stimulating general survey of Jerome Hall, " Prolegomena to a Science of Criminal Law " (*Pen. Law Rev.*, 1940, pp. 549–80) and his book *Theft, Law and Society* (1935).

SECTION II : THE FOUNDERS OF THE SOCIOLOGY OF LAW

A. THE FOUNDERS IN EUROPE

I. *Durkheim*

In the Introduction, we gave some general indications of the place held within Durkheim's sociology by the sociology of law. Here we will give a concrete summary of his sociology of law. Aside from the two principal works in which he takes up legal questions—*De la division du travail social* (1893, Engl. transl. 1915) and " Deux lois de l'évolution pénale " (in *Année Sociologique*, vol. IV, 1900), all his works, as well as the important notes published in the *Année Sociologique* (the third part of which was devoted to the sociology of law), contributed to the clarification of this field. Any serious analysis of his studies leaves no doubt that he was far from reducing the sociology of law to merely genetic problems. In fact, he made a serious contribution to the development of systematic legal sociology (by studying the relation of types of law to the forms of sociality) and of the differential legal sociology of inclusive societies. Only, since he believed he had to link these two fields of research to the study of filiation throughout archaic society considered as the key to the explanation of all evolution, his genetic legal sociology emerged as the basis of all the solutions he found. Let us analyse the interconnection of the three basic problems of Durkheim's sociology of law.

The *Division du Travail Social*, 1893, properly selects as the starting point for its study the problem of the relation between forms of sociality and kinds of law. " The visible symbol of social solidarity (conceived as a solidarity in fact, that is, a form of sociality) is the Law." " Hence we can be sure of finding all the essential varieties of social solidarity reflected in the Law." And, inversely, an objective classification of the kinds of law, a classification valid for sociological research, can be only accomplished through a classification of the forms of solidarity ; in fact, the distinction between public and private law " accepted among jurists serves only practical purposes " and designates only law privileged or not privileged by the State, whose dispositions in this respect are essentially variable. Private law often includes jural structures quite analogous to those included in public law (for example, family or trade union law are not by nature different from constitutional law) ; the State itself did not exist in all epochs of social life, nor has it always since its inception played the same rôle. Thus, sociology of law must distinguish between the kinds of law. The first necessary classification will be that between law corresponding to a " mechanical solidarity " or solidarity through similarity, and law corresponding to " organic solidarity ", or solidarity through dissimilarity. The law corresponding to mechanical solidarity is penal law ; that corresponding to organic solidarity is family, contractual, commercial law, the law of procedure, administrative, and constitutional law. All law which can be defined as " rules with organized sanctions " stands in contrast to the " rules with diffused sanctions ", characteristic of morality. Thus the two main types of jural regulation, parallel to the two opposed types of solidarity, are manifested in two different kinds of organized sanctions : law arising from mechanical solidarity is accompanied by repressive sanctions and law arising from organic solidarity is accompanied by restitutive sanctions. " The repressive sanction is a sanction implying a blame inflicted by society, a dishonour, whether it take the form of capital or corporal punishment, privation of liberty, etc., or simply of a public reproach. The restitutive sanction consists merely in restoring matters to their former status, disturbed relationships to their normal form, whether this be done by recalling the infraction deed to the type from which it deviated or by annulling it, that is, depriving it of all social validity."

Durkheim finds evidence for the parallelism between repressive law and mechanical solidarity, restitutive law and organic solidarity. Indeed, repressive sanctions and the penal law which they accompany protect the most essential social similitudes. The repressed crime is a rupture of the mechanical solidarity, " an offence against the intense state of the collective consciousness, against a collective ideal identical in all ". Moreover, " the more the mechanical solidarity predominates " in a society, and " the more the individual is integrated in a homogeneous society without any intermediary, the more repressive law will prevail over restitutive law. On the contrary, restitutive sanctions protect the differentiation of society in specialized functions, in subgroups, in individualized personal activities. Restitutive law guarantees the free division of social labour, of which it is itself an effect : it is associated with a more flexible collective ideal, which admits of its particularization." In a society where organic solidarity, a solidarity among the dissimilars, becomes predominant, a great part of the law liberates itself from the penal law and even begins to prevail over it. In particular, the parallel development of the Contract and the State, both accompanied by sanctions of a restitutive tendency, is the most precise manifestation of the reinforcement of organic solidarity and its jural symbols.

A more detailed analysis leads Durkheim to distinguish certain sub-types within these two main types of jural regulations and forms of solidarity. Thus, within the restitutive law, Durkheim contrasts contractual law and law which goes beyond contract (domestic law, trade union law, constitutional law, etc.). He notes furthermore that " in the contract not all is contractual," and that often " our voluntary co-operation creates for us duties which we did not desire ", i.e., there often arises under the form of contract the autonomous statutory law of numerous groups which cannot be reduced to the sum of their members, or what, since Durkheim, has been called " *actes-règles* " (regulatory acts) or " contracts of adhesion ". Likewise, the organic solidarity seems, according to Durkheim, to break down into what he himself calls " contractual " or delimitative solidarity, and a more intense and more positive solidarity which might be designated as solidarity by interpenetration or partial fusion (cf. below, Chapter II). On the other hand, he finds that restitutive law includes a law " of purely negative character, amounting to a pure abstention " (such as real law) to which no type of solidarity seems to correspond, and the " law of positive co-operation ", which alone symbolizes organic solidarity and which breaks down into the two sub-types just mentioned.

In themselves, these considerations would not overcome the sphere of " microsociology of law ", if Durkheim limited himself to examining the relations between the different forms of solidarity and the different kinds of law, as elements coexisting within each inclusive society and each special group. But he saw fit to transpose mechanical solidarity and organic solidarity, as well as repressive and restitutive law, into historical phases of the development of the inclusive society, and even came to consider these phases as degrees of moral progress, attributing to organic solidarity and restitutive law a higher value than to mechanical solidarity and repressive law. It is here that Durkheim's systematic microsociology seeks its foundation in genetic macrosociology, and finally even in a theory of progress bound up with the belief in a preconceived ideal.

To justify this thesis, Durkheim calls on legal history. He maintains that the more archaic a society is, the more prevalent are repressive sanctions of an extremely vigorous and intense nature ; the more highly evolved a society is, the milder are punishments, until repression is almost entirely displaced by restitution. Thus, in the Old Testament and in the laws of Manu, severe repression is dominant, the codes protecting religion being pitiless in exacting expiation of sin. The Law of the Twelve Tables, however, relates to a society much more highly evolved, and rests on far gentler sanctions, not to mention the considerable limitation of punishment by restitutive sanctions. Comparing the first codification of customs in Christian societies (Salic law, laws of the Visigoths and Burgundians, etc.) with the laws of the Middle Ages and the latter with those of modern times, the situation is as follows: punishments become ever milder and re-stitutive sanctions tend increasingly to replace repressive sanctions.

On the other hand, the parallel development of the contract and the State, a repercussion of the progressive predominance of organic solidarity, leads, according to Durkheim, to the realization of equality, liberty, and justice in the domain of law and to the disappearance of domination in favour of collabora-tion. The members of society are no longer regarded " as things over which society has rights, but as co-operators with whom it cannot dispense and towards whom it has duties ". The growth of State influence consists only in the increase of its functions, which it realizes in a fashion continuously less oppressive, through public services which administer but do not command. Durk-heim believes with Saint-Simon that the State increasingly " administers " and decreasingly " governs ", and that its ever-broadening administrative functions require only restitutive and not repressive sanctions. The transformation of the State into an equalitarian association of collaboration, favouring both the multiplication of its contractual relations and the affirmation of individual law, seems to him the surest manifestation of the benefits of organic solidarity, which progressively eliminates mechanical solidarity.

In his later researches, however, Durkheim tempered his initial optimism about legal evolution. Even in his *Deux lois de l'évolution pénale* (1900), he separated the State from any necessary tie with organic solidarity and emphasized its in-dependent rôle as a factor in the evolution of punishments to the extent that it is based on domination.

The intensity of the punishment [we now read] becomes greater, the lower the type of society and the more absolute the central power.

[In fact], the structure of the social type and of the governmental organ must be carefully distinguished. That is why there are two independent factors in penal evolution. And since they are independent, they act independently, sometimes even in opposite directions. For example, it sometimes happens that, in passing from an inferior type to other higher types, one does not see the diminution of punishment one might expect, because, at the same time, the governmental organization neutralizes the effects of social organization. The process is very complex.

Thus repressive sanctions do not necessarily evolve as a function of mechanical solidarity nor is the State necessarily a manifestation of organic solidarity. Moreover, " when punishments involving the privation of liberty replace corporal punishments ", the mitigation of punishments due to the progress of organic solidarity can be accomplished without any limitation of repression through restitution.

In his *Suicide* (1897) and in the preface of the second edition of his *Division*, Durkheim went further in rectifying his original thesis, emphasizing the fact that the reinforcement of the State, far from always being an effect of the intensification of social cohesion by the development of organic solidarity, can on the contrary be the effect of social amorphism, of disintegration leading to unilateral domination. He has forcefully described the gulf created between the centralized State of the eighteenth and nineteenth centuries and the mass of citizens deprived of intermediary corporations and transformed into an atomic dust ; he regards this gulf as one of the factors causing the increase of suicides. He also points out that the development of modern armies, side by side with the disintegration of economic life, has greatly limited the dominance of organic solidarity in favour of a situation strongly resembling mechanical solidarity. It is therefore not surprising that Durkheim's most qualified successor, Marcel Mauss, wrote as follows :

The problem is more complex. First, in certain points, individualism has led our own societies to veritable amorphism. Durkheim has often spoken of this almost pathological void existing between our morality and our law, between the State and the family, the State and the individual. There is something mechanical even in our idea of equality. Inversely, there was much of the organic in archaic . . . societies. But this organic element is different from our own.

What do these lines mean if not a recognition of the failure of genetic sociology of law as a basis for the microsociology of law ? This in no way excludes the value of genetic studies as long as they renounce disproportionate pretensions and limit themselves to the framework of a single type of inclusive society.

Durkheim raised the problem of the differential sociology of law by establishing a classification of the " social types qualitatively distinct from one another " and studying the " legal systems " corresponding to each of these types. Here, of course, he is dealing with the jural typology of all-inclusive societies, quite distinct from the microsociology of law, studied in his *Division du Travail*. Originally, however, he believed he could distinguish a type and structure of all-inclusive society completely identified with mechanical solidarity and having a " legal system " coinciding entirely with repressive law : this is the " horde " or unisegmentary society. Durkheim designates the horde as " the veritable social protoplasm " and he establishes " as many fundamental types of inclusive society as there are forms in which the horde can combine with itself in giving birth to new societies, and ways in which the new societies can in turn combine ". Thus he distinguishes : (1) the type of simple polysegmentary society, formed by a repetition of clans (a horde integrated with a larger whole)—such as may be observed among the Australians and the Iroquois ; (2) the type of simply composed polysegmentary society, in which several tribes fuse (e.g., Iroquois or Kabyle confederation) ; (3) the type of doubly composed polysegmentary society, such as cities, unions of confederations, tribes (e.g., Roman curiæ) ; (4) in opposition to all these types of segmentary society, there is a type of organized society " constituted not by a repetition of similar and homogeneous segments, but by a system of agencies. In this society, individuals are integrated into groups, not by virtue of their hereditary relations, but through the special nature of their social activity ". This fourth type is obviously the broadest and qualitatively the most distinct from the others ; it corresponds, on the whole, to any evolved society.

Each of these types of all-inclusive society possesses its own religious, legal, and economic structure. For example, totemism prevails in the first, tribal religion in the second, national religion in the third and partially in the fourth, where it subsequently became universalized. The legal system in the first type is confused with taboos, and sovereignty remains in diffusion ; in the second and third types law is partially laicized and territorialized ; finally, in the fourth type, law is entirely separated from religion and sovereignty is definitively centralized in an organization.

In his investigation " of qualitatively distinct social types " and corresponding legal systems, Durkheim wanted to free himself from the prejudices of unilinear evolutionism, by differentiating the legal typology of inclusive societies from genetic sociology of law. He wrote, in fact, that

if there is only a single social type, societies can differ from one another only by degrees. If, on the contrary, there are qualitatively distinct social types, no effort at juxtaposition will make them fit together exactly like the homogeneous sections of a geometrical straight line. Thus historical development loses the ideal and simplistic unity which had been attributed to it ; it breaks down, so to speak, into a multitude of fragments which, being specifically different from one another, could never be combined in a continuous line.

—Yet if we take a closer look at Durkheim's classification of social types, we find that no more than in his microsociology of law was he able to eliminate the predominance of genetic considerations and, finally, the prejudice of unilinear continuity of development. In fact, aside from his two excessively broad and summary main types—" segmentary society " and " organized society "— all the others which he established are entirely quantitative (repetition of segments) and not qualitative ; they represent, as he himself said, " a hierarchy of phases of development ". Thus, sociology of law, hardly founded, loses itself in the hasty generalizations of old-time genetic sociology, whose essential fallacy Durkheim retains in his typology : the identification of the " simple " (or elementary) and the " primitive ". This idea has been eliminated by all modern sociological and ethnographical research, which points to the enormous complexity of primitive society, a complexity radically different from our own.

It must be added that Durkheim, himself not satisfied with his first classification of social types, which he felt to be too quantitative and genetic, made certain essential corrections in *l'Année Sociologique* (1910, vol. XI ; 1913, vol. XII). Here he distinguishes : (1) societies formed of totemic clans (Australian type) ; (2) societies differentiated on the basis of partially effected totemic clans (North American Indians : here the differentiation consists " in a more or less complex system of classes, military orders, colleges of priests, diverse social agencies ") ; (3) tribal societies with male filiation, in which there is a development of local groups (village communities) and permanent central govern-

ment (Nigritians, Sudanese, Bantus, etc.) ; (4) national societies
(nations, among which several types must be distinguished).
Although this second classification brings out the qualitative
aspect of the types and their essential discontinuity much more
clearly, there persists a suggestion of continuous genesis.

The problems of genetic sociology of law proper (that is, the
factors governing the transformation of law) occupied Durkheim
in a twofold aspect : first, the morphological and particularly
the demographic factor (volume and density of the population)
and second, the religious factor, more precisely the influences of
beliefs in the Sacred (implying, according to Durkheim, Magic,
aside from Religion). Durkheim saw links between these two
factors—the first intermediate, since " material density " cannot
be detached from " moral density " with which it is impregnated,
the other direct—with the states of collective consciousness, whose
variations are the ultimate foundation of the transformations of
legal institutions. Towards the end of Durkheim's career, this
statement led him to the important conclusion that Law, like
Religion, Morals, Economics, Æsthetics, in brief all the principal
social phenomena, are " systems of values, arising from collective
ideals ". The variations of this ideal of collective consciousness
constitute the basis for the movement of legal institutions ; for
" society cannot create or re-create itself, without at the same
time creating an ideal ", and by this creation, " it periodically
makes and remakes itself " (Philosophie et Sociologie, 1924 ; Formes
Elémentaires de la Vie Religieuse, 1912).

Durkheim applied his general views on the development of
law only to a single type of society : that constituted by totemic
clans. This limitation was the great strength of his genetic
sociology of law, for the latter is possible, as we have several
times repeated, only within a single qualitative framework, since
the different factors of transformation are combined within each
type in an incommensurable fashion.

For example, Durkheim affirms that the division of social
labour, and with it the jural regulation, " vary directly with the
volume and density of societies ", since the societies which have
become regularly more dense and generally more voluminous,
" are also the most highly developed ". But this statement,
certainly correct for the type of society composed of totemic clans,
is inapplicable, not only to contemporary but to any evolved
society. It is obvious that volume and density do not always go
hand in hand (extremely voluminous societies may present an

amorphous mass with very little density, e.g., the empire of Genghis Khan ; and extremely dense societies may be very limited) ; migrations, the fall of the birth-rate may depopulate a society ; the legal control may take up an offensive against demography, either by combating density or by seeking to put a stop to depopulation. Numerical densities in themselves are incommensurable, for everything depends on the level of technical production. The interpenetration of the factors affecting the volume and density of a society is so complex, its relations with the law so unstable that, in attempting generalizations, we always run the risk of mistaking effects for causes. In this field, we must limit ourselves to the analysis of concrete cases, never forgetting that the sole cause of social and hence legal transformations is always to be sought in the social type as a whole, in " total social phenomena ", as Mauss in France and Cooley in America so well expressed it (see below, Chapter V).

The influence on the transformations of jural institutions worked by variations of belief in the Sacred, Durkheim discusses only in relation to the totemic clan and tribal society. Since law is essentially bound up with religious interdictions, the violation of which is accompanied by blame, by social reprobation, it becomes more flexible and leaves room for individual initiative, when the magic interdictions, the violations of which involve only technical consequences, begin to compete with and limit the religious taboos. The sacred, impersonal, and anonymous force of the *Mana* is at first represented exclusively by the totemic principle—the clan God. But, in the course of time, the exclusively religious totemic *mana* is generalized, and this gives rise to tribal religion on the one hand and to magic on the other.

The differentiation of collective from individual law runs parallel to the differentiation between religion and magic. Religion is doubly social : by content, the Sacred, which is only a projection of the ascendancy of society, and by exercise, which is always collective and which presupposes the existence of a church. Magic, on the contrary, which is born of religion and subsequently opposes it, is social only in its content, the *mana* ; in its exercise it is much more individualistic and diffuse. Magic contributes to the separation of the magician from the group, in permitting the manipulation of the *Mana* by the individual will and for individualist aims. The collective law, bound up with religion, is thus limited by individual law, associated with magic. Paul Huvelin, Durkheim's disciple, broadly developed this idea, going so far as to define magic in its consequences for law " as a deviation of the power arising from the Sacred by the individual who uses it for his own profit " (see *La Magie et le Droit individuel*, *Annuaire Sociologique*, 1906 ; *Les Tablettes Magiques et le Droit Romain*, 1900. See also *infra*, Chapter IV).

In concluding this exposition of Durkheim's sociology of law it should be noted that his researches on the religious and magic factors in the transformation of law in archaic society, lead him to introduce a new classification of the kinds of law : " collective law " and " individual law ". This classification does not exactly correspond to the opposition between repressive law and other types (domestic, contractual, constitutional), based on two solidarities ; for it is obvious that certain kinds of " restitutive law " (e.g., domestic and constitutional, law of procedure, etc.) emanate from " collective law ", and others (e.g., contractual) emanate from " individual law ". His first sketch, already retouched by the distinction, within restitutive law, between contractual law and law passing beyond the contract, is further complicated by being interwoven with a classification based on a new criterion.

We cannot stop here to discuss the valuable achievements of Durkheim's disciples, Mauss, Fauconnet, Bouglé, and Davy. Extensive use will be made of them in Chapters IV and V, devoted to a discussion of the legal typology of all-inclusive societies and the factors governing the transformation of legal systems.

Let us sum up here as succinctly as possible the necessary reservations with regard to Durkheim's sociology of law. We have attempted to bring out the richness and scope of his endeavour, at the same time criticizing his reduction of jural micro-sociology and typology to genetic considerations. Having most aptly raised the problem of the relations between forms of sociality and kinds of law, Durkheim was prevented from arriving at definitive results by three factors : his classification of the forms of sociality is too simplistic ; the connection he established between law and organized constraint is highly questionable ; finally, law is not the symbol of all forms of sociality, but only of certain forms, corresponding to precise conditions, since other forms of sociality may turn out to be sterile from the jural point of view.

The similarity and dissimilarity may be more rough or more subtle, they may designate an affirmation or a negation of identities, or simply equivalences, they may relate sometimes to

entire subjects, sometimes to certain of their aspirations, sometimes to values and objects through which relations are established
between the subjects. Finally, we do not find forms of sociality
or of solidarity in which at one and the same time certain affinities
and certain differences are not implied. In this sense, only
" organic solidarity " is real, and it is therein that the plurality
of forms of sociality must be sought. Durkheim himself recognized this fact in the end, though he did not pursue it to any
conclusion.

The connection between law and organized constraint excludes from the reality of law one of its most important sectors,
and one which is of special interest to sociology : the spontaneous,
dynamic law, which is constantly being modified, the life-giving
source of organized law, with which it is constantly coming into
conflict. Any organization of constraints presupposes this
spontaneous law, serving as a basis for organization, and all
laws equipped with sanctions, even diffuse sanctions (yet, contrary to Durkheim, remaining law : such as regulation sanctioned
by the boycott or the vendetta, etc.), finally rests on an un-
sanctioned law which serves as a basis for the jural sanctions.
If all law is certainly socially guaranteed, and the real effectiveness of the law is verified by the reactions of disapproval, this
social guarantee is something quite different from jural coercion,
that is, precise and predetermined measures taken against the
delinquents, regardless of whether the constraints be organized
or diffuse (see our Introduction, sect. V). For this reason alone,
it is impossible to make a type of constraint correspond to a precise
form of sociality, since the same jural structure can be accompanied by different types of constraint, or in certain circumstances
by none at all. The question is further complicated by the fact
that the distinction between repression and restitution overlaps
with that between unconditional constraint which one cannot
evade, and conditional constraint which one can evade by leaving
the circle in question.[1] Moreover, the violence of constraints
depends on the relation between the organized sociality and the
spontaneous sociality, a matter which Durkheim does not take
into consideration. If the former is penetrated by the latter,
the constraints become milder, if, on the contrary, the former is
detached from the latter, they become more severe. It is, furthermore, these relationships, between the organized superstructure

[1] See below, Chapter III, sect. III, and *l'Idée du Droit Social,* pp. 25 et seq. See
also MacIver, *The Modern State* (1926), pp. 272 et seq.

and the spontaneous infrastructure, which lead in some cases to
a law of collaboration, in others to a law of domination (see below,
Chapter II).   In brief, Durkheim was wrong in identifying, on
the one hand, repressive law, law sanctioned by unconditional
constraint and law of domination, as opposed to restitutive law,
on the other hand, law sanctioned by conditional restraints and
law of collaboration.

In reality, where Durkheim sees identity, there are multiple
combinations : law of collaboration, for example, may be repressive and sanctioned by unconditional constraints ; law of
domination can be sanctioned by restitutive sanctions and conditional constraints (internal law of business concerns, trusts, and
factories to-day).

The different forms of sociality are symbolized by law, only
if they are active, if they have a common task to accomplish.
The different socialities between friends, between lovers, between
followers of a doctrine, between people speaking the same language, engender neither jural regulation nor organization.   To
establish the kinds of law through the forms of sociality, we must
therefore, without neglecting the others, extract those forms which
might be symbolized by law.

To conclude our criticism, let us note that Durkheim, who
elsewhere insisted strongly on the rôle of the multiple sub-groups
in social life, concerned himself very little in his sociology of law
with the fundamental problem of the jural typology of particular
groups, e.g., the specific nature of domestic law, trade union and
association law, State law, church law, etc.   Only in archaic
society did he point out the conflict between the mystico-kinship
group of the clan and the local group, a point later developed by
his disciple Davy (Davy and Mornet, Des Clans aux Empires,
1923).   The jural typology of inclusive societies absorbed all
Durkheim's attention.   Thus, in considering the evolved society,
he did not analyse the problem of the opposition between the
legal order of society and the legal order of the State (on which
certain forerunners of the sociology of law so strongly insisted),
and, in general, he omitted the problem of jural pluralism.   This
fact is the more striking in view of his pronounced interest in the
new flowering of the trade union and corporative movement,
which he took into account in his ethics, devoting a special posthumous study to professional morals (Revue Métaphysique, 1930).
This omission may be attributed to several reasons.   In the first
place, the predominance of genetic sociology of law naturally

concentrates Durkheim's attention on inclusive society ra[ther than]
on sub-groups. But the truth is that opposite developm[ents]
occur within sub-groups : organic solidarity and the law [corres-]
ponding to it can prevail in local groups, and at the sam[e time]
mechanical solidarity and its corresponding law can prevail in
economic activity groups (eighteenth and nineteenth centuries).
What is more, this contradictory movement can occur in groups
of the same type. Among economic activity groups at the end
of the nineteenth and the beginning of the twentieth centuries,
we saw the development of trade unionism, co-operatives, social
insurance, etc., bring about reinforcement of organic super-
contractual solidarity and statutory law, while the development
of large-scale industry and the growth of unemployment brought
about a simultaneous reinforcement of mechanical solidarity.
Durkheim was inclined to pass over these diversities too rapidly,
in order to bring out the tendencies of the all-inclusive society,
which, however, cannot be determined without taking into consideration the equilibrium of the frequently opposing develop-
ments of the particular groups which constitute a society.

In the second place, Durkheim tended towards a certain
social and legal monism : he arranged his sub-groups in a stable
hierarchy, the professional groups always subordinate to the State,
which also held primacy over international society. This view,
so contrary to sociological relativism, was bound up with his
conception of a unique collective consciousness, replacing the
plurality of conflicting collective consciousnesses which we find in
the life of society as a whole and even within each special group.
From this follows his interpretation of religion and collective law
—principles of social unity—in archaic society as the sources of
magic and of individual law, which are only succedaneous for
them. From this likewise follows his conception, with regard to
evolved societies, of the constant development of the State and
the Contract, and his failure to envisage the possibility of their
common decadence in favour of legal institutions of other types.

The final reason for the indicated difficulties in Durkheim's
sociology of law : this is the predominance of genetic questions,
the concentration on organized constraints, and the hidden
tendency towards a social and legal monism, resides certainly
in his irresolution with regard to the spiritual content of jural
experience. The ideals of Justice he sometimes regards as simple
projections and products of the collective subjectivity, sometimes
as contents *sui generis*, grasped only by it and resisting it. The

two conceptions he unites, by raising the collective consciousness to the rank of a metaphysical spirit.[1] Durkheim clearly saw the necessity, in the sociology of law, of a synthesis between idealism and realism, or rather of an " idealist-realist " foundation. But while he never abandoned the idea of substituting the sociology of law for the philosophy of law and the systematico-normative study of jural patterns, he never arrived at the desired synthesis. In his concrete studies on sociology of law, his realism dissolved his idealism, threatening to lead him back to the conception of law as a simple epiphenomenon, a subjective projection : hence the predominance of genetic research. In his general conceptions, on the contrary, his latent metaphysical " hyper-spiritualism " led him towards the juridization and moralization of all social reality.

II. *Duguit, Levy, and Hauriou*

The three other French founders of the sociology of law, Léon Duguit (d. 1928), Emmanuel Levy, and Maurice Hauriou (d. 1930), came to this science not from sociology but from jurisprudence. While the first two can be regarded as disciples of Durkheim, the last considered himself rather his adversary. It is Hauriou, however, who continued to seek a synthesis between idealism and realism as a basis for the sociology of law. Duguit, on the contrary, claimed to be exclusively " realistic and even naturalistic " in his orientation, while Levy inclined towards an excessive idealistic subjectivism. As for their treatment of concrete problems, they concentrated attention on the jural typology of particular groupings, a study which Durkheim had somewhat neglected ; further, they complemented this research by the study of the transformations of the present legal system, that is, they applied their differential and genetic research to the legal type of the present-day inclusive society. On the other hand, they insisted on the rôle of spontaneous and dynamic law, as the basis of the social reality of law. In all three, however, what was lacking was the study of the problems of microsociology of law, as well as the differentiation between the three fundamental aspects of legal sociology ; in this, from the methical point of view, they were inferior to Durkheim, although superior to him in grasping the complexity of the present-day reality of living law.

(A) *Léon Duguit* concerned himself less with the study of the

[1] See my criticism in *Essais de Sociologie* (1938). The analogy with Cooley's conceptions was indicated in the Introduction, sect. III,

sociology of law proper than with its utilization in jurisprudence —that is, the technical art of systematization of law actually in force, particularly constitutional law (cf. his *Traité de Droit Constitutionnel*, 1st edition, 1908, 2nd edition, 1920–7, in five volumes). At the same time, he spoke incessantly of " a sociological theory of law ". This could only compromise the sociology of law, which has a totally different aim from the philosophy of law and can by no means claim to replace it. In order to bring out the contribution of Duguit in the development of our discipline, we must eliminate that part of his work which is related to a new dogmatization of law. Among the works of Duguit most directly touching the problems of the sociology of law, *L'État* (1901–3) is devoted predominantly to general questions. His *Le Droit Social, le Droit Individuel et les Transformations de l'État*[1] (1911) ; *Les Transformations générales du Droit Privé depuis le Code de Napoléon* (1912) ; *Les Transformations du Droit Public* (1921) ; *Souveraineté et Liberté* (1922), are concerned mostly with the legal typology of present-day society and the regularities of its development.

Like Durkheim, Duguit associates all law with *de facto* solidarity, that is, sociality. But instead of distinguishing the different types of law through a classification of the forms of solidarity, Duguit, having found that, in civilized society, which alone interests him, there can be only organic solidarity, concentrates all his attention on the relation between the law engendered by this solidarity (which he calls " objective law ") and the State. By identifying solidarity and real collective units —groups (microsociology and macrosociology), and by citing the nation and international society, in their opposition to the State, as incarnations of solidarity, Duguit utilizes the bond between law and sociality to liberate positive law from all dependence on the State. To consider law as a function of solidarity means, for him, to oppose extra-statist society and its jural order (objective law) to the State, which expresses not a solidarity but a relationship of pure force between the governing and the governed. Thus, on the one hand, the problems of microsociology of law are identified with those relating to the legal typology of groups, and on the other hand, the State is excluded from the number of real groups, and is regarded as a fiction masking a relationship of mechanical forces.

The " objective law " emanating from the solidarity which exclusively governs the social *milieu* opposed to the State, is

[1] See also the English translation, *Law and the Modern State* (New York, 1919).

independent of the expression of any will ; it is pre-existent to the will, since the will can do no more than acknowledge it and can produce jural effects only by putting itself at the service of the " objective law ". More than that : since all organizations (organized superstructures), like the State, are only relations of force, they stand outside of the life of law. They can produce no law, and within them there is no jural relationship. The organized superstructures represent only an assemblage of in-dividuals " in which the stronger individual wills impose them-selves on the less strong ". From this it follows that " no relation exists between the supposed corporation and its supposed organ. The idea of representation is fallacious, since it is based on a fallacious idea : the jural structure of the organization." If, however, all organizations and all actions of their supposed agencies are nothing but pure violence, having no relation to law and the solidarity from which all law emanates, these acts of violence may be *legitimate* or *illegitimate* ; this depends on whether they correspond to or contradict the exigencies of the objective law emanating from the social solidarity. This con-formity or non-conformity can be acknowledged only after the action, since no government, agent, or organization has the right to act in the name of the governed, the represented, the members of the organization.

In Duguit this individualistic anarchism towards all organized superstructures of social life, astonishing in a thinker who regards himself as a sociologist, flows from a negation of all rights (*droit subjectif*) : " To speak of the rights of individuals, of the rights of society, of the rights of groups, is to speak of things which do not exist." From the point of view of " subjective " rights, " there is neither social law nor individual law ". Objective law, emanating from social solidarity " excludes both the notion of a right of the collectivity to command the individual, and of a right of the individual to impose his personality on the collectivity and on other individuals ". In this, Duguit is reacting against the individualist interpretations of rights " as the *a priori* superio-rity of one will over another ", " qualities inherent in an individual (*dominium*) or collective (*imperium*) will, giving them the right to command, because they are wills ". This reaction is certainly sound, but it draws him much too far. Instead of demonstrating that " rights " are impossible without objective law and cannot under any circumstances serve as its basis or source, since these result from law (for jural subjects are immanent in the objective order of law, as points of imputation), Duguit denies the existence of jural subjects and of their legal attributions. From this follows the impossibility of recognizing any jural tie, even more any organized superstructure. Indeed, organization, from the jural point of view, is nothing but a linking of differentiated and distributed competencies and offices, that is, an interpenetration of rights, granted for the accomplishment of definite functions. In denying the existence of " subjective " rights, in order the better to affirm the impossibility of detaching law from social reality, Duguit is led to eliminate one of the most important sectors from this reality and from the life of law attached to it : to wit, the sector of organized superstructures.

Yet this paradoxical conception, though it leads Duguit to a number of contradictions, also has its positive result : it impels him to reveal, in its full scope, the rôle of spontaneous and un-organized law, which he wrongly identifies with all jural regulation. It is this law which Duguit designates as objective law, emanating from the social solidarity and pre-existent to the expression of any will. Unorganized and spontaneous law " is anterior and superior to the State ", superior not only to the power of the State, but also to the State-order and State-institution themselves. The limits and the number of functions of the State depend on the variations of the spontaneous and unorganized law of the inclusive society ; likewise, the relationships and the hierarchy between the various other groups are modified, trans-formed, and transposed through the movement of this unorganized and spontaneous law. " The State (like all other groups) is subordinated to the law superior to it, which it does not create and which it cannot violate." " There cannot exist at one and the same time a law arising spontaneously and imposing itself because it corresponds to the social solidarity, and another law arising from an independent source." " The intervention of the legislator is powerless " to modify the spontaneous and un-organized law : " all it can do is more or less to formulate this pre-existing and mobile law, which will always overflow its limits."—Under these conditions Duguit obviously cannot accept the definition of law which attaches it to an organized compulsion and more generally to a rigid and predetermined constraint. " The notion of law is alien to the notion of constraint and existed at a time when constraint was impossible, at a time when it was even inconceivable." " What constitutes a jural regulation is not the existence of a constraint but the social reaction which provokes the violation of this regulation ", in other words, the social guarantee of the real. effectiveness of a ruling, and this cannot be adequately expressed in any predetermined measure against the delinquent.   It is for this reason that Duguit justly refuses to take the criterion of constraint as a fundamental pivot of his sociology of law.

Before going on to Duguit's differential and genetic sociology of law, the most instructive part of his work, we must consider two points. First, how does Duguit interpret the structure of the social solidarity in its relations with the law ?   Second, does he solely recognize a spontaneous and unorganized common law, emanating from the nation and international society, or does he also recognize a particularist spontaneous law ?

As to the first point, Duguit had started out by excluding from social reality, and also from solidarity, everything which we cannot observe by our " external sense " ; not only aspirations towards values and ideas (the spiritual level and the symbolic level of social reality) are eliminated by his analysis, but so are all psychic elements, either of collective or individual psychology. The solidarity was for him a pure " necessity ", " an exterior, physical, and vital necessity ", " an equilibrium of physiological needs and of services exchanged in consequence ".   Moreover, the law arising from this solidarity was only an " indicative " and not a norm ; it included neither obligation, nor appreciation, nor any element of redress.   Under these conditions it is very difficult, if not impossible, to understand how Duguit could oppose to the force and violence of the governing groups solidarity as well as the objective law emanating from it.   Thus, towards the end of his career, Duguit was forced, when he spoke of solidarity and law, to take into account the psychological element and aspirations towards justice.   " What makes law is the belief, profoundly penetrating the masses of men at a given epoch and in a given country, that a certain regulation is imperative, that is to say, just in accordance with the sentiment of justice prevalent at that moment."   " Law, in one word, is above all a psychological creation of society, determined by its material, intellectual, and moral needs."   But if Duguit concludes by admitting the psychic basis of solidarity and law and even the intervention of beliefs in justice, he persists throughout all his works in denying the existence of any collective mind and in recognizing the reality only of the individual consciousness.   This individualistic and nominalistic intransigence towards the psychological in a scholar who insists with so much vigour on " the primary and irreducible fact of society ", who brilliantly combats all aspects of individualism, and who went so far as to deny the existence of rights, might seem incomprehensible.

It can be explained, on the one hand, by his sensualism, which led him to the idea of a closed consciousness, shut up within itself, and drove him to consider the collective mind, if it did exist, as entirely transcendent, isolated from individual consciousness and turned in upon itself. Indeed, every possibility of an immanent collective mind, presupposing the interpenetration of awakening individual consciousnesses, is excluded by his premises. On the other hand, he introduced in his theory an unconfessed ideal, which incessantly substitutes in his thought for real solidarity, ideal solidarity consisting in the vision of a " perfect society " as " a vast co-operative workshop ", based on an equalitarian and anti-hierarchical mutualism. And this ideal does not admit any domination of the totality over the individual, any type of hierarchical totalitarianism, which seemed to him the inevitable consequence of recognizing a collective mind. " If there are only individual consciousnesses and wills," wrote Duguit characteristically, " we do not see how some could be superior and others inferior." The paradox of Duguit's nominalistic individualism, which has assuredly played a rôle in his negation of the legal reality of organized superstructure, is thus explained by the fact that in this way alone could his sensualism ward off the authoritarian totalitarianism which profoundly repelled him.

Duguit has sometimes been reproached with harbouring the naïve conception of a pre-established harmony in the social *milieu*, governed by a solidarity, engendering a common objective law, and thus excluding all antinomy and all conflict between groups (for example, the struggle between classes and professions). In this form the reproach is certainly not justified, for Duguit recognized narrow circles, each giving rise to its own " objective law " ; and this implies the possibility of conflict between equivalent frameworks of law and opens the path to a certain pluralism. Thus within the solidarity which constitutes a nation, there are " narrower solidarities " such as the union of the different branches of industry joined by collective conventions of labour, trade unions, co-operatives, public services, etc. ; and the autonomous frameworks of objective law which they engender may be called equivalent. Duguit, however, envisages only " concentric circles of solidarity ", and this permits him without difficulty to establish a stable hierarchy, such as is impossible for circles of the same magnitude, distinguished not quantitatively but by a difference in their functions (e.g., political group, economic group, religious group ; or within economic society, a group of producers or consumers, or groups made up of different professions, etc.). In this respect a certain tendency towards monist "harmonism" cannot be denied in Duguit, and this strongly debases his jural typology of groups, already rendered confused by the absence of all microsociological analysis and by the negation of the reality of organized superstructure.

The legal typology of present-day all-inclusive society, as elaborated by Duguit, proposes to describe the transformations of the system of law in the second half of the nineteenth and in the twentieth century. These transformations, according to the author, tend to show the decadence of State sovereignty in the domain of public law and, at the same time, of the autonomy of will in the domain of private law. These tendencies are particularly manifested in the progressive limitation of the rôle of the statute and of the contract.

The "Roman, Royal, Jacobin, Napoleonic, collectivist form" of State, associated with the principle of sovereignty, "which is only another name for the subjective right of the State to command", "is dying out", to be replaced by "functional federalism of decentralized public services", administering themselves under the control of the governings. Professional unions tend to be integrated in this co-operative federation of public services which will be the regime of to-morrow. This concretely realizes the substitution of the "government of men by the administration of things", foreseen by so many thinkers ; this substitution, as Durkheim already indicated, occurs at the same time as the scope of State functions increases. On the other hand, the "statute" as the predominant fashion of acknowledging the spontaneous and unorganized law, is strongly limited by other procedures of acknowledgment, equivalent to it, such as collective labour bargains, codes of various associations, special standards of various public services, etc.

The autonomy of the will is at the same time curtailed in numerous aspects : present-day law often protects social aims having no relation to an individual or collective subject (Rockefeller, Carnegie, Goncourt Foundations, philanthropic and municipal hospitals) ; "objective responsibility", not for a tort but for the risk imposed on workers by their labour, replaces subjective responsibility ; property is no longer a "*jus utendi et abutendi*", but a "social function", limited by an obligation to employ the ownership productively. This social function is often directed towards objective ends, in which case the property no longer belongs to a property subject. Most conspicuous, however, is the limitation of the contractual relation as a free accord between individual wills. A whole series of highly important obligations and relationships have arisen independently of such agreements between equivalent wills. The transactions, which are still called "contracts", such as transport contracts, contracts for gas, electricity, shipping, labour, public concessions, represent only unilateral adhesion to jural orders established in advance, without any will on the part of the supposed "contracting party". The contracting party merely accepts a jural order imposed on him and which he cannot modify ; he merely accepts integration into an already constituted group.

Thus, in our epoch, thanks to the parallel decadence "of the imperialist conception of public law", and "the individualistic conception of private law", there arises "a legal system which is realistic, socialistic and objectivistic", and which is itself "the product of a day in history. Even before the edifice is completed, the attentive observer will perceive the first signs of its destruction and the first elements of a new system." Is the system which is to-day being constituted "progress or retrogression ? We do not know. In social science, there is little meaning in such questions."

In attempting a critical appreciation of Duguit's sociology of law, let us, at the outset, note that a certain contradiction between its systematic part and its typological and genetic part seems obvious. On the one hand, indeed, Duguit states that State sovereignty never existed, on the other hand, that it is in the process of disappearing in our epoch ; in one place he says that the autonomy of the will was always a metaphysical fiction, in another he describes how it is being progressively limited by other means of establishing jural ties.

There is no doubt that the general tendency of Duguit's research is too dogmatic, too little impregnated with the principle of relativity. On the other hand, his genetic descriptions are obviously not free from a certain preconceived bias, a desire to prove that the present evolution of law confirms in all points of view his theoretical premises, his sensualist realism, the absence of rights and of jural subjects in the reality of law, etc. Other qualitative types of legal systems are thus presented as errors and aberrations, and the present type as the incarnation of truth, which conforms to Duguit's unconfessed ideal of a federalist and equalitarian mutualism. These deviations in Duguit's analyses and descriptions, contrary to his own methodological precepts, have certainly done great harm to his research, often preventing him from grasping the true sense of transformations and from describing them impartially. But to do Duguit justice, it must be said that sometimes the dogmatism and absolutism of his systematic conceptions are more apparent than real. For example, when Duguit says that the sovereignty of the State is always subjected to a law superior to and independent of the State, we might think that he was opposing to the dogma of the absolute sovereignty of the State, another dogma which takes no better account of the reality of facts, as his own. Yet if we distinguish between *jural sovereignty* (primacy of one framework of law over another) and *political sovereignty* (a State monopoly on unconditional constraint), as Duguit implicitly does, we are immediately aware that most important variations can intervene in the relationship between the State and the Law. When spontaneous and unorganized law, to which belongs jural sovereignty, attributes particularly broad competencies to the State (especially that of being the sole agency for formally acknowledging law), the State plays a considerable rôle in jural life ; and the combination of this rôle and of its political sovereignty leads to the wrong idea of absolute sovereignty. On the contrary, when the variations of spontaneous and unorganized law of the inclusive society give to groups other than the State competence to acknowledge common law, the rôle of the State in jural life diminishes, and we then speak of the " decadence of its sovereignty ". This, however, in no way affects its monopoly of unconditional constraint (political sovereignty), which it retains within the limits of its competence. Such examples might be multiplied.

We should pause to consider one point of Duguit's thinking which inspires more fundamental reservations. This is his negation of rights and of the jural reality of organized superstructures, and his consequent identification of the three following oppositions which in reality cross each other and do not correspond : organized and unorganized law, rights and objective law, individual and social law. Instead of bringing our author closer to social reality, this identification constantly removes him from it. In order to maintain contact, he finds himself obliged to recognize " constructive rules of law " fixed by formal methods of acknowledgment, as opposed to " normative rules of law ". This brings organizations back into jural life, for these procedures of acknowledgment are eminently associated with organizations. Moreover, he directly re-introduces organized law in speaking of the autonomous codes of organized groups and in attributing a prominent place in his typological and genetic sociology of law to " the co-operation of public services ", whose body is obviously rested on organized law. Organizations excluded from the law as pure mechanisms of violence, thus find themselves reintegrated in the jural sphere. And with the organizations reappear rights of which the organizations are the crystallized interpenetrations ; this takes place in Duguit under the form of recognizing " subjective jural situations ". Nor is this concept distinguished from the habitual concept of " subjective rights ", except by their greater dispersion and the absence of any tie between them. In reality, since rights of subjects are no more than attributions and competencies distributed by objective law, they vary according to its variations ; the more the objective law becomes organized, the more rights appear multiplied and interlocked. On the other hand, the more social law prevails over individual law, the more social rights of subjects prevail over individual rights of subjects.

Duguit's merit lies more in pointing out the existence of certain problems which have escaped Durkheim (spontaneous and unorganized law, law and the State) than in having solved them. Basically he continued, and applied to his time, the researches of the doctrinaires who pointed out the existence of a jural framework of society opposed to the State (particularly the " historical school of jurists " and Proudhon). Duguit's contribution to the sociology of law lies rather in his struggle against certain consecrated dogmas, and in his description of the recent transformation of law, than in a methodical study of the problems.

(B) If Duguit sought to turn the sociological synthesis of Durkheim towards a radical naturalistic realism, going as far as sensualism, *Emmanuel Levy*, on the contrary, tried to give it an exclusively subjectivist and idealist orientation. His books, *L'Affirmation du Droit Collectif* (1903), and *Les Fondements de Droit* (1929), present a sociology of law based solely on " collective beliefs ". Not all Levy's work belongs to the sociology of law. His systematic considerations underlining the mystical, alogical, supra-intellectual element in collective jural beliefs (" limited, however, by measures " springing from reason) are bound up with a description of immediate jural experience, approached only via the philosophy of law. On the other hand, Levy pursues the practical aim of developing a " socialist vision of law ", of finding the spirit of a future law in conformity with his convictions. These two aspects of his thought will not be touched upon here [1] as they are no part of his contribution to the sociology of law proper.

The effort of E. Levy bears almost exclusively on the problems of the genesis of law, applied to the present time. He describes recent transformations of law through variations of collective beliefs. In other words, he analyses the present evolution of the collective psychology of law. Touching neither the problems of microsociology of law nor of the jural typology of groups, Levy, in so far as he attempts a systematic sociology of law, limits himself to bringing out most vigorously the preponderant rôle of spontaneous, unorganized law, of which crystallized, rigid, organized law, always laggard, is no more than a reflection. This spontaneous law presents itself to Levy, on the one hand, exclusively in the form of " collective law ", on the other, as a phenomenon of consciousness, " our nature, our absolute ". This is a collective consciousness, to be sure, penetrating individual consciousness and realizing itself through " contacts " (we would say through interpenetrations of consciousnesses), free currents of the collective mind. Other strata of social reality (morphological basis, varied external behaviours, symbols, values, and ideals) are given no consideration.

Levy's total " dematerialization of law ", understood as the reduction of all jural life to beliefs alone, takes the form of an interpretation of all legal institutions under the aspects of " confidence ", " good faith ", " expectation ". Property, responsibility, contract, law of property and law of transaction, constitutional law, civil law, and penal law, thus all have the same purely psychological foundation. Property is only a possession of good faith ; responsibility arises from confidence abused ; contracts, whether individual or collective, are based on the confidence of the parties, reflecting the collective confidence in the validity of the contract ; public power also is only the result of the same collective confidence. Levy goes even further : confidence, good faith and the expectation arising from them, are reduced to credences. The psychology of " measured collective

[1] See concerning the whole doctrine of E. Levy, my *Expérience Juridique et la Philosophie Pluraliste du Droit* (1936), pp. 170–200.

beliefs " resolves itself, according to the author, entirely into " the horizon of credences "—the foundation of the unity of all the legal institutions which are in this way exclusively reduced to the law of transactions. Thus all jural relationships were dissolved into relations between persons sharing *credences,* essentially delimitative and negative relations presupposing isolated and opposed subjects ! Failing to envisage the problem of the forms of sociality, Levy ends by reducing all forms of sociality to " relations with others *(alter ego)* ", to relations of interdependence and convergence, ignoring partial interpenetrations and fusions and thus coming back to traditional individualistic conceptions.

His description of the present transformations of law suffers considerably from this double narrowness of viewpoint : from his reduction of all the social reality of law, of all society in general, to collective psychology alone, and his limitation of this psychology to a psychology of credence, a notion emanating from inter-individual and inter-groupal (inter-mental) psychology rather than from collective psychology in the true sense. The present transformations of law tend to replace the personal obligation of the debtor by the obligation of his property, and the right of property by the right of values, independent of all possession. " First the man was seized ; then his property, then his possessions, then goods to which he has only rights of credence, finally only values." " The domain of values is that of influences," and the right over values rests on essentially unstable law, the flux and reflux of the collective confidence in this or that factory, enterprise or industry, this or that national economy, this or that class, incessantly upsetting all rights and creating and destroying acquired riches and social situations.

The jural regime of values profoundly modifies the meaning of the contract and the structure of the State which evolve together. It likewise transforms responsibility, by everywhere reinforcing the collective character of these institutions. Thus the individual contract is entirely identified with collective bargains. " The contract does not concern only the relations between contracting parties, it influences all like values, merchandise, titles ; the principle that jural acts do not concern third parties is dead ; there is no longer any jural limit." " The collective bargains which engender credences of labour (considered as a value) on capital do not form an institution apart " ; when the collective bargain made by the trade union " projects its ray directly on all, members and non-members, present and future ", it only realizes the general tendencies of the evolution of the contract " under the legal regime of values ". Responsibility, under the same regime, becomes essentially a collective insurance against professional or other risk ; now it is only " an evaluation of the risk ". Finally, " the State, which has a well-defined existence in a society based on individual property, where its violence limits and unifies isolated right, participates (to-day) in the instability of values and resolves itself into collective acts of credence. " It is not possible to constrain values." " The State goes forward to the extent that credence, belief, hope, and assurance, which time makes and unmakes, apply to the future." The development of economic groupings, in turn, disperses the State, which at the same time is attacked in its traditional forms by the international organizations with which it is identified. " Thus the State develops until it destroys itself. We might say that it is everywhere." The State becomes " every social contact which causes and protects the law ". But under a regime of values, the contract possesses the same characteristics. Hence, at present, " there is a unity of the State and the contract ; the contractual State of capital and of labour mobilizes the territorial State and, like it, envelops us ". From this point of view, Levy protests against those who speak of a decadence of the contract and the State. They merely assume new forms as they become mutually identified and fuse directly with the collective acts of credence which triumph universally.

Levy has incontestably given us an extremely subtle description of the transformations of property and of responsibility in modern capitalist society, moving towards a law based on unstable values, influenced by and dependent on collective confidence and insurance against the risk arising from this instability. The " sphere of credence " and his limitation to collective (or rather inter-mental) psychology, however, have proved themselves far too narrow frames for an objective description of the modern evolution of law in all its complexity. Credences correspond only to a particular form of sociality—" relations with others (*alter ego*) " based on delimitation and equation—and cannot serve as a principle for explaining the different types of law secreted by the groups, which rest on the multiple forms of sociality by inter-penetration and partial fusion in the *We* : State law, autonomous group law, law of collective bargaining, etc. The identification of the individual contract with the collective bargains, and of both with the State, contradicts the most obvious jural and sociological realities. It creates an artificial harmonious unity in a sphere where are actually manifested the sharpest antinomies, conflicts, and struggles. At the same time it fails to resolve any concrete problem (e.g., of the reciprocal validity of the individual contract and the collective bargain, of the free trade unions or corporations integrated into the State as its organs, etc.). Levy's exaggeration of Durkheim's and Saint-Simon's thesis of the transformation of the State into an agency which administers only without governing, going so far as to identify it with all social contacts which engender law, reveals his monist and unitarist tendencies. Finally, his concentration on collective psychology alone, or rather on inter-mental psychology, eliminating all the conflicts between the different levels of depth of social and jural reality (in particular, between organized superstructures and spontaneous infra-structures) leads him to ignore the complex and varied equilibria between the principles of domination and of collaboration. All this confuses his notion of " collective law " and his description of the jural transformations moving towards the triumph of this kind of law. The incertitude and imprecisions are increased by the absence of any microsociological analysis, which would reveal within the spontaneous collectivity itself a struggle between mass, community, and communion (see below, Chapter II).

(C) In opposition to the sensualist realism of Duguit and the subjectivist idealism of Levy, *Maurice Hauriou* sought, like Durkheim, to achieve an " idealist-realist " basis for his sociology of law. Unlike Durkheim, however, he resolutely affirmed the irreducibility of the level of values and ideas intervening in social life, with regard to the collective mind which grasps them but which, affirming themselves as objectives, they resist. " It seems to me most important ", he wrote, " for social science to break with philosophical subjectivism and to rest on objective idealism, even if this should involve going back to Platonic idealism." These ideas and values, however, cannot be found by construction or demonstration, for they are particularized and incorporated in the facts which surround us. Only a broadened immediate experience enables us to grasp them. At the same time, the spiritual element of social life is not stable and immutable, but moving within Bergson's " creative duration ". This element, penetrating and spiritualizing all other dimensions of social life, gives the latter an accent of qualitative dynamism linked with creative duration. By applying these principles, combined with that of the essentially antinomic and pluralistic character of the social reality whose life consists of equilibria essentially mobile, unstable, and constantly upset (influence of Proudhon), Hauriou was able fundamentally to reconcile the sociology of law and the philosophy of law, without confusing the two. The point of junction between them is, according to him, the *institution*, and it is to this that Hauriou consecrated his principal efforts. From the philosophical point of view, it is in the institution that we must seek the objective jural values and ideas, in particular the multiple manifestations of the ideas of justice and order, constituting the ideal element of all law. From the sociological point of view, it is in the *institution* that an unstable equilibrium is reached between behaviours and between forces, and it is there that we observe the interpenetrations and convergences of consciousnesses in the service of ideas. It is in the institution that occurs " the transformation of the situation of fact into a jural situation ", that the reality of law becomes differentiated into several levels of depth ; that in several steps, " the drama of the personification of social groups " proceeds ; that the order of social law and the order of individual law are opposed, through the opposition between the " communion-institution " (" group-institution ") and the " relation-with-others " institution (" thing-institution "). Finally, from the point of view of jurisprudence, it is in the institution and the relations between institutions that the problem of the sources of positive law is resolved, the problem of primary or material sources, as well as of formal or secondary sources (procedures of acknowledgment).

Hauriou's sociology of law concentrating on an analysis of the levels of depth and the equilibria constituting the " institution ", that is, the social reality of law, is directed, on the one hand, towards systematical problems (conflicts and compromises between spontaneous dynamic law and organized, more rigid law, legal order of society, and legal order of the State), on the other hand, towards the problems relating to the jural typology of groups, the latter, unfortunately, not distinguished from the microsociology of law. Among Hauriou's numerous works, those most directly relating to the sociology of law are his *Science Sociale traditionnelle* (1896), *L'Institution et le Droit Statutaire* (1906). *Principes de Droit Public* (1st ed., 1910, 2nd modified ed., 1916), *La Souveraineté Nationale* (1912), *La Théorie de l'Institution et de la Fondation* (1925, in *Cahiers de la Nouvelle Journée*). His *Précis de Droit Administratif* (numerous editions) and his *Précis de Droit*

Constitutionnel (1st ed., 1923, 2nd ed. 1928) have, on the contrary, a more technical character. Moreover, his works after 1916 renounce the sociological relativism and, in direct contradiction to the most valuable contributions of his thought, mark a return to Thomist conceptions (stable hierarchy between the groups, *a priori* predominance of the State, the idea of the " personal founder " of the institution). Since we are concerned exclusively with sociology of law, we may properly ignore the dogmatic retrogressions of his later career.[1]

The institution, " this jural idea of a task or enterprise which realizes itself and endures in a social structure ", represents in its proper sense the purely spontaneous, dynamic and concrete element of all law ; it is the profoundest and least crystallized level of the social reality of law, opposed to all intellectual schematism, to any conceptual crust, just as " the idea of the task " (dynamic values) is opposed to the " aim ", which expresses it but incompletely, and just as the " urge " (*élan*) is opposed to the finality. The institution—this ever-renewed outpouring of spontaneous law—represents the " qualitative duration, the continuity, in brief, the real in the life of law ", its true " ontological " element. It is by digging down to this depth of reality that we find " an authority which neither appears personified " nor formulated. It is no longer either will, organization, constraint, or rule, but the institution itself " more objective than all rules ", even the most flexible—a spontaneous social guarantee of all jural ties. The more superficial levels of the social life of law, not having the same density of reality, the same degree of existence, are superimposed on the institution, which is their nourishing and lifegiving root, their primary source. These levels are the following : (1) the most superficial layer is that of rigid legal rules, fixed in advance by technical procedures of acknowledgment (such as statutes, codes, custom, judicial precedents, collective bargains, etc.) ; (2) next come the more flexible rules established *ad hoc* for concrete cases (rules established by " juridical police " or discretion and disciplinary law) ; (3) finally comes the institution itself manifesting the fact that " all law cannot be reduced to the rules of law ", which would remain chimerical if they were not rested on the impersonal and spontaneous authority of the institution, " materializing ideas and values in facts ", particularly the ideas of " Justice and social Peace ".

---

[1] See the detailed study of the evolution of Hauriou's thought in my *Idée du Droit Social* (1932), pp. 647-710.

Hauriou contrasts two types of institutions : " group-insti-tutions "—social bodies, and " thing-institutions "—" relations with others ". In this distinction he touches on the problem of forms of sociality as the cradles of different kinds of law, but since he does not distinguish between the microsociology and macro-sociology of law, he immediately abandons the question to identify it with that of " the internal and external jural life " of real collec-tive units. The group-institution " is a phenomenon of the *interpenetration* of individual consciousnesses, haunted by a common idea and thinking (more precisely grasping) one another ". This partial fusion of consciousnesses is qualified by Hauriou as the *communion*, a term to which he gives a threefold sense ; it desig-nates : a particularly intense collective mind ; a form of sociality realized in the " We " ; the necessity of participating in a spiritual element to arrive at this result. It is " the manifestations of com-munion among its members, interiorized in the framework of the idea of the task ", which make the institution a whole irreducible to the sum of its members, which is capable of binding them by law without their individual consent and thus engendering an order of " social law " or " institutional law " in the strict sense of the term. At the same time, the internal equilibrium of behaviours and forces, put at the service of the communion in the " idea ", gives birth to a " social power ", which is only an objective function of the group as an " irreducible whole ", pre-supposing in itself neither organization nor personification of the group, since it is pre-existent to them. Often a group-institution is concealed beneath a contractual form. Such is the case with " contracts of adhesion ", among others : labour contracts as well as collective bargains. In the latter case, the contracting parties (unions of workers or employers) are only agencies of the group-institution, their agreement being only a form of acknowledging the order of the pre-existing social law. In the former case the worker merely integrates himself within a pre-existing factory body and is subjected to its legal order.

The group-institution, to enjoy jural existence and to engender its autonomous framework of social law, does not have to be recognized in its exterior action as a " juridical person ". Thus, a circle of producers or consumers, an industry, a factory, a family are group-institutions not less than trade-unions, trusts, joint-stock companies, churches, States, etc. More than that, even when regarded as illicit and persecuted by the State, the group-institu-tions remain jural realities, for their interior life is independent of outside recognition. The conflicts between the autonomous orders of social law arise, then, from all sides, and there follows an intense social and jural pluralism. Thus Hauriou, in direct opposition to Duguit, proclaims the fundamental reality of groups as subjects of law, and seeks a sociological explanation for " the phenomenon of the juridical personification of wholes ". Here he again has recourse to his sociology of levels of depth, distinguishing four superimposed acts of the " drama of the personification of the group ", corresponding to four profundity levels of the same. The deepest layer of the group is the spontaneous " foundational communion ", underlying all organization and personification as " an objective individuality ". Next above is the organization emanating from it, representing the social power, whose competencies it distributes. This is the act of " incorporation " ; when the drama of personification stops here, the organized superstructure becomes an association of domination, insufficiently rooted in the " foundational communion " and transcending it. Thirdly comes the " interiorization " of the " incorporation " through its penetration by the underlying " communion " ; this implies the triumph of democratic collaboration within the organization and transforms the organized superstructure into a " collective moral person " enjoying the free adhesion of its members. This " moral person of the group " functions only for its internal use, as the subject of an order of law which it engenders. Finally, last act of the drama of the personification of the group, is the attribution to the group of a " juridical personality " for external use. Here the group presents itself " as a simple unit " subject to " relations with others ". This is the most superficial level of the jural reality of the group, its outer crust. " It is like a stage set in a theatre : the perspective is calculated to be seen by the audience, that is, from outside. But as soon as one enters the wings, i.e., the inside, the entire effect is confused." That is to say that because we were considering only this most superficial level of group reality and wrongly sought to apply it to its internal life, ignoring the sociological basis of the problem, we were induced to consider the personality of groups as fictitious and even to seek to eliminate this " fiction ". Hauriou's legal sociology in depth-levels, continuing and perfecting the work of Gierke, restores to groups their jural reality and personality, taking as a starting point the spontaneous group-institution " communion ", from which arise the principal stages of personification.

The thing-institution or " jural commerce " (transactions)

realizes, like all group-institutions, " objective ideas ", particularly the idea of commutative Justice. But its sociological foundation is different. Here we are concerned with " relations with others ", outside the group institutions, i.e., relations between groups or individuals remaining essentially distinct from one another, reciprocally separated, their tie going no further than *communication* as opposed to communion. Here we have to do more with inter-mental psychology than with a collective mind. A whole does not arise from " relations with others " from which no power can emanate. These inter-individual and inter-group relations with others, however, spontaneously realize ideas " having duration in a social *milieu* " and they, too, engender their own order of law, " the framework of individual law " manifested in contracts, transactions, credits, properties, etc. Individual law is a more superficial gradation of social reality of law than social law, for the former presupposes the latter. " The layer of group-institutions is the deepest and most primitive, it plays the same part as the granite stratum in the earth : it is its bony frame, which sustains the more recent layers resulting from alluvial deposits of relations with others." Of course, the contrast between objective law and rights is not involved here, for they are interwoven with individual law and social law. Moreover, the equilibrium between these two last orders of law (both simultaneously implying objective law and rights) is unstable and " has been several times reversed in the history of law ". The reversal itself springs from the variations of social law, which in this sense retains primacy. Here is an essentially relativist and sociological point of view, to which unfortunately Hauriou did not remain faithful in his last works.

The energy with which Hauriou insisted on the capacity of each group-institution to engender its own framework of law, the force with which he presented the problem of legal pluralism, inevitably led him to study the jural typology of particular groups. Indeed, at the very beginning of his career, he had raised the problem of the specificity of the types of group, such as territorial institutions (the State), institutions of economic activity and religious institutions (both non-territorial) and, finally, of institutions such as the nation and international society which embrace all others. The opposition between organized superstructures as " incorporations " and " moral persons ", the distinction between public services and " associations of public interest ", indicated a tendency towards complementary differentiation between the corresponding frameworks of law. On the other hand, the distinction between " political sovereignty ", belonging to the State and consisting in a " commanding power ", and " jural sovereignty " (sovereignty of law), belonging to extra-statist society, particularly to the nation, made it possible for Hauriou to envisage without prejudice reversals in the hierarchy of jural types of groupings.

This typology of groups, however, was not greatly developed by Hauriou and represents no perceptible progress. This fact is due to a number of causes. First, there is the total absence of microsociological consideration which, within each group, would take into account a plurality of forms of sociality combating and equilibrating one another in a particular way. Since the frameworks of law which correspond to the type of group are complexes of different kinds of law engendered by the forms of sociality, they cannot be characterized without taking the forms of sociality into consideration. In other words, since the true spontaneous institutions are not the groups but the microsociological elements, Hauriou deprived himself of the possibility of fruitfully studying the jural specificity of groups by reducing them to a single form of sociality—the " communion ". Finally, the same absence of microsociological analysis made him hesitate to admit that the general interest could be represented by other groups than the State, and towards the end of his career this hesitation led him (under the influence of St. Thomas) dogmatically to proclaim the State as " the institution of institutions ", the most perfect and eminent institution " embodying the common good ". Finally, retreating from his own earlier conceptions, he refused to consider economic society *en bloc* as a group-institution and identified it *a priori* with " jural commerce " (system of transactions), proclaiming rather unexpectedly that " the centre of gravity lies in the bourgeois State, presupposing the inviolability of private property and the freedom of the market ". It is, consequently, no surprise that the jural typology of groups is not the strong point of Hauriou's sociology of law, whose merit lies rather in his analyses in depth of the reality of law, revealing its " vertical pluralism " far more accurately than its " horizontal pluralism ". If, to these reservations, we add the fact that it is useless to seek in Hauriou a study of the legal types of inclusive society, let alone an examination of problems of a genetic order ; if we observe, moreover, how incessantly he falls back into traditional conceptions concerning the performance and immutability of the spiritual world (whose functional relations with the collective conducts embodying them remain unknown to him, just as he fails to take into account the distinction between objective ideas and values and those symbols which express them and which are directly dependent on the social medium in which they function), we can grasp the limits of Hauriou's sociology of law, which oscillates between a consistent functional relativism and an equally recurrent traditionalist dogmatism.

III. *Max Weber and Eugene Ehrlich*

Although the sociology of law of Max Weber (d. 1922), expounded in Chapter VII of Part 2 of his *Wirtschaft und Gesellschaft*, was published several years later than the works of the Austrian scholar, Eugene Ehrlich (d. 1923), Ehrlich's conceptions may be regarded as an anticipatory response to Weber's tendency to subordinate the sociology of law to dogmatic-constructive systematizations of jurisprudence. In fact, as we indicated in our Introduction, all sociology of law, according to Weber, is reduced to the study of the probabilities or " chances " of social behaviour, according to a coherent system of rules elaborated by jurists for a given type of society. Weber's contribution to the legal typology of inclusive societies, which he accomplished under the guidance of these principles, we will use in our systematic exposition of the problems of differential sociology of law. Weber's approach to the application to sociology of the method of interpretative understanding of the inner meanings of acts, a method conducive to a reconciliation and mutual collaboration of the sociology of law and the philosophy of law, was analysed in the Introduction.

Here, then, it will suffice to recall Weber's name, the better to emphasize the significance of Ehrlich's positions. They constitute a demonstration of the fact that, if the sociology of law takes its point of departure solely in systematization of the jurisprudence, it will not succeed in grasping its proper object, the integral jural reality which transcends any scheme of " abstract legal propositions " or rules of conflict. The method of posing the problem reveals a kinship between the sociology of law of Ehrlich and that of Hauriou. Without knowledge of each other, both sought the institutional base (*Einrichtungen*, Ehrlich called it) of the life of law. Ehrlich, however, is favourably distinguished from Hauriou by his more consistent, more relativist, sociological viewpoint, which is more deeply penetrated by history and freer from prejudices. On the other hand, Ehrlich is inferior to Hauriou in that, although he never falls into the sensualism which marked Duguit, he has a too unilaterally realistic tendency, which takes account neither of collective psychology nor of the spiritual strata of social reality.

In his three major works, *Beiträge zur Theorie der Rechtsquellen* (1902), *Grundlegung der Soziologie des Rechts* (1st ed. 1913, 2nd ed. 1928), and *Die Juristische Logik* (1919), Ehrlich sets himself a two-fold task. In the first place, he aims at showing that the so-called " science of law " elaborated by jurists is simply a relative " technique " aimed at transitory practical ends and, owing to its factitious systematizations, incapable of grasping anything except the most superficial crust of the effective reality of law. Secondly, Ehrlich aims at describing methodically and objectively, by a method apart from all technique, the integral and spontaneous reality of law in all its levels of profundity. But even more than in Hauriou, the vertical pluralism of levels replaces in Ehrlich any study of the horizontal pluralism of forms of sociality. This to the extent that Ehrlich winds up by connecting the problem of the differentiation of jural regulation exclusively to that of levels of depth, as though every kind of law did not have its own series of superimposed strata !

The fact that the dogmatic-normative " science " of law is not a science but merely a technique serving transitory ends of courts, becomes particularly obvious when it is recognized that certain principles habitually regarded as springing from an immutable " jural logic " are in reality only adaptations to quite concrete historic circumstances. Such are the three " postulates " of the " so-called logic of law " which, in reality, has nothing to do with a true logic. These are : first, the negation of freedom of judges, who are bound by propositions fixed in advance ; second, the dependence of all law on the State ; third, the " unity of law ", identified with the systematic coherence of jural propositions. Ehrlich shows that, as far as these points are concerned, we are dealing only with procedures of fiction, " mask " applied to the effective reality of law, techniques which make sense only at certain historical epochs of the life of law, the better to serve the needs of a centralized State and its benches (e.g., the Justinianian epoch or the eighteenth to nineteenth centuries). Far from depending on this " jural logic ", the sociology of law is called on to unveil its crude symbolism and to circumscribe its validity by revealing its provenance.

The first postulate—the binding of judges by abstract legal

propositions fixed in advance—is simply the result of the artificial absorption of foreign (Roman) law by a group of Continental European countries. Entirely unknown even in the Roman republic, not to speak of other types of societies (archaic, Oriental) this postulate also has not any validity in Anglo-Saxon countries. Under the influence of entirely novel and unforeseen institutions and cases confronting judges, it is being universally abandoned. The second postulate—that all law depends on the State—was adopted only with a view to the needs of absolute monarchy (*quod principi placuit habet legis vigorem*) and subsequently passed over into constitutional and republican regimes. One cannot hold Roman law entirely and solely responsible for this conception (e.g., as Duguit did). Ehrlich showed that Roman law of the classic republican period was as far as possible from the statist conception, which finds no expression until the epoch of the Cæsars. Mediæval jurists, on the one hand, contemporary jurists, on the other, under the combined influence of autonomous groupings inside the State and of international organizations outside it, have been forced to abandon this old fiction. The final postulate—the monastic unity of law—has been nothing but a technique favouring hypertrophic centralization of the State, a procedure consciously fictive and based upon deductive rationalism. This postulate so obviously conflicts with the living reality of law, wherein arises the jural autonomy of multiple social groups and the plurality of frameworks of particular circles, that in order to win acceptance for this fiction, recourse was made to the artificial constructs of *Begriffsjurisprudenz*, which boasted of transforming lawyers into " men who regard the essence as an accident and an accident as decisive ". In fact, even when the first two postulates had been accepted, as in the seventeenth and eighteenth centuries, the third secured a foothold only with difficulty and to-day has no use at all. In order to find a new technique, one adapted to circumstances, in order to apply new symbolic postulates, even lawyers are anxious that legal sociology should not be enslaved to a so-called " jural logic " which could only obstruct the field that must be surveyed.

Underneath the " abstract propositions " of law (*Rechtssätze*) usually elaborated by the State, underneath the concrete rules serving for the solution of conflicts (*Entscheidungsnormen*) among individuals and groups, elaborated generally by judges and jurisconsults (and which, because of their independence of abstract propositions, have been called " free law "), there exists a "law which rules society as an inner pacific order". This law, serving as a basis for all legal rules and being much more objective than any rule, constitutes the direct jural order of the society (*gesellschaftliches Recht*). The study of this order is the specific task of the sociology of law, which thus is marked off from jurisprudence, not only by its purely disinterested method, based on observation alone, but even more by its subject-matter. While jurists are concerned with the systematization of the first two levels of the reality of law, composing the surface, legal sociologists take for their point of departure the most profound layer of that reality, the spontaneous and direct inner pacific order of society itself, explaining the conditions which must intervene if superimposed rules are to emerge from this order. It is thus that the sociology of law makes obvious the thesis that " the centre of development of law in our epoch, as in every other, must not be sought in statutes, nor in jurisprudence, nor in doctrine, nor more generally in any system of rules, but in society itself".

" The pacific and spontaneous order of society " is defined as a criss-crossing of a plurality of inner jural orders of particular groups, exclusive of the State. Here Ehrlich approaches problems of the jural typology of particular groupings. He does not pursue the analysis, however, being devoted solely to a study of the layers of profundity of inclusive society. He gives only a very general characterization. " The inner order of groups is not only the primary historical form of all law, but this order is now, as always, a fundamental basis." " To-day, as always, the effectiveness of law depends chiefly on the mute action of associations which bind individuals together. Expulsion from an autonomous circle, whether it be church, trade union, party, family, trust or any other group, loss of a job, of credit, of a clientèle, are the most real means of fighting infractions of law." " Whatever the State does in addition, to sanction law on its own part, has infinitely lesser importance, and one could maintain with much reason that the jural order of society would not be threatened in the least if these sanctions simply did not exist." Furthermore, abstract legal propositions formulated by the State, " comparable to the foam that appears on the surface of water " are addressed essentially only to State courts and other State organs. Groups and individuals live in total ignorance of the content of these propositions. They know only the spontaneous jural order of society, composed of " institutions ", in regard to which every rule is simply a superficial crust, a projection. It is, then, " only a tiny part of the jural order of society which may be affected by State legislation, and the greatest part of spontaneous law develops quite independently of abstract legal propositions ''. The latter, constituting the most static level of law, even when they affect a sector of spontaneous law of society, always lag behind it. Thus the most important events of jural life—abolition of mediæval serfdom, liberation of the English peasants, transformation of the law of private property into a law of commanding and governing masses of wage-earners, the formation of trade unions and trusts, the development of collective bargaining, etc., have taken place quite independently of the abstract propositions of law. For long, they were altogether ignored by State legislation, which began to be aware of them only after considerable delay. In the last analysis, State law is not only impotent with respect to the law of the society, but in cases of conflict it invariably winds up by curbing itself; here we are dealing with nothing less than a tension between the most superficial and the most profound layers of the reality of law.

The superimposition on the pacific and spontaneous jural order of society of rules for reaching decisions in cases of conflict, and the superimposition on top of these rules of abstract legal pro-positions, as well as the variations in these relations among the three levels of the reality of law, have to be explained sociologi-cally, according to Ehrlich. Here he touches on the problems of the jural typology of all-inclusive societies, although he does not stress the point. Rules for decisions presuppose conflicts among groups and individuals, whose interests and competences they delimit. Here we are dealing more with a question of war than of peace, with collective or individual subjects confronting each other as disconnected units. In order that these rules may clearly detach themselves from the spontaneous and pacific order of society, there must take place a differentiation between the individual and the group and there must arise a multiplicity of equivalent groups. On the other hand, these rules for reaching decisions being more precise, more fixed, more abstract than the spontaneous jural order, they presuppose a certain development of rationalism, of reflective thought based on logic. The measure of the isolation of the individual from the group and the plurality of equal groupings being a relative phenomenon admitting a series of nuances and degrees, the relations between the rules of decision and spontaneous law are different in different societies and his-torical circumstances. This fact Ehrlich also fails to stress. The superimposition on the rules of decision of abstract legal propositions (which do not directly correspond to the establishment of the State, for even after its arising, the State had not a long time to intervene in the life of law), presupposes the need of the highest possible degree of jural stability and generality. This need shows itself, for instance, in the struggle of the territorial State against feudalism and in the development of modern capitalism based on reinforced rationalism claiming to deduce all the particularities of concrete rules from a single principle. Of course, stability, unity, and generality allow varying nuances and degrees, and never achieve any but very relative results ; thus the rôle of abstract legal propositions and of the State which formulates them, is very different in different societies and epochs. We live, according to Ehrlich, in an epoch in which this rôle tends anew to be diminished.

The essential defect in Ehrlich's sociology of law, a very interesting one and one which has had a particularly profound influence in the United States,[1] is the total lack of microsociological and differential analysis, that is to say any accounting for the forms of sociality and jural types of groupings. Ehrlich's sociological and jural pluralism is an exclusively vertical one. It leads him to confuse under the terms " law of society " (*Gesellschaftsrecht*) a series of different kinds of law, and this confusion is repeated with respect to rules of decision and abstract propositions. According to him, whatever is " institutional " or spontaneous in law, comes from society opposed to State and has the character of internal law of associations (*Verbandsrecht*). Contractual law, law of property, and law of unilateral domination are only masked forms of law of society and the objective and spontaneous order of individual law (interindividual and intergroupal) does not exist. At the same time, the State is seen only under the form of abstract legal propositions, as though there were not levels of depth within the order of the State and as though there did not exist a spontaneous political union distinct from other spontaneous unions (economic, religious, etc.). The absence of microsociology and jural typology of groupings leads in Ehrlich to sharply monistic conceptions. Moreover, the law of society is artificially impoverished by being confined solely to the sphere of the spontaneous, as though it did not have its own abstract propositions in autonomous statutes of groups, and its

[1] See the English translation of Ehrlich's *Sociology of Law* (1935), with introduction by Roscoe Pound.

own rules of decision elaborated in the functioning of boards of arbitration and similar bodies.

After a denial of opposition between law corresponding to the We and law corresponding to relations with others (I, you, he, they), this opposition reappears under the form of rules of decision in cases of conflict, distinct from the inner pacific order of society. But this identification of kinds of law with levels of depth is seen to be artificial and unfortunate. Indeed, it neglects the fact that every kind of law has its own levels, and that courts are concerned with the " inner pacific order " of groups as well as with inter-individual (or inter-groupal) law. This latter has itself an institutional and spontaneous foundation. Instead of studying the mutual crossing of levels of depth of the reality of law, with kinds of law differentiated according to the forms of sociality, and with frameworks distinguished according to the types of groups, Ehrlich has recourse to parallelisms and artificial identifications. Thus he simplifies the complex web of the life of law. No doubt his indifference to the spiritual elements of social and jural life, i.e., to the symbolic patterns, values and ideas inspiring the collective conduct (particularly to the various aspects of the ideal of Justice), in short, his excessive positivism, con- tributed to this uniformization of the subject matter of the sociology of law. This is also the reason why he did not reach any precise definition of law, differentiating it from moral, religious, æsthetic, and educational regulations. The failure of this indispensable differentiation, which was not connected with his principal discoveries in the field of the sociology of law, but only with his philosophical prejudices, has nevertheless com- promised some of his important conclusions.[1]

B. THE AMERICAN FOUNDERS

In the introduction we studied the stages in the approach of American sociology towards the inclusion of problems of sociology of law. The very development of this discipline in the United States is due to the efforts of jurists.

I. O. W. HOLMES. The preparatory phase is linked with the name of Mr. Justice Holmes, a close friend of the great American philosopher, William James. Already in his *Common Law* (1881), and again in a series of important studies (of which the principal one is *The Path of the Law*, 1897, reprinted in *Collected Legal Paper*,

[1] For criticism of the conceptions of Ehrlich see my *Le Temps Présent et l'Idée du Droit Social* (1932).

1921), Holmes gave the signal for what Professor Aronson has aptly called " the sociological revolt in jurisprudence " in the United States. Rejecting with equal vigour both the logical-analytical and the historical schools, Holmes insisted on the necessity for jurists to lean in their work on the disinterested and empirical study of living and actual social reality, such as is made by the social sciences, and particularly by sociology. " If your subject is law, the roads are plain to anthropology, the science of man, to political economy, the theory of legislation, ethics." " It is perfectly proper to regard and study the law simply as a great anthropological document. The study pursued for such ends becomes science in the strictest sense." This science in the strictest sense from which the sound jurisprudence " should draw its postulates and its legislative justification ", and which can be only sociology, is not, however, limited to the study of external conduct. " It is proper to resort to it to discover what ideals of society have been strong enough to reach that final form of expression (which is law) of what have been the changes in dominant ideals from century to century." Thus " the scientific study of the morphology and transformation of human ideas in the law " enters in the field of positive sociological study of the latter. And how could it be otherwise if " the first requirement of a sound body of law is that it should correspond with the actual feeling and demand of the community ", and if " the very considerations which judges most rarely mention, are the secret rule from which law draws all the juice of the life. I mean, considerations of what is expedient for the community concern." " We live by symbols and what shall be symbolized by any image of the right depends upon the mind of him who sees it." " A law embodies beliefs that have triumphed in the battle of ideas and then have translated themselves into action." After these quotations there can be no doubt about the exact significance of the well-known sentence of Holmes : " The life of the law has not been logic, it has been experience ", experience the content of which must be described by the sociology of law. This experience includes not only external sense data and not only behaviour, but also symbols and spiritual meanings inspiring social conducts.

How does it come about, however, that the ideas of Holmes have inspired not only representatives of " sociological juris-prudence " (Pound, Cardozo, Brandeis, and Frankfurter, etc.), but equally partisans of " legal realism " who hold to the exclusive description of " official behaviour ", " of that which judges do " and decide in each concrete case, and that even a philosopher, an adversary of behaviourism, has felt obliged to accuse Holmes of succumbing to that temptation? [1]   Three elements in Holmes's thought pushed him in a direction contrary to his major inspiration.   First, his definition not only of jurisprudence but of law itself as a " prophecy of what the courts will do " limited his vast programme of legal sociology by concentrating his attention on the description of a single level of depth of the social reality of law, that related to the activity of courts.   On the other hand, his insistence on the entire independence of law from any moral credo, due both to this purely technical conception and his exclusively individualistic interpretation of morals, permitted misinterpretations of Holmes's position, against which he protested in vain.   Finally, the identification of law and jurisprudence, the latter being regarded only as a generalization of the former, entailed a lack of clarity as to the relations of jurisprudence and legal sociology, which he was inclined to identify with each other.   Desiring to make of jurisprudence, which is an *art*, a descriptive science in the narrow sense of the term, Holmes rather transformed involuntarily the authentic science of legal sociology into an art, while eliminating the aims of the effective art of jurisprudence.

These internal difficulties, which in some measure are characteristic of the whole development of legal sociology in the United States, were, however, much mitigated by the incomparable finesse and flexibility of Holmes's thought and particularly by his conception that tribunals themselves deal with the spontaneous law of society, which imposes itself on them.

II. Roscoe Pound.   The sociology of law in the United States has had its most elaborate and detailed, its most broadly conceived and subtle expression in the rich scientific productions of Dean Pound, the unchallenged chief of the school of " sociological jurisprudence ".   Pound's thought was formed by a constant confrontation of sociological problems (problems of social control and social interest), philosophical problems (pragmatism and experimental theory of values), problems of legal history (the various measures of stability and flexibility in the types of jural systems), and, finally, problems of the work of American courts (the element of administrative discretion in judicial process). This multiplicity of centres of interest and of points of departure aided Pound to broaden and clarify ever more the vast per-

[1] See M. R. Cohen, *Law and Social Order* (1933), pp. 204-6.

spectives of legal sociology and to develop gradually its different aspects.

In his earlier programme for this discipline, Pound, despite the broadness of his views, gave preference to practical aims : " (1) To make study of the actual social effects of legal institutions and legal doctrines ", and consequently " to look more to the working of the law, than to its abstract content " ; (2) To promote " sociological study in connection with legal study in preparation of legislation ", and consequently to regard " law as a social institution which may be improved by intelligent effort discovering the best means of furthering and directing such effort " ; (3) To make " study of the means of making rules effective " and " to lay stress upon the social purposes which law subserves rather than upon sanction " ; (4) The study of " sociological legal history ", that is " of what social effect the doctrines of law have produced in the past and how they have produced them " ; (5) " To stand for what has been called equitable application of law " and " to urge that legal precepts are to be regarded more as guides to results which are socially just and less as inflexible moulds " ; (6) " Finally, the end, towards which the foregoing points are but some of the means, is to make effort more effective in achieving the purposes of law " (see " The Scope and Purpose of the Sociological Jurisprudence ", *Harvard Law Review*, 1912, vol. 25, pp. 513–16). Incontestably, but two of the six points of this programme relate to theoretical judgments concerning the social reality of law : " the study of social effects of law " and the " sociological study of legal history ". All the other points are applications of results of the sociology of law to the art of judge or legislator. Certain studies of Pound which followed his first programme, particularly " A Theory of Social Interest " (*Proceedings of the American Sociol. Soc.*, vol. 25, p. 361, 1913), " The Administration of Justice " (*Harvard Law Review*, vol. 26, 1912–13), " Courts and Legislation " (*Amer. Pol. Rev.*, vol. 7, p. 361, 1913) reinforced the impression of the concentration of Pound's attention on the art of jurisprudence, which he interprets in a consciously teleological way, believing that the connection of jurisprudence, as " social engineering ", with sociology is best realized by social ends held by the jurist. Pound's insistence on social interests, which has sometimes altogether mistakenly been regarded as a leaning towards social utilitarianism, a view he has always really rejected, as evidenced by his opposition to Ihering, has in fact been for him only a method of inducing courts to heed the reality of particular social groups and their specific orders. The conflicts among these groups can be resolved only by jural procedures which combine administrative discretion, flexible law of standards, and the application of more rigid rules of common law.[1]

This original orientation of Pound's sociology of law on practical ends has, moreover, been considerably surmounted by the first series of Pound's important works. In these works [2] he has forcefully shown the sociological relativity of jural techniques, categories, and concepts. He has described this relativity with reference to types of inclusive societies and of the particularity of their cultural traditions. Thus he has provided a sociological analysis of the English and American types of common law, now classic. He has brought out the variations in the concepts of law itself, as a function of types of society and corresponding legal systems. He has described the variation of theories on the relation between law and morals as a function of the social types. He went even further in posing the problem of the sociological foundations of the knowledge of law. At the same time, Pound undertook a study of the actual transformations of law, paralleling that of Léon Duguit but less dogmatic. Thus he has advanced the genetic sociology of law as applied to the type of contemporary society.

Here are some of his conclusions. " Our common law policy presupposes an American farming community of the first half of the nineteenth century ; a situation as far apart as the poles from what our legal system has had to meet in the endeavour to administer justice to great urban communities at the end of the nineteenth and in the twentieth centuries." " Demand for socialization of law in the United States has come almost wholly, if not entirely, from the city." But " through all vicissitudes the supremacy of law, the insistence upon law as reason (and not arbitrary will) to be developed by judicial experience in the decision of cases and the refusal to take the burden of upholding right from the concrete each and put it wholly upon the abstract all . . . have survived. These ideas are realities in comparison whereof rules and dogmas are ephemeral appearances " (*The Spirit of the Common Law*, pp. 124, 129, 216). The various definitions of law and the various philosophies of law " were in the

---

[1] See " Jurisprudence ", in H. E. Barnes, *History and Prospects of the Social Sciences* (1925), pp. 468–74.

[2] *The Spirit of the Common Law* (1921), *Introduction to the Philosophy of Law* (1922), *Interpretation of Legal History* (1923), and *Law and Morals* (1924).

first instance an attempt at a rational explanation of the law of the time and the place or of some striking elements therein. These theories necessarily reflect the institution which they were devised to rationalize even though stated universally." To-day " judicial empiricism and legal reason will bring about a workable system along new lines ", but generally we can observe that law and law definitions and theories are " a continually wider recognizing and satisfying of human wants and claims or desires through (jural) social control with the less sacrifice (of them) " (*Introduction to the Philosophy of Law*, pp. 68–9, 16–49, 283, 99). The concrete relations of law and morals, which are always linked, but the intensity of whose connection constantly varies, as well as their reciprocal positions in the system of social control, depend on the types of society and corresponding jural and moral beliefs (*Law and Morals*, pp. 115–17 and *passim*).

The different interpretations of legal history (ethical, religious, political, ethnological, economic, pragmatic, etc.) are themselves conditioned by concrete situations of a type of society (*Interpretation of Legal History, passim*). The transformations of our actual legal system are the following :

(1) Limitations of the use of property ; (2) Limitations upon freedom of contracts ; (3) Limitations on the power of disposing of property ; (4) Limitations upon the power of the creditor or injured party to secure satisfaction ; (5) Transformation of idea of liability in the sense of a more objective base ; (6) Judicial decisions in regard to social interests, by limiting general rules to profit of flexible standards and discretion ; (7) Public funds should respond for injuries to individuals by public agencies ; (8) Reinforced protection of dependent members of the household.

All these transformations are " roads to socialization of the actual law ". (*The Spirit of the Common Law*, pp. 185–92).

While thus giving us a deep insight into the jural typology of inclusive societies and genetic sociology of law, Pound simultaneously contributed to problems of systematic sociology of law. By routes other than those of Hauriou and Ehrlich, he arrived at the distinction among various levels of depth in the social reality of law. He has distinguished between (*a*) administration of justice or the judicial process, (*b*) law, (*c*) legal order, and (*d*) jural values (" the ideal element of law "). He has brought out that, in law itself, the level of rules (rigid law) is other than the level of principles, conceptions, and standards (flexible law) or, finally, discretionary law based upon intuition (*Introduction to the Philosophy of Law*, pp. 114–41 ; *Interpretation of Legal History*,

pp. 153–7 ; *History and System of the Common Law*, pp. 4–16).
Thus he has shown the fact, paramount for sociology of law,
that the reality of law is not reducible to abstract patterns, and
that to study it in full it is necessary to go beyond symbols and
into that which they symbolize.

In a more recent series of works [1] Pound has insisted with
particular vigour on the fact that social reality, and especially
the social reality of law, is penetrated by " ideal elements ",
" spiritual values ".[2] Thus sociology of law is impossible for
him except as part of what we have proposed to denominate the
sociology of human spirit or of the noetic mind.   Since, according
to Pound, there are combined in the social reality of law " social
utility " and " ideal elements ", " social needs, interests, and
adjustments " and " spiritual values ", he arrives with Hauriou
at an *ideal-realistic* conception of law.   A synthesis of idealism
and pragmatism here comes to his help and guides him towards
visualizing jural values in their concrete particularizations and
their functional relations with historical social structures and
situations.

Despite all these rich sociological suggestions, however, and
despite the tenacity of his functionalist, relativist, ideal-realist
orientation, it does not seem that Pound, here sharing Hauriou's
fate again, arrives at an entirely accurate definition of the aims
and methods of the sociology of law.   Firstly, in all his works
he has been faithful to his initial identification of the sociology
of law with jurisprudence, the jural art or technique.   Now,
even that jurisprudence which is oriented on sociology (" sociological jurisprudence ") remains an art, bound to a particular
situation, a particular system of law.   Pound well takes account
of this fact as well as of the necessarily teleological nature of all
jurisprudence, the " sociological jurisprudence " even more than
all other types of jurisprudence.   But instead of clearly setting
apart the sociology of law which, as a science based on reality

---

[1] *The Formative Era of American Law* (1938), *The History and the System of the Common
Law* (1939), *Contemporary Juristic Theory* (1940), as well as his polemical articles against
the legal realists, " The Call for a Realist Jurisprudence ", *Harvard Law Review* (1931),
pp. 697–716 ; " Twentieth Century Ideas as to the End of Law ", *Harvard Legal
Essays* (1934), pp. 357–75 ; " The Ideal Element in American Judicial Decisions ",
Harvard Law Review, vol. 45 (1932), " Century of Social Thought ", in *American Juristic
Thinking in the 20th Century* (1939), pp. 143–72.

[2] The idealistic element in Pound's thought has been well stressed in M. Aronson's
article, " Roscoe Pound and the Resurgence of Juristic Idealism ", in the *Journal
of Social Philosophy* (1940), vol. VI, No. 1, pp. 47–83.   Aronson, however, somewhat
exaggerates the idealistic element in Pound's thought and does not sufficiently bring
out the latter's orientation towards " ideal-realism ".

judgments, must be independent of all estimation and goals of jurisprudence, he attributes, on the contrary, practical ends to the sociology of law itself and thus makes it, too, teleological. He even conceives of profiting from his valuable demonstrations concerning the ideal-realistic structure of the jural fact, to conclude that one cannot deal with law, even sociologically, except in a teleological fashion. Contrary to Durkheim and Weber (who particularly clarified this question [1]), Pound does not notice that one can deal with the values which realize themselves in social facts and still abstain from pronouncing judgments of value and appreciation. He fails to see here the difference between the object and the method of handling it. Nor does he distinguish between philosophical reflection which verifies the objectivity of spiritual values, and sociological description which abstains from discussing the authenticity and objectivity of values whose realization it observes. A certain confusion of value judgments and reality judgments thus creeps into Pound's sociology of law. It is reinforced by the fact that, when he speaks of the ideal elements of law, he does not distinguish clearly between jural and moral values. Or, we might better say that he is inclined, following a well-founded tradition, to push justice towards a moral ideal. The consequence in his thought is an opposition between justice and "social order" (security, stability), the latter acquiring with him, moreover, the character of an absolute, non-relative principle, a unique and monistic "order". From all this there arises a certain dogmatic and simultaneously moralizing trend directly menacing to the viewpoint of the method in the sociology of law. If we add Pound's tendency to look for the best medium between extremes (justice and order, reason and experience, uncertainty and security), conscientiously following where Aristotle trod, in order to achieve a harmonious and stable wedding of irreducible antinomies, we have an account of the danger to which Pound's sociology of law is exposed by his method. As one fruit of this teleological orientation may be cited Pound's refusal to abandon the belief in the necessary and *a priori* pre-eminence of the State over other groups. This goes so far that he identifies "legal order" with the State order, for all civilized society, and, more generally, in speaking of order and security in law, thinks of a unique and absolute order. His sociology of law does not take sufficient account of particular

---

[1] Cf. Introduction *supra* and Weber's famous essay, " Über die ' Wertfreiheit ' in Sozialwissenschaften ", in *Abhandlungen zur Wissenschaftslehre* (1922).

groupings except in the formula " of social interests ", which must be harmonized and balanced by this unique order. He overlooks the fact that each group has its order, its framework of law, its own jural values, as well as the fact that relations among these orders are constantly changing according to the types of inclusive society, in regard to which the State itself is merely a particular group and a particular order! This conception even prevents him from visualizing problems of the micro-sociology of law and differential legal typology of particular groupings. Even when Pound seems to overcome this view he returns to it directly by proclaiming the *a priori* supremacy of the State order.[1] Here we reach the limits of relativism and of the functional point of view, which have marred the otherwise so subtle and rich sociology of law of Roscoe Pound.

III. BENJAMIN CARDOZO. Like that of Holmes and Pound, Justice Cardozo's sociology of law sets out from reflections on the need for renovating actual juridical technique by closing the gap between it and the living reality of contemporary law. As with them, and even more so, his attention is first of all concentrated on the activity of the courts. His first work, significantly entitled *The Nature of the Judicial Process* (1921, 8th ed., 1932), aims at showing that " the growing uncertainty of the judicial decision " is an inevitable manifestation of the fact that the judicial process is "not discovery, but creation", creation intensified by the actual situation of the life of law (pp. 166, 115). This situation consists in the fact " that for every tendency one seems to see a counter-tendency, for every rule its antinomy " (p. 25). These antinomies are imposed on courts not only by fissures and gaps in legal rules, not only by the fact " that there are few rules, there are chiefly postulates, standards and degrees " (p. 161), but also by the spontaneous conflict of regulations in society itself. For " back of precedents are the basic juridical conceptions, which are the postulates of juridical reasoning, and further back are the habits of life, the institutions of society, in which these conceptions had their origin and which by a process of interaction they have modified in turn " (p. 20). Thus it is sociology of law

---

[1] The following text is typical of Pound : " We must not forget that law is not the only agency of social control. The household, the church, the school, voluntary organizations, professional associations, social clubs and fraternal organizations, each with their canons of conduct, do a greater or lesser part of the social engineering. But the brunt of the task falls on the legal order—the regime of ordering human activities and adjusting human relations—through political organized society—by application of its force " (see *Contemporary Juristic Theory*, 1940, p. 80 ; *Introd. to Philosophy of Law*, 1922, p. 99 ; *History and System of Common Law*, 1939, pp. 3–5.)

alone which, by seeking the " living law " at its source, in the life of society itself, can explain the difficulties actually facing judges. All the more so since the freedom of judges to make creative decisions is strictly limited by rules and codes, " the accepted standards of the right conduct " which " find expression in the *mores* " of society and of particular groups (pp. 73, 112). " Life may be lived, conduct may be ordered, it is lived and ordered for unnumbered human beings without bringing them within the field where the law can be misread " (p. 130). Thus, finally, not the judges but " life itself fills open spaces in the law " (p. 113). " If judges have woefully misinterpreted the mores of their day, or if the mores of their day are no longer those of ours " they can only submit to new spontaneous regulations springing out of society itself (p. 152). " I do not mean to range myself with the jurists who seem to hold that in reality there is no law except the decision of the courts " (p. 124). Thus, Cardozo arrives at this conclusion : " Law and obedience to law are facts confirmed every day to us all in our experience of life. . . . We must seek a conception of law which realism can accept as true " (p. 127).

The quotations which I have given, show, it seems to me, that, already in his first work, Cardozo constantly goes beyond the conception of the sociology of law as being exclusively a subsidiary art of judges for the introduction into interpretations of social goals inspired by value judgments.

It is, moreover, through this narrow conception of " sociological method " complementing logical method by analogy, as well as the method of tradition in the judicial process, that Cardozo starts his book and at some points (pp. 10–31, 76, 94) returns to it. It is this teleological-sociological tendency which drives Cardozo to seek, by calling on judicial precedents, a point mediate between the extremes of movement and stability, uncertainty and security. On the other hand, the tendency towards the description of the spontaneous law of society itself, drives him to recognize that in social reality of law " nothing is stable, nothing is absolute. All is fluid and changeable. There is an endless becoming. We are back with Heraclitus " (p. 28). The hesitation of Cardozo between these two tendencies is due not only to the fact that he did not separate sociology of law from " sociological jurisprudence ", but also and more fundamentally to the fact that he did not recognize " the accepted standards of the right conduct in the society and the particular groups " as belonging to the domain of law properly so called.　After having brought out their primordial rôle in the "judicial process" and in the life of society, he designates them by the ambiguous term, "mores", which he contrasts with law properly so called. Though, in polemizing with Austin and Holland, he stresses that the distinction between "strict law" and broader and more flexible regulations is more or less a "verbal disputation" (p. 133), and he wrote : "Not for us the barren logomachy that dwells upon the contrast between law and justice and forgets their deeper harmonies" (p. 134).　He hesitates, however, to include the "mores of society", which he recognizes himself as the deepest level of law in the realm of law.

From this point of view, his second book, *The Growth of the Law*, 1927, is especially typical.　On the one hand, the tendency towards the sociology of law in the true sense increases.　Cardozo writes : "The inquiry about mores is a branch of social science calling for a survey of social facts", rather than a branch of philosophy and jurisprudence themselves ; "yet the two subjects converge and one will seldom be fruitful unless supplemented by the other.　The method of sociology involves with growing frequency the approach from other angles" (pp. 112–13).　The different juridical techniques themselves are conditioned by the ages and the situations in the society (p. 108).　At the same time, justice itself "may mean different things to different minds and at different times" (p. 86).　"We can learn whether a rule functions well or ill by comparison with a standard of justice or equity, known or capable of being known to us all through an appeal to everyday experience" (p. 123).　Even more "often. the question before the courts is concerned with the rules that are to regulate some business enterprises or transactions.　The facts of economic or business life are the relevant considerations." Thus, "the principles and rules of law have their roots in the customary forms and methods of business and fellowship, the prevalent convictions of equity and justice, the complex of belief and practice which we style the mores of the day" (p. 53).

But despite all this, Cardozo refuses to follow the example of Duguit, Krabbe, and Ehrlich and to include the deepest social reality of law in law itself !　Criticizing the authors cited, he states that "mores" become law only by being sanctioned or being capable of sanctioning by courts (pp. 48–52).　He leans on Holmes's definition of law as a "prophecy of what the courts will do" (pp. 33–46).　In order not to limit too much the field of study of the sociology of law, however, he gives a broadened interpretation of this conception. It suffices, according to Cardozo, to establish with sufficient probability that mores may be and some day will be " embodied in a judgment " to consider them as law (pp. 30–8). " They may lack an official imprimatur, but this will not always hinder us from resting on the assumption that this omission will be supplied when occasion so demands " (p. 53), "what permits us to say that the principles are law when there is the force or persuasiveness of the prediction that they will or ought to be applied " (p. 43). If this means only that a distinction must be made between mores having a jural structure and those lacking it, and that the possibility of their application by the bench is only an external verification of the mentioned internal difference, Cardozo's conception represents a considerable portion of truth. It does not, however, show that the difference between jural regulation, in all its levels of depth, and other kinds of regulation, lies in the difference in the values served, and that there are jural regulations so diffuse as to be unable ever to reach the bench. One may, however, interpret Cardozo's thought in a narrower sense to mean that the quality of law is effectively given to a regulation by the court as an organ of the State. Now in a more subtle way this conception relapses into all the difficulties of those who forget that the bench, as well as the State itself, presupposes a law which organizes them and determines their jurisdiction. Nor can we overlook the fact that the rôle and activity of the courts in the life of law is essentially variable. From this viewpoint, Cardozo's hesitations are only the result of his orientation of the sociology of law on problems of juridical technique, when the inverse orientation alone would be logical. These hesitations limit his deep vision of the social reality of law and, in the domain of the sociology of law proper, lead him back to teleological considerations. There results a desperate effort to hold " the balance between flexibility and certainty " (p. 109). As though this balance itself were not absolutely variable and conditioned sociologically according to the different types of "normative facts" of law, which our discipline is to study with complete objectivity and independence !

Cardozo's last book, *Paradoxes of Legal Science* (1928), the most impressive of all his works, takes one more step towards a sociology of law independent of juridical technique (jurisprudence) and serving as a basis thereof. The sociology of law must be guided by the consciousness, writes Cardozo in this book, that " law defines a relation not always between fixed points but often, indeed, oftenest between points of varying position " (p. 11). In it must dominate " the principle of relativity ". This relativism is augmented further by the fact that " the reconciliation of the irreconcilable, the merger of antitheses . . . are the great problems of the law ". " Manners and customs (if we may not label them as law) are at least a source of law " (p. 15). " The pressure of the mores may fix direction of the law " (p. 30). The description of the relations between strict law and mores, and even of those between jural norms and moral norms (pp. 37–41), must be freed " from the tyranny of concepts. They are tyrants rather than servants, when treated as real existences and developed with merciless disregard of consequences to the limit of their logic. Here as elsewhere tyranny breeds rebellion, and rebellion breeds emancipation " (p. 61). Thus, relativistic dynamism and anti-conceptualism begin to dominate the last thoughts of Cardozo, supported by a reflection on the particularism of concrete values (pp. 52 et seq.) and by a more pronounced sociological pluralism. " The group is not a constant quality. It is subject to Protean changes. We have, along with others, the clan, the church, the club, the guild, etc., each evoking loyalties, of varying intensity at different times and places " (p. 87).

Does there not follow from all these methodological considerations the necessity of detaching the sociology of law from the teleological art of jurisprudence, related above all to the needs of the courts in a given epoch, and to free the notion of law from all limitations by particular types of legal system ? It is impossible for us to judge what final orientation Cardozo would have given his sociology of law had death not cut short his labours. All we can say is that, having set out from a much narrower basis than Pound and having left without consideration the problems of the jural typology of inclusive societies and of genetic legal sociology, Cardozo brought out with incomparable penetration the complexity of the social reality of law, of which he saw with singular clarity the plurality of levels of depth and their mutual conflicts. Thus he contributed largely to systematic sociology of law, all the more because of the flexibility of his philosophical mind, which enabled him to emphasize the character of our discipline as a branch of the sociology of human spirit. Teleological-practical orientation, however, persisted in Cardozo's sociology, and prevented his conceptualistic relativism from bearing all its fruits.

We can but mention here the valuable contributions of other outstanding representatives of sociological jurisprudence, above all those of Justice Felix Frankfurter [1] and John Dickinson.[2] These authors concentrated their attention even more than did Pound and Cardozo on the practical application of the sociology of law to actual juridical technique.

IV. LEGAL REALISM AND BEYOND : K. N. LLEWELLYN AND THURMAN ARNOLD. The neo-realistic school which developed during the last ten years represents a violent reaction against the dominantly teleological and moralizing orientation of " sociological jurisprudence ". Associated with the names of K. N. Llewellyn, Thurman Arnold, Walter W. Cook, H. E. Yntema, L. Green, Underhill Moore, H. Oliphant, Max Radin, Jerome Frank, E. W. Robinson, and Charles E. Clark,[3] this current is united only in the negativism of its spokesmen. They strive to eliminate teleological considerations and value judgments not only from sociology of law but also from jurisprudence itself. As for positive conclusions, still largely fragmentary, the various " realists " diverge widely from each other. Some turn towards a sociology of law based exclusively on reality judgments and freed from dependence on jurisprudence of which the sole task is reduced to applying the results of reality judgments without any consideration for ends and values (Llewellyn, Arnold). Others would eliminate jurisprudence in general, to replace it not by sociology, but by a naturalistic psychology which describes the minds of lawyers (Robinson) or even by psycho-analysis of lawyers (Frank). Still others, while proclaiming the necessity of applying purely scientific and descriptive methods to jurisprudence, are really concerned solely with the elaboration of a new juridical technique, exclusively based on an inductive generalization of " official behaviour " (among others, Radin). At bottom, only the works of Llewellyn and Arnold, which otherwise differ widely from each other, have any direct relation to the problems of the sociology of law proper. They alone need concern us here, but since the final orientation of their works apparently goes beyond " legal realism ", we shall begin by characterizing some of the points of departure which,

[1] *The Business of the Supreme Court, a Study in the Federal Judicial System* (1927), *The Public and its Government* (1930), *Justice Brandeis* (1932), *Justice Holmes and the Supreme Court* (1938), *Law and Politics* (1939).
[2] *Administrative Justice and the Supremacy of Law in the United States* (1927), " The Law behind Law ", *Columbia Law Review*, vol. 29, pp. 113-46, 285-319.
[3] For a serviceable bibliography of " legal realism " and its critics, cf. E. W. Garlan, *Legal Realism and Justice* (1940), pp. 135 et seq.

at least, were common at the outset of the discussion, to all spokesmen of this current.

The " legal realists " all start with a very narrow and certainly abusive interpretation of Holmes's definition of law as a " prophecy of what the courts will do ". Eliminating from their considerations rules, principles, standards, values, opinions of judges, finally law imposed on courts directly by society, the realists primitively reduce law exclusively to decisions of judges and more precisely to their behaviour. Thus Llewellyn wrote in an early work : " What the officials (judges or sheriffs or clerks or jailers or lawyers) do about disputes is, to my mind, the law itself " (*The Bramble Bush*, 1930, p. 3).

Also Frank : " The law is a decision of a court. Until a court has passed on those facts, no law on that subject is yet in existence " (*Law and the Modern Mind*, 1930, p. 46). Simply by describing such " official behaviour " as it is externally perceptible and observable, realistic jurisprudence claims to become objective and natural science.

Not the reason given by any individual judge for his decision ; not even the cumulative body of rules which have grown up through the ages under the stress of historical circumstances, but the actual conduct, the reflex action of all the parties involved in the solving of a dispute, that is the proper subject for any study which undertakes to be scientific. These ways can be observed empirically, tabulated statistically and interpreted inductively by the scientific jurist precisely as the scientific entomologist describes and classifies the ways of the ants. . . . Guided by a purely empirical behaviourism, forswearing the quest for rationality and purpose, jurisprudence will at long last escape the rut of metaphysics and enter triumphantly upon the highest stage, the scientific stage of its development.[1]

Some realists go still further. They stress the idea that all which is not visible and tangible in law, such as rules, principles, standards, values, opinions, beliefs, is but philosophical imagination, and that here as elsewhere the only reality is the sensual one. That is to say, in every legal case the gestures and externalizations of officials made by means of spoken and written words are the sole reality. Apparently they do not see the extreme difficulty into which they and, at bottom, more moderate realists, fall. It is the difficulty we indicated when criticizing behaviourist conceptions. Everything which is not an automatic reflex in

---

[1] I quote this quite precise characteristic of the basic thesis of " legal realism " from one of its distinguished critics, M. Aronson ; cf. his " Tendencies in American Jurisprudence " in the *Toronto Law Review* (1941), vol. IV, No. 1, p. 103.

human conduct is impregnated with inner meanings and significant noetic symbols which the observer must understand and
interpret in order to grasp the sense of the behaviour. I do not
believe that the realists, even the most extreme, would agree to
consider as " legal " the fact that a particular judge wipes his
nose during a trial ! To speak of " official behaviour " is to
introduce the entire realm of noetic symbols and inner meanings
associated with the term " official ", and thus to undermine the
logical consistency of this conception. Hence the term " realism "
in this trend has a tendency to take very different significances,
none of which, however, has any precise relation to realism or
neo-realism in the philosophical sense of these terms. Legal
realism has now the sense of " naturalistic sensualism ", now
that of a simple exigency of replacing value judgments by reality
judgments, now that of an " empiricism ", which term can
assume numerous meanings, now that of anti-conceptualism,
now that of decisionistic and actualistic irrationalism [1] which
need be neither sensualist nor realistic, etc. From the viewpoint
of its application to jurisprudence, this decisionist trend, which
dissolves law in administrative arbitrariness, predominates among
realists in the last analysis. Its danger, from the viewpoint of the
existence of law itself, as a specific social regulation, has already
been denounced forcefully by Dean Pound in his severe, but, from
this viewpoint, unquestionably deserved criticism of legal realism. [2]

Except for the elements cited, the realistic trend is marked
above all by a desire to make jurisprudence itself purely scientific,
or at least to base it solely on science. Thus realists who distinguish jurisprudence as an art from science properly so called,
like Llewellyn [3] and also like Radin, [4] strive to show that it can
get along without any goal and any philosophical reflection.
They forget that even techniques based on authentic natural
sciences have also precise goals to be achieved. Medicine aims at
the health of the sick, engineering at the building of bridges which
shall span rivers and bear heavy loads. They forget, furthermore,

[1] Pound has already rightly indicated the lack of preciseness in the term realism
as recently employed by legal scholars, cf. *Contemporary Juristic Theory* (1940), pp. 46–8.

[2] See " The Call for Realistic Jurisprudence " in *Harvard Law Review*, vol. 44
(1931), pp. 707 et seq., and *Contemporary Juristic Theory* (1940), pp. 1–29.

[3] " We have to do primarily with law as a science of observation, and secondarily
with law as an art. We are presented in law, as in every other discipline, with the
fierce distinction between a science and an art " (" Legal Tradition and Social
Science ", in *Essays on Research in Soc. Science* (1936), pp. 90, 192, 104, and *Präjudizien-
recht und Rechtssprechung in America* (1933), vol. 2, pp. 89 et seq.)

[4] *Law as Logic and Experience* (1940), pp. 54–6, 125, 136–7, 145–65. On certain
inconsistencies in the conception of Max Radin cf. Introduction, above,

that goals, without which no jural technique can get along, while
conditioned by the type of legal system in question and by the
social structures and situations to which it corresponds, are
simultaneously linked with particular spiritual values embodied
in them.   The view of the legal realists, even of the most subtle,
like Llewellyn, being neither clear nor precise on this question,
all interest in their work seems to me to be concentrated in the
domain of science, entirely detached from value judgments, on
which they propose to base the jurisprudence.   To the extent
that this science is conceived simply as a naturalistic psychology,
as in Robinson (*Law and the Lawyers*, 1935), or an even more
dubious psycho-analysis as in Frank, it lies outside of our domain.
Here it suffices to note that no kind of individual psychology can
generally lead to a contact with the problems of law as phenomenon essentially constituted by collective experience and linked
to the social whole.   But to the extent that this science is conceived as sociology of law (Llewellyn) or simply as sociology
(Arnold), we must consider the doctrines of this current in greater
detail.

K. N. Llewellyn declares even in his first writing that the
scientific basis of jurisprudence can be only the sociology of law :
" It is indispensable to give the sociology of law the possibility
to achieve its own work, without disturbance, before its sure results
can be applied to Jurisprudence " (*Praejudizienrecht, etc.*, 1933,
vol. 2, p. 119).   The first step of this sociology of law must be
" the fierce distinction between science and art ".   At the same
time, it must take account of the fact that it is not law which
creates society, but that the pre-existing society being richer than
all regulations gives birth to law.   " Law and the law officials
are not therefore in any real sense what makes order in society.
For them society is given and order is given because society is
given " (*The Bramble Bush*, 1930, p. 12).   " The law is not all,
nor yet the major part of society " (" A Realistic Jurisprudence ",
Col. Law Rev., 1930, No. 30, p. 443).   Legal sociology presupposes
" the conception of society in flux, and in flux typically faster
than the law, so that the probability is always given, that any
portion of law needs re-examination to determine how far it fits
the society ".   " The conception of law in flux, of moving law "
is but one consequence of the fact that it is society which engenders
law and not law which engenders society (" Some Realism about
Realism ", *Harvard Law Review*, 1931, No. 44, p. 1236).   Mobility
like stability, always relative in law, is only a result of concrete

social situations. " Our society is changing and law, if it is to fit society, must also change. Our society is stable and law, which is to fit it, must also stay fixed " (*The Bramble Bush*, p. 63). " Law is the organ of society's woe when order is not working " (ibid., p. 149). To study it sociologically, one must begin with " observable behaviour " and continue " in terms of the way in which persons and institutions are organized in our society and of the cross bearing of any particular part of law and of any particular part of the social in the social organization " (*A Realistic Jurisprudence*, p. 464).

All these statements, acceptable in themselves and reminiscent of Cooley's polemic against Ross's nominalist conception of social control as the creator of the social bond, leave open and unresolved, however, a series of basic questions. First, is law only the unilateral product of society or in part also the producer of society ? The first conception, transforming law into a pure epiphenomenon, would eliminate from law all regulative function. The second conception presumes a bond between law and spiritual values, that is, clear consciousness that the sociology of law is a branch of the sociology of human spirit. Quite typically, Llewellyn, despite all his " realism ", does not claim so much descent from behaviourism as from the combined influences of Sumner and Weber. But he merely fails to explain what he takes from each and how he reconciles them. He shows, moreover, such hostility against all collaboration between sociology and philosophy as to hinder every possibility of following Weber's method of interpretative understanding of the spiritual meanings of behaviours. Thus, as a consequence, the reality of law is threatened to be wiped out in Llewellyn's sociology. There arises, moreover, the pressing question of how Llewellyn reconciles his conception of law as a direct product of society and his definition of law as that which " the officials do about disputes ". The contradiction would here seem to be flagrant, for " official behaviour " might be in total conflict with the life of society, might struggle against its movement, just as jural regulation in harmony with the rhythm of society might fail to find any expression in decisions of the courts. If Llewellyn were to reply that for him officials, the courts, etc., are " organs of society ", that would first of all be tantamount to recognizing that here is no question of the simple external behaviour of judges, but of the significant noetic meanings of their behaviour. This would further imply that " what the officials do " is not law in its

entirety, for courts being " organs " presuppose a pre-existent
law which organizes them and gives them their jurisdiction.
Llewellyn certainly had a sense of the impasse he was facing.
And he tried to escape by adding in some of his studies to his
original definition of law the statement that not simply official
behaviour, but also " the laymen's behaviour is a part of law "
(*A Realistic Jurisprudence*, p. 457) or, as he wrote elsewhere, that
" the law is what courts *or people* are actually doing " (*Some
Realism About Realism*, p. 1237).   But here the difficulty is not
solved at all ; it is merely driven to its extreme.   For obviously
not all conduct of people is to be regarded as law, but only a
certain kind of conduct, that guided by jural patterns and symbols,
and inspired by jural values (a fact which Llewellyn's master,
Weber, expressed in an over-simplified fashion—whose terms we
criticized in our Introduction—by saying that the conduct which
interests the sociology of law is that which follows or transgresses
legal rules and their systematization).   In any case, here we are
back at the point of departure, and we must conclude that
Llewellyn faces the alternatives of abandoning his ultra-realist
point of start, or of renouncing the sociology of law, which can
develop only as a branch of the sociology of spiritual meanings.

Since Llewellyn's penetrating thinking remains unfinished,
standing at a crossroads of development, we should not be
astonished that in his most recent studies, " On Reading and
Using the New Jurisprudence " (*Columbia Law Review*, vol. XI,
pp. 581–614, 1940) ; and above all in his very important article,
" The Normative, the Legal and the Law-Jobs : The Problem
of Juristic Method, Being also an Effort to Integrate the ' legal '
into Sociological and Political Theory " (*Yale Law Journal*, 1940,
pp. 1355–1400), he re-examines the whole question and arrives
at new results.   This last article is extremely compact and rich ;
it develops an entire new programme of sociology of law and
really deserves a book.   It is the most positive outcome of
Llewellyn's research and one of the most important texts of
American legal sociology.   After having formally renounced the
definition of law as a prediction of official behaviour, not solely
because it is " an incomplete way to see law ", but still more
because it threatens to eliminate the problem itself (*On Reading*,
etc., pp. 593–603, and note 17), and after having severely criticized
the extremist conceptions of Frank (pp. 598–603), Llewellyn raises
anew the problem of defining law acceptably to the sociology
of law.   The latter, he now insists, must take into account the

most different kinds of society (Llewellyn has announced a book in collaboration with A. Hoebel on *Law-Ways of the Cheyenne Indians*) and the rôle of particular groups in the life of law : " The legal must be studied in any group and needs light on every known type of social interaction." Thus the object of the sociology of law cannot and must not be linked with the existence of courts or of the State (" Normative, etc.", pp. 1352, 1360, 1365, 1374, 1386, 1393-4). " The Law-Jobs and Law-ways, I repeat, go to the essence of any group." They do not " presuppose of necessity the existence of any tribunal at all. . . . They are implicit in the concept of groupness. . . . They are part of the living of men-in-groups." Thus the legal systems of an inclusive society are " always somewhat pluralistic, instinct with diverse and warring premises of growth. . . . The pluralistic vari-tendencied system is kept at work on the digestion or assimilation of the constant in-flow of new law-stuff and new trendings into it from the re-adjusting areas of the culture." It implies " the clash of rival " law-regulations. " This requires to be made explicit because the law concept of modern thought goes only to that great unit called the State, or to such other political whole as may come in question. But in a functional view a newly wedded couple, a newly formed partnership, a two-child casual playgroup have each, *qua* group, the problems to deal with, which are here our concern." Even more, " the aspects which those problems take on in the modern State are clarified and not obscured by observing them within such simpler groupings, taken as each, for the moment, a unit of observation " (p. 1374). On the contrary, by detaching the definition of law and the description of the structure of its reality from any orientation on the needs of actual juridical technique one obtains " a flood of new light " for jurists themselves. Indeed, " no analysis which is capable of general use for all groups can, unmodified, get into perspective all the official law phases of a developed modern society. That once admitted, however, I yet insist, that no quantity of modern technical complexity alters the nature of the basic functional problems, nor does it cause them to disappear " (p. 1379).

After having established that " the bridge between sociology and the legal " is " the human behaviour in the realm or in the aspects which we regard as legal ", Llewellyn proposes to call this " group legal behaviour " " law-ways ", which he opposes to " law-stuff " (pp. 1357-9). " Law-ways is used to indicate any behaviour or practice distinctively legal in character, flavour, connotation or effect." " Law-stuff " is used to mean any phenomena in the culture which relate discernably to the legal ; it includes rules of law, legal institutions of any kind, lawyers, law-libraries, courts, habits of obedience, a federal system : in short, anything in the culture whose reference is discernably legal " (p. 1358). This last field, whose existence was denied by the legal realists at the beginning of the discussion, causes to reappear clearly the realm of the significant noetic meanings of legal conduct, and drives towards a need for fixing exactly the difference between the jural meanings and "religious", "moral", " economic ", " recreational " meanings. Llewellyn believes he can arrive at this without any contact with philosophical analysis, that is to say, " regardless of the inherent rightness or justice " (pp. 1364, 1370–3). The sociological description, or rather what he takes for sociological description, seems to him to be enough. The legal, according to him, pre-supposes " a socially significant normative generalization ", but a normative generalization of a specific type. " All socially significant normative generalization which is in original an eternal process of emergence from the mere living of any group ", consists in " a projection and idealization " of " right patterns " of different degrees in precision and generality (pp. 1357–64). The legal is this patterned normative generalization, in so far as it is bound to " authority " and regularity in the law-ways, as well as in the law-stuff. If the authority, or the regularity, is not sufficiently expressed, we are in a sphere close to the legal or pre-legal, which Llewellyn proposes to call " jurid " (pp. 1358, 1366–7). Authority in law-ways has different aspects : " effectiveness or existence as a part of the entirety concerned ", " recognition ", " enforcement or sanction ", " supremacy " over competing standards and authorities. One of these aspects is sufficient to give to the normative generalization the authority necessary to be legal, which sum in the law-stuff is expressed by imperativeness of some degree or other. The other element, " the regularity of patterns ", is expressed, in its behaviour aspect, by " going expectations, quantum of procedure, quantum of certainty of remedy " and, in its imperative aspect, in " limits, devices, understandable character " (pp. 1367–70). The " law-jobs " in all particular groups and in whole societies consist " in the disposition of trouble cases, in the preventive channeling, in the allocation of authority and the arrangements of procedures, in the net organization of the group or society as a whole, so as to provide direction and incentive " (pp. 1373–83). The "juristic method ", i.e., juristic technique, or in developed legal systems jurisprudence, as the solution " of the problems of keeping the legal institutions and its stuff in hand and on their law jobs ", is itself a law-job. As such it can be discovered in an embryonic stage in all groups and societies, but it takes clearer contours when courts come into recognized existence (pp. 1392–7). Thus juridical techniques can and must be made relative, integrated into the concrete situations of legal frameworks and explained sociologically.

It would seem to us to be indisputable that Llewellyn's programme of the sociology of law and his description of the complex structure of its social reality is making very considerable progress. His analyses reveal the antinomic and pluralist complexity of the reality of law, the levels of whose depth he describes (an aspect of the study we have proposed to call systematic micro-sociology of law). He poses also the problem of the jural typology of particular groups and inclusive societies. Even his definition of law, which insists on the necessity of the interpenetration of the normativeness and of the effectiveness, etc., and which reveals its characteristics of determination and generality (Llewellyn says " regularity ", but the term is not clear) of jural regulation, would seem at several points to agree with our definition. One fundamental point remains obscure in Llewellyn's analyses, however. Exactly what is the meaning of " normative generalization ", and how can we speak of it and continue to deny its connection with spiritual values ? We have sufficiently insisted in the Introduction on the necessity of distinguishing between symbolic-cultural patterns and technical patterns, as well as on the impossibility of differentiating these cultural-symbolic patterns from one another without relying on a differentiation among the spiritual values (permeating them). By eliminating the appeal to specific jural values of justice, Llewellyn shuts off the possibility : (a) of connecting the intermediate character of the validity of law, which is placed between autonomy and heteronomy, to the internal structure of its regulation, as contrasted with that of religion, morals, and æsthetics ; (b) of penetrating the deepest levels of the social reality of law, which transcend the corresponding patterns and are concentrated around symbols proper,[1] collec-

---

[1] Llewellyn mentions the rôle of symbols in social life, but does not dissect their structure. He regards them fundamentally " as something outside from legal " (pp. 1390–1).

tive values, and beliefs. His conception of juridical technique makes it relative exclusively to social structures and not to values realized therein. Therefore his notion of jurisprudence remains very disputable. Moreover, while giving the sociology of law a task which it cannot accomplish (to define law without the help of philosophy), Llewellyn does not avoid the danger of limiting its subject. He excludes from the sphere of the sociology of law the functional study of particularized jural values and the collective beliefs and intuitions which grasp them.

In his new orientation Llewellyn has certainly broken the narrow circle of legal realism in which he was first imprisoned, but he has not yet succeeded in working out an " ideal-realism " which takes account of the fact that the sociology of law is a branch of the sociology of the noetic mind studying the functional relations between spiritual meanings and social structures. Here is the limit of his standpoint. But his thought is still in the process of formation, and there is every reason for hope. In order to appraise his contribution more precisely, one must await the completion of Llewellyn's new programme in a book.

The use by Thurman Arnold of legal realism as a point of departure for the sociology of law has taken a form quite different from that of Llewellyn. Like the latter, Arnold has entirely overcome the narrow conception of law held by the realists, but in quite another direction : that of a conviction that all social life is linked with collective illusions, beliefs in ideals. In his two works, *The Symbols of Government* (1935), and *The Folklore of Capitalism* (1937), he has tried to show that " social institutions require faith and dreams ", irrational and illusionary beliefs in ideals and principles, " which are everywhere inconsistent ", but the " social effectiveness of which cannot be ignored ". The dogmatic rationalization of these illusory symbols makes them " obstacles and not aids ", and feeds " the social disease of slavery to symbols ". On the contrary, scepticism towards symbols, accompanied by a consciousness of the fundamental rôle which they play and cannot but play in social life, has a liberating character. That is why " the anthropological approach towards social ideals, their dissection without judging as to whether those stimuli are sincere ", is simultaneously the basis of all objective social science and can have the practical effect of a revolt against their degeneration into oppressive idols.

Applying these considerations to discussions about law and jurisprudence, Arnold writes :

" Law is primarily a great reservoir of emotionally important symbols." It " consists of a large number of mutually contradictory symbols and ideals " (*Symbols of Government*, pp. 34, 49). All symbols being " inconsistent ", " obviously law can never be defined " (ibid., p. 36). " It is a sort of heaven which man has created for himself on earth " (p. 33). " It is a part of the function of law to give recognition to ideals representing the exact opposite of established conduct. The principles of law are supposed to control society, because such an assumption is necessary to the logic of the dream. The observer should constantly keep in mind that the function of law is not so much to guide society, as to comfort it " (p. 34). But at the same time " the student . . . needs to understand that while the presence of the ideal element in law is a confusing factor, its omission leads to a spiritually unstable institution, backed by the harsh exercise of power, lacking that permanence and strength which come from unquestioning public acceptance " (p. 71). This mistake was made especially by the sociologist, Pareto, whose conceptions, in some measure close to Arnold's, are compromised by a dogmatic adherence to the " ideal of power itself ", which makes the social scepticism of this reactionary thinker inconsequent and unilateral (ibid., pp. 250–1).

Jurisprudence, " jural technique ", " *the mystery* " of which Arnold proposed to dissect along with that of the law, is, according to him, a symbol itself, but one of the second degree, " the holy of holies " (pp. 47 et seq.). It is the expression of a " great emotional need " for a rational unity of what cannot be harmonized. " We may describe jurisprudence as the effort to construct a logical heaven behind the courts wherein contradictory ideals are needed to seem consistent " (p. 56). " We may define jurisprudence as the shining but unfulfilled dream of a world governed by reason " (p. 58). " A sort of heaven, if it is to be successful, must be far away " (p. 223). Thus the " holy of holies ", which jurisprudence seeks is linked with " the escape from reality ", " which constitutes not its weakness but its greatest strength " (p. 44). The true social function of jurisprudence in action in courts as well as in the writings of jurists, is " ceremonial and ritualistic ". " Both are necessary to create faith and loyalties concerning governing forces " (p. 45). Thus " jurisprudence should be considered as ceremonial observance rather than as scientific observation " (ibid.).

The realists do not take sufficient account of this situation, and finally fall into the same errors as the idealists against whom they rebelled. For if the idealists take for reality symbolic illusions rationalized into principles and doctrines, the realists, while denying the intervention of principles and doctrines, take existing symbolic ceremonies for reality (pp. 10–15). Both " ignore the structure of the institution before them, except as it illustrates their theories " (p. 24). " No realist or sceptic ever quite escapes the influences of the symbols of his time, because most of his own conduct, and the conditions under which he maintains his own prestige, are based on the symbols " (pp. 42–3). " It is child's play for the realists to show that law is not what it pretends to be and that its theories are sonorous rather than sound." " Yet the legal realists fall into great error when they believe this to be a defect in the law " (p. 44). Seeking to correct this " defect ", which is nothing less than the sense and strength of law, " realism in law schools tends to become only the same old jurisprudence with a new terminology " (p. 53).

The conclusion of all this is, for Arnold, the necessity (granting the impossibility of defining and differentiating symbols) of basing all social sciences solely on sociological description of social symbolism, conceived, despite their effects, as illusory crypto-grams, emotionally charged. " This would require the abandon-ment of separate sciences of law, political theory, and economics, for the study of the moving stream of humanity before their eyes, in which law, political science, and economics are so inextricably mingled, that there can be neither truth nor wisdom in their separation" (pp. 22, 76–103). Such a dissolution of the particular social sciences into a sociology of symbols is, according to Arnold, particularly urgent in our epoch, because never before has so great and fatal a rôle been played by symbols degenerated into idols and obstacles hampering the spontaneous movement of society (*Folk-lore of Capitalism, passim*).

Arnold's conceptions, which have attracted much attention and provoked wide discussion, are extremely instructive from the point of view of the sociology of the human spirit. For Arnold, having grasped with particular force the decisive importance of symbols in social and especially in jural reality, has been pre-vented from reaching acceptable conclusions because of deficiency in his conception of symbols themselves. Emphasizing rightly that social symbols are heavily charged with emotion and even with mysticism, he feels justified in concluding that they are entirely subjective projections, fantasies, meaningless illusions.

This conclusion has been reinforced in him by an intellectualist prejudice, according to which all that is not subjective is necessarily rational. As though emotional-volitional values, inspiring symbols, could not be considered objective and spiritual, no less than logical ideas ! Thus he has confused the study of objective values with the dogmatic rationalization of symbols. The result has been scepticism, not solely with regard to symbols (a scepticism partly justified in so far as they constitute an intermediate and relative sphere), but also with regard to particularized spiritual elements embodied therein. Hence his negation of all possibility of differentiating symbols, his return to the earlier imperialism of sociology, with its claim to be able to absorb and dissolve all social sciences and the refusal to admit even any differentiation of branches within sociology itself (sociology of law, knowledge, religion, economics, general sociology, social psychology, etc.). Thus Arnold finally cannot find a specific place either for law among social symbols, or for the sociology of law within sociology.

Contrary to his premises, however, Arnold goes on to define law, which he has declared indefinable, and he even links symbols, which he calls illusory, to objective spiritual values. This he does involuntarily and, so to speak, unconsciously. In fact, after all his insistence on the inconsistency of law, he writes as follows : " Law preserves the appearance of unity while tolerating and enforcing ideals which run in all sorts of opposing directions. And herein lies the greatness of the law " (*Symb. of Gov.*, p. 247). " The law fulfils its functions best when it represents the maximum of competing symbols " (p. 249). Does this not mean that law is a preliminary reconciliation of different and conflicting values, embodying itself in social reality by means of symbols ? And does this not constitute a return to a definition of law, rather analogous to that which we gave in the Introduction (V) ? On the other hand, after having denied any need for studying the spiritual and objective elements which express themselves in symbols, and while regarding symbols as pure illusions, Arnold writes: "We suggest that the formula of the new social philosophy may be the fundamental axiom that man works only for his fellow man " (ibid., p. 263, and *Folklore, passim*). But then objective and spiritual values exist after all, and their particularizations must be sought in symbols, variable and relative, of course, but quite clearly something other than illusions.

All the interest of Arnold's writings lies, it seems to me, in his approach to this conception, whose development his philosophical prejudices prevent. And that is why his writings, despite their suggestive and seductive force, remain only essays, open to very varying interpretations and chiefly misinterpretations.

SECTION III : SOME OTHER PRESENT-DAY CURRENTS

In France the most recent studies in the field of the sociology of law (except for those of the Durkheim school) have concentrated generally on a description of actual transformations in law and on a study of the characteristics of trade-union law contrasted with that of the State.   Maxime Leroy, in his now classic books, *Le Code Civil et le Droit Nouveau* (1906) ; *Les Transformations de la Puissance Publique* (1907) ; *La Loi* (1908) ; *La Coutume Ouvrière*, 2 vols. (1913) ; *Les Tendances du Pouvoir et de la Liberté en France au XXe siècle* (1937), contributed a model for this type of study, based only on the descriptive observation of empirical variations and liberated from all dogmatic claims and tendencies. But this purely descriptive method, to the extent that it pierced through to spontaneous levels of jural reality, could not but raise problems of systematic sociology of law.   This it did by revealing the multiple conflicts which move the actual life of law, conflicts between rules fixed in advance and flexible principles, between frameworks of law corresponding to diverse types of groupings and even between different kinds of social regulation.

Other writers followed the same type of investigation.   Among them have been Cruet (*La Vie du Droit et l'Impuissance des Lois*, 1914) and, above all, Gaston Morin (*La Révolte de Faits contre le Code*, 1920, and *La Loi et le Contrat* ; *La Décadence de leur Souveraineté*, 1927).   They, too, show serious concern for problems of systematic sociology of law.   Their conclusions might serve as a rallying-point and a background for the deeper objective description of actual transformations in the law.   The systematic analysis of problems of the sociology of law on an ideal-realist basis and as a branch of the sociology of human spirit, chiefly under the aspect of the microsociology and jural typology of groupings, inspired the works of the present writer.[1]   But these had mainly another aim.   They were concerned either with a study of the collaboration of the sociology of law and the philosophy of law in defining a particular kind of law (social law), or

---

[1] *L'Idée du Droit Social* (1932), *Le Temps Présent et l'Idée du Droit Social* (1932), *L'Expérience Juridique et la Philosophie pluraliste du Droit* (1936), and " Les Formes de la Sociabilité " (1938), in *Essais de Sociologie*.

with an analytical approach to the problems of microsociology in general. That is why in the works cited, the interrelations of the branches of the sociology of law were not sufficiently analysed, and the social reality of law itself somewhat simplified, lacunæ which the present work tries to fill in.

In Anglo-Saxon countries, the development of pluralistic theories in political science has paralleled the more recent trend of the sociology of law in France. Defined for the first time in G. D. H. Cole's *Social Theory* (1920) and Harold J. Laski's *Authority in the Modern State* (1919), as well as in J. A. Hobson's *The Guilds and the State* (1918), this trend attracted attention primarily by its connection with " guild socialism ". Political pluralism has had its most detailed expression in Laski's *Grammar of Politics* (1926), and has found some partisans in the United States (cf. W. F. Shepard, " Political Science ", in H. E. Barnes, *History and Prospects of Social Science*, 1925, pp. 396, 443, and to some extent also Mary P. Follet, *The New State*, 1918, *Creative Experience*, 1924). It has, moreover, concentrated its efforts particularly on the teleological and practical questions of the reorganization of the present-day's State and society on the basis of a new equilibrium of groups [1] rather than on a disinterested description of the jural typology of groups, to which, however, it has certainly contributed.

Much more important from the viewpoint of the sociology of law proper has been the contribution of John R. Commons in his remarkable work, *The Legal Foundations of Capitalism* (1924). As its title shows, this book is dedicated chiefly to the sociological description of the present-day legal system, that is to the legal typology of the inclusive society of to-day. Commons describes in an impressive and thoroughgoing fashion the transformation which has taken place in meanings of such legal institutions as property and transactions which are to-day founded on "expectations of invisible things ", thus confirming some of the points made by E. Levy in France. He shows forcefully the rise of an " industrial government " (pp. 306–12) competing with the State government, as well as the rôle of the law of labour unions and trusts in contemporary jural life. But Commons's book does not stop here. It contains important reflections on the systematic

[1] Cf. my critical analysis of English political pluralism and guild socialism in *L'Expérience Juridique et la Philosophie pluraliste du Droit* (1935), pp. 287 et seq. See also G. N. Sabine, " Pluralism, A Point of View ", in the *American Political Science Review*, vol. XVII (1923) and S. W. Coker, " The Technique of the Pluralist State ", ibid., vol. XV (1921).

sociology of law, concentrated around the " *working rules* " which govern " groups of associated individuals in *going concerns* " (pp. 6 et seq., 134 et seq., 298 et seq., 331 et seq.). " Each going concern is, indeed, a government, employing its peculiar sanction " and regulated by its own framework of working rules. Under the influence of traditional concepts, however, Commons does not regard these " working rules " as law, except when they impose themselves on the official courts and can serve as a " basis of prediction of the probability of official behaviour " (pp. 90, 127). This leads him to the conclusion that " law, ethics and economics " are all aspects of " working rules " of the same structure, being differentiated only according to the degree of probability of external behaviour which they can determine. He would consequently be inclined to base their studies on a unique discipline, and falls into the same difficulties we have pointed out in analysing " legal realism ", of which, in one sense, he is a forerunner.

Much less typical of current tendencies in American legal sociology is the recent *Introduction to the Sociology of Law* (1939) of N. S. Timashev. This highly informed and learned book contains a " sociological theory of law " of the old type, rather than the sociology of law properly so called. The author's attention is concentrated on a definition of law in which are united collective moral conviction and the heteronomous power which enforces it, a very disputable definition since it ignores the fact that jural conviction (if it is generally a conviction !) is different in structure from moral conviction. It likewise ignores the fact that power, in so far as it is linked with law, is itself based upon law. Timashev adds general considerations on the evolution of law and the relation of law and other manifestations of culture. These considerations are interesting in themselves, but do not sufficiently take into account either the qualitative discontinuity of types of inclusive societies, or the jural typology of particular groupings, not to speak of a total lack of jural microsociological analysis even under the aspect of conflicting levels of depth (rigid, flexible, spontaneous), an aspect so much stressed by other current authors.

In Germany the book of Hugo Sinzheimer, *De Taak der Rechtssociologie* (Dutch, 1935), was preceded by a multitude of important preparatory works by the same author on labour law, particularly *Die soziale Selbstbestimmung im Recht* (1916), *Grundzüge des Arbeitsrechts* (1st ed., 1921, 2nd ed., 1927), as well as *Die*

Soziologische Methode in der Privatrechtswissenschaft (1909). Sinz-heimer, drawing simultaneously on Gierke, Ehrlich, and Weber, posed the basic problem of the differentiation and hierarchization of the various parts of our discipline. He proposed to distinguish between (*a*) descriptive sociology of law, (*b*) critical sociology of law, (*c*) genetic sociology of law and (*d*) theoretical sociology of law. Critical sociology of law studies the problem of the realization of norms in effective collective conduct. Theoretical sociology of law studies the action of the spiritual elements, as well as of the morphological and economic aspects, on the constitution of the reality of law. Descriptive sociology of law merely assembles facts about the life of law in various societies. Genetic sociology of law follows the transformations of law according to concrete spheres and epochs. Critical sociology of law presupposes descriptive, genetic leans on the two, and theoretical sociology of law crowns the edifice.

If we can only approve the idea of clearly distinguishing and arranging the various orders of study which constitute our discipline, we must nevertheless regard as questionable the way in which Sinzheimer does so. In fact, " description " would seem to us impossible without precise criteria ; " criticism " is rather too closely linked to Weber's prejudice, separating stabilized systems of rules too much from their realization in practices and conducts. Sociological " theory ", finally, seems to be with Sinzheimer simply a study of factors in the genesis of law.

Among other central European writings on genetic sociology of law, applied to contemporary society, note must be taken particularly of the work of the Austrian, Karl Renner, entitled *Die Rechtsinstitute des Privatrechts und ihre soziale Funktion* (1929),[1] the first draft of which appeared under the title " Die soziale Funktion des Rechts " (1904) in *Marxstudien*, vol. V. This book contrasts the immutable " legal framework " with its economic and social repercussions under the regime of developed capitalism. It concludes that a radical transformation of society does not always imply a concomitant modification of legal structure ; consequently, economic evolution has not always law as a factor, nor does the transformation of social economy always have direct repercussions in law. For example, the structure of property has to-day thoroughly changed and has become " socially and

---

[1] English translation to be published in " the International Library of Sociology and Social Reconstruction ". Edited and introduced by O. Kahn-Freund, LL.M., Dr. Jur., Lecturer in Law (University of London) under the title *The Institutions of Civil Law and their Social Functions*.

economically" a power of command over masses of wage-earners subjugated to an authoritative organization. But "juridically" the law of property has remained purely individualistic. Obviously Renner, in analogy with Weber, subordinates the sociology of law to a study of the realization of the rigid rules of law in effective conducts. But this he does without observing that there are deeper levels of law, varying in direct and immediate functional relation with the totality of social life, the transformation of the structures of jural institutions being in action independently and even in opposition to abstract propositions of law. The latter form only the rigid crust, the surface of the reality of which is in perpetual flux. Renner's conceptions are, nevertheless, very instructive from the viewpoint of the limits which Marxist sociology finds itself forced to impose on itself when it seeks to deal with jural phenomena. From a simple epiphenomenon of productive forces, law becomes an autonomous sector of social life interacting with other sectors, the productive forces themselves being interpreted by some recent Marxists as identical with " total social phenomena " embracing the spiritual and psychological strata.

Thus Marxist sociology in general, and its sociology of law in particular seem increasingly to be escaping naturalistic and realistic temptations (see also N. Bukharin, *Historical Materialism*, 1922, American ed., 1925 ; Paschukanis, *Allgemeine Rechtslehre und Marxismus*, 1927 ; and, as mentioned above, Karl Mannheim's fusion of the methodology of Weber and Marxism in *Ideology and Utopia*, enlarged English ed., 1936). On the other hand, Franz Oppenheimer, an independent German sociologist inspired by both Marx and the Austrian L. Gumplowitz (*Grundriss der Soziologie*, 1886 : *Die soziologische Staatsidee*, 1902 ; *Grundriss der Soziologie*, posthumous ed., 1926), falls once more into naturalism. In his voluminous *System der Soziologie* (1923–33), whose second volume is devoted to the sociology of the State and of law, he reduces these elements to relations of forces which reveal themselves in struggles of races (social, not biological), classes and groups. Minute descriptions of historical types of inclusive societies are here employed to establish a philosophy of history, to predict a future conforming to the author's federalist ideal, and to erect a skeleton of a sociologico-naturalistic theory of law. Here we witness a return to the very beginnings of sociology, to long-transcended errors which once barred the road to the development of the sociology of law properly so called.

Relatively more fruitful tendencies emerge in the recent work of the Hungarian scholar, Barna Horvath, *Rechtssoziologie* (1934) ; see also the author's summary in French, " Sociologie Juridique et Théorie Processuelle du Droit ", in *Archives de Philosophie du Droit et de Sociologie Juridique* (1935, Nos. 1–2). Following Weber, Horvath sees the social reality of law as effective conducts corresponding to coherent systematizations of rigid norms. In exaggerating this conception, under the influence of the logical formalism of Kelsen, he bases the sociology of law on a " synoptic method " which, without confusing or connecting them, would compare " ought " to " is." The problems of sociology of law are reduced to the relations between law and other social phenomena, economy, different kinds of struggle, power (*Macht*) and knowledge. For each of these relations, he studies the historical variations, then the mutual social function of two confronted phenomena, finally the variations of logical and axiological (value) principles which inspire them. In every case these confrontations lead Horvath to the conclusion that the spheres of law economy, struggle, power and knowledge, while supplementing and interpenetrating one another, are in a relation of inverse progression and correspond fully only as far as the degrees of average intensity are concerned. Law as a social phenomenon is, then, relatively autonomous. Only with respect to different " procedures ", procedures linked to litigations before the bench or extrajural procedures, does law find itself entirely engaged and placed in a relation of direct progression with them. That is why Horvath thinks he can conclude that law, from the sociological viewpoint, is " the historical, social, logical, and axiological function of procedure, which in itself is the technical means of combining liberty with social compulsion ". " The mutual relation of the most developed procedure and law is not inverse, but direct. Law is only a superlative of procedure " ; the sociological study of law would, then, in the end show itself capable, the author believes, of " establishing a procedural theory of law ", which has something in common with the American " legal realism " (see above).

The first defect in Horvath's sociology of law consists of his synoptic method, which denies to our discipline capacity to have its own subject, and which reduces it to a combination of subject-matters borrowed from other sciences ; thus this method eliminates the possibility of studying full reality of law, in which the spontaneous jural life plays a basic rôle. The other defect shows itself, it seems to us, in an insistence on problems lying on the periphery of the sociology of law—relations between the social reality of law and other social phenomena (which, moreover, inexplicably include neither morality nor religion). But these can be studied only after the principal analyses of the sociology of law are achieved (cf. our study of factors, *infra*, Chapter V). Horvath begins, so to speak, at the end, and although his analyses often have interesting results, they suffer, despite all treatment of historical variations, from an extreme generalness which eliminates all genuine typology. The differentiation of law according to qualitative types of forms of sociality and groups is ignored as is the differentiation of social reality in layers of profundity. Now the different kinds, frameworks and systems of law thus distinguished will be found by us in extremely varied relations to economics, struggle, power and procedure. Horvath sees only the legal typology of inclusive societies, but even this does not halt his trend towards excessive generalization. It finally comes to serve as scaffolding for a procedural " theory of law ", as dogmatic as any other, and capable only of compromising the true sociology of law, since it transcends the latter's competence. Horvath's failure, despite the breadth of his learning and his penetrating analyses, is instructive. It shows how dangerous it is to undertake the study of the sociology of law without having sharply differentiated its distinct and interdependent sections, and without having defined the specificity of the social.

It is impossible to conclude this brief survey of current tendencies in the sociology of law without mentioning the rich development of legal ethnology and comparative law, disciplines which have constantly become more circumspect, more modest and more hostile to the simplistic thesis of evolutionism. More and more, their study has tended to limit itself to the establishment of discontinuous types. In legal ethnology, it is indispensable to mention the works of the Franz Boas school in America : the many important contributions to the ethnology of the Kwakiutl Indians of F. Boas himself (containing the discovery of the jural institution of potlatch), as well as his books *The Mind of Primitive Man* (1922) ; *Anthropology and Modern Life* (1928) ; *General Anthropology* (1938) ; the books of R. L. Lowie, *Primitive Society* (1920), *The Origin of the State* (1922), *An Introduction to Cultural Anthropology* (1934), as well as the works of Alexander Goldenweiser. In Britain, as well as in America, the books of Bronislaw Malinowski enjoy great authority ; particularly concerned with primitive law are : *Argonauts of the Western Pacific* (1922), *Crime and Custom in Savage Society* (1926), *Myth in Primitive Psychology* (1926), *Sex and Repression in Savage Society* (1927), *The Sexual Life of Savages in North-Western Melanesia* (1929), *Coral Gardens and their Magic* (1935), *The Foundations of Faith and Morals* (1936).

In Germany, the most important contribution in this field is Thurnwald's book, *Die Menschliche Gesellschaft in ihren ethnologisch-soziologischen Grundlagen* (especially vol. V, 1934, devoted to law). In France, after the important works of Durkheim's followers : Paul Fauconnet, *La Responsabilité* (1920) ; Marcel Mauss, *Le Don, Formes archaiques des échanges* (1923) ("Année Sociologique", Nouvelle Série) and Georges Davy, *La Foi Jurée* (1922), the publications of the "Institute of Legal Sociology and Ethnography of Paris", edited by René Maunier must be cited, as well as his own books, *Mélanges de Sociologie Nord-Africaine* (1930), and *Coutumes Algériennes* (1935). For comparative law, as the greatest achievement must be cited John Henry Wigmore's work, *A Panorama of the World's Legal Systems*, I–III, vol. I (ed. 1928, II, ed. 1936). In France the numerous very important volumes published by the "Institute of Comparative Law at Lyon", under the direction and inspiration of Édouard Lambert, represent the best achievements in this field.

The *International Institute of Sociology of Law* (Paris, 1931–40, General Secretary Georges Gurvitch) has in its two series of publications : *Archives de Sociologie Juridique* (25 volumes) and *Annuaires des Congrès* (4 volumes), made an effort to give a complete survey of all recent researches in sociology of law.

CHAPTER II

SYSTEMATIC SOCIOLOGY OF LAW
(THE MICROSOCIOLOGY OF LAW)

Systematic sociology of law has the task of studying the functional relationship between social reality and kinds of law. It is necessary to distinguish clearly between *kinds of law, frameworks of law, and systems of law.* The real collective units only, e.g., groups, give birth to the frameworks of law, the latter representing already the syntheses and the equilibria among different kinds of law. The analogy is perfect with the structure of every group constituted by synthesis and equilibrium among different forms of sociality. At the same time the all-inclusive societies only, i.e., the syntheses and equilibria among the multiplicity of groups, engender " the systems of law " ; in these systems compete and combine different frameworks of law, each of which itself represents a synthesis of different kinds of law. For example, the " State law ", " trade-union law ", " co-operative law ", " family law ", etc., are only frameworks of law, into which compete and combine different kinds of law. The " feudal law ", " bourgeois law ", " American law ", " French law ", " actual law ", " archaic law " are systems of law into which many frameworks of law oppose and seek equilibria.

This is the reason why the problem of kinds of law is independent from that of types of groups and of types of all-inclusive societies and is linked with that of forms of sociality and layers of depth, i.e., it is bound up with the microsociology.

In modern physics a distinction is made between " macrophysics ", dominated by constants founded on the calculation of probabilities, and " microphysics " of electrons, waves and " quanta ", in which the indeterminate is infinitely greater. So in sociology it is possible and desirable to come down to the simple and irreducible, so to say, microscopic elements of which each real collective unit is composed. Such microsociological elements are not at all individuals, *but the ways of being bound to the whole and by the whole, the forms of sociality.*

It is in regard to these " social electrons " that the pluralism, the moving variety and the indetermination in the social life are the most strongly pronounced. Thus, it might appear very paradoxical to link the " kinds of law " to the " forms of sociality " and the layers of profundity in social reality, that is to the most unstable and " anarchical " elements in the social life. Are we not accustomed to see in law the principle of unity and stability, the rule of solution, at least provisional, of social conflicts ? From this point of view jurists and sociologists often agree in the statement that all jural regulation presupposes a centre of unification on which it rests ; elsewhere they seek the latter not so much in a particular group, as in the all-inclusive society, unfortunately often identified, without any reason, with the State. From here it is only one step more to binding the fate of law with that of the State and to considering the distinction between public law and private law as the solution of the problem of kinds of law. But this distinction depends on the variable disposition of the State which grants privileges, varying by epochs and circumstances, sometimes to one, sometimes to another sector of law ; it is inapplicable to the immense sea of law not subjected to the State. Thus, the distinction between public and private law is not based on any internal criterion and does not solve at all the problem of jural differentiation as a function of social reality.

It is indisputable that in the real social life law has a true regulative firmness only while it is relatively unified in a jural framework, and even more in a legal system. In this sense the synthesis and equilibrium realized through the groups and the all-inclusive societies enjoy a pre-eminence in the jural life over the forms of sociality. This observation can be verified in the field of constraint, law, as we know admitting the possibility of constraint, but not requiring it necessarily. Jural constraint, in the sense of precise measures determined in advance and taken against the delinquent, can only be exercised by real collective units, groups and all-inclusive societies, but not by forms of sociality. Thus, constraints protect the frameworks or systems of law rather than the kinds of law, which can profit from the former only in an indirect way.

But to constraint in the strict sense is opposed in jural life the broader and more flexible concept of sanctions, i.e., of different sorts of reactions of disapprobation ; moreover, the sanctions in the larger sense themselves are only the external manifestation of the basic category of *social guarantee* on which is founded the effectiveness of all law (see Introduction). This is that social guarantee of the effectiveness of law which represents the indispensable true mark of all law ; for the correspondence of the duties of some with the claims of others (the imperative-attributive character of law) is not possible without this social guarantee.

Now every form of sociality is capable of becoming, under certain conditions, the basis of a guarantee of this kind, consequently the birthplace of law, protected or not by constraints which are imposed by the unity of the group. We can also express these observations in the following statements. Having designated as "normative fact" each manifestation of social reality capable of engendering law, i.e., to be its primary or material source (see Introduction above), we can conclude : the normative facts of the all-inclusive societies possess in the jural life primacy over the normative facts of particular groups ; and the latter possess primacy over the normative facts of forms of sociality. But this does not at all hinder each form of sociality from giving birth to its own peculiar kind of law ; the forms of sociality play, beside and inside groups and all-inclusive societies, in which they are integrated, the rôle of primary sources of law, and this rôle is a very important and decisive one ; for it is impossible to understand the jural life of groups and inclusive societies without referring to the jural life of forms of sociality.

Thus, the microsociology of law is definitely possible on the sole supposition that the distinction between kinds of law, frameworks of law, and systems of law is clearly made.

The general conditions to which a manifestation of social reality must correspond in order to produce law, i.e., to be a normative fact, are the same for microsociological elements (forms of sociality), for real collective units (groups) and for all-inclusive societies. The first condition is the capacity of these social facts to embody positive values by their very existence ; this capacity as we know (see Introduction and Conclusion) is certified by the collective acts of intuitive recognition, acts in which the participants yield to a social fact realizing one of the multiple aspects of the idea of Justice. The second condition is that in these facts prevails the active element, a task to be accomplished. Not only some forms of sociality (for instance unions of people speaking the same language, relations founded on sex-appeal, or worship), but even some types of groups (groups of friends, escorts of chiefs, Humanity as distinguished from International Society, also partially the conjugal family, and so on, see further) in which the passive element prevails, show sterility from the jural point of view. On the contrary, all manifestations of active sociality (interpretations having work to realize ; relations with others consisting of exchanges, contracts, relations of property, conflicts, finally struggles) and all active groups (Nations, States, cities, villages, factories, industries, trade unions, co-operatives, classes, international society, and so on) are productive from the jural point of view, i.e., they engender their proper law and are controlled at first by their own jural regulation.

Moreover, only the active interpenetrations and groupings possess the capacity to engender organized superstructures ; for the social organization is always a product of social action and represents the agency of this action. Not each manifestation of active sociality and not each active group possesses an organization, and law which they produce can affirm itself and be valid independently of all organization, whether the latter is born or only in formation. But the virtuality of an organized superstructure can directly serve as criterion of every active sociality and of every active group, and, consequently, also of their capacity to be producers of law.[1] If, as we see, there are social links incapable of engendering law, of becoming normative facts, as well as of being regulated by law, this incapacity has nothing to do with the distinction between microsociology and macrosociology. The opposition between forms of sociality on the one hand, types of groups and all-inclusive societies on the other, reveals its capacity to be applied to the analysis of jural life.

The kinds of law which are in competition inside the same jural framework or inside the same legal system can be differentiated under a twofold aspect : horizontal and vertical. The horizontal point of view considers the kinds of law as functions of forms of sociality located on the same layer of depth ; the vertical point of view considers the kinds of law as functions of the superimposed layers of depth in jural reality. To each form of active sociality, realizing an aspect of the ideal of Justice, and to each layer of depth of the jural reality corresponds a peculiar kind of law. Thus, these two classifications, the horizontal one and the vertical one, criss-cross.

Consequently, the microsociology of law has a double task : (1) to study the kinds of law as functions of different forms of sociality ; (2) to study the kinds of law as functions of layers of depth which can be found within every form of sociality when it becomes normative fact.

---

[1] See for more detailed analysis of this question my books *Essais de Sociologie*, (1938), and *Expérience Juridique* (1936).

Section I : Forms of Sociality and Kinds of Law

(a) *The Classification of the Forms of Sociality*

I. The horizontal classification of the forms of sociality develops on two different levels of profundity : direct, spontaneous sociality, and organized, reflected sociality. Spontaneous sociality is manifested in immediate states of the collective mind, and also in collective behaviours, whether they be practices guided by more or less flexible patterns or collective acts of innovation and creation. Organized sociality, on the other hand, is linked with collective behaviours in so far as they are guided by patterns crystallized in deliberate schemes, which are fixed in advance and impose hierarchized and centralized conduct. Thus organized sociality resists the mobile spontaneity of the collective mind and is separated from it. The different types of spontaneous sociality exert only more or less interior *pressures*, acting simultaneously within our consciousness as the pressure of one state of this consciousness on another, and in collective life as the pressure of one form of spontaneous sociality on another. Organized sociality, on the contrary, exerts *sanctions* and *constraints* from outside. It is remote, distant, separated by a greater or lesser gulf from the spontaneous infrastructure to which, under certain circumstances, it can become transcendent. The character of the organized superstructures depends on the measure of their embeddedness in the spontaneous infrastructures and in their peculiar forms. Thus spontaneous sociality always underlies organized sociality, and does not entirely express itself in the latter. At the same time, since spontaneous sociality is more mobile and dynamic than organized sociality, conflicts and tensions are incessantly arising between these two profundity-layers of social reality. Congealed schemes of the organized superstructures always lag and have again and again to be broken by the explosions and eruptions of spontaneous sociality. More or less this is even the case where, as in democratic regimes, organizational frames remain wide open to the influence of spontaneous sociality.

Taking into account the fact that the spontaneous layer is fundamental and that distinctions between organized superstructures can be made only by considering the extent to which they are rooted in the spontaneous infrastructures, we must postpone these latter distinctions to the next section, which treats vertical strata of jural reality.

II. Within spontaneous sociality, one may first observe sociality by interpenetration or partial fusion in the " *We* ", as opposed to sociality by simple interdependence between me, you, him, them, i.e., " relations with others ". This is the opposition between integration and co-ordination, between collective intuition and symbolic communication, between union and delimitation. When a " We " arises (" we-Americans ", " we-Frenchmen ", " we-Englishmen ", " we-Proletarians ", " we-intellectuals ", etc.), this We constitutes an irreducible whole, a new unity which cannot be decomposed into a sum of members. But at the same time this whole is not opposed to their members. Here the whole is immanent to the parts and the parts are immanent to the whole. This reciprocal immanence, which might be designated as mutual participation of the unity in the plurality and of the plurality in the unity, is always present in the We, at least to a certain degree. The We means an interiority and intimacy of the union in an awakened state. It has an intuitive basis. Its foundation is actual collective intuitions. The actuality of the intuitive foundation of sociality by interpenetration in the We is determined by the fact that patterns and symbols here play only a subordinate rôle for, in the last analysis, they presuppose a We already existing to a certain degree. Let us take the example of language. No one will entirely contest the very great importance of language for the *rapprochement* of consciousnesses and for their interior bond (the rôle of language in the formation of national unity is well known). But in order that the signs and symbols of a language should induce the same effects in all who speak it, in order for the language itself to be formed, it must be based on a previous union of consciousnesses. Thus language is only a means of reinforcing the interpenetration of consciousnesses ; it is not the foundation of their partial fusion in the We, for it presupposes that fusion. Hence, sociality as participation in a We can dispense with symbolic intermediaries ; by making possible precisely a mediation by signs, patterns, and symbols it dominates them, thanks to the actuality of the collective intuitions which serve as their effective base.

Quite different is sociality by simple convergence and interdependence. Here consciousnesses and behaviours, though forming a new reality by their co-ordination, are relatively closed to each other. Despite their mutual bond, they remain essentially distinct ; their convergence, so to speak, does not reach to their interior. Though they orient themselves on one another, they continue to remain reciprocally transcendent and opposed to the whole. Instead of fusing, even partially, they reciprocally delimit one another, or even enter into conflict. The sole actual intuition in this form of sociality is that of the " reality of other selves ", (whether " the other " be an individual or a group, a totality), who are primarily felt as an obstacle, a shock. But the link itself is by no means experienced intuitively. For it to be knotted and reinforced, the " I, you, he, they " must appeal to inter-mediary signs, patterns, symbols, which here dominate the bond. Under these conditions, consciousnesses and behaviours only *communicate* among themselves, and no communication can occur without the mediation of signs : words, gestures, declarations, outward marks, significant behaviours. Thus intermediary signs, patterns, symbols, serve as the primordial foundation of this form of sociality. For example, in exchanges, contracts, relations of property, only gestures, declarations oral or written, outward marks on an object and so on, can serve as an effective basis for the bonds established.

III. The second criterion for distinguishing forms of sociality is that of the intensity of a spontaneous sociality by partial fusion. When this fusion is very weak and integrates only superficial states of individual consciousnesses, which open only on the surface but remain closed in their more profound and more personal aspects, we are dealing with the *Masses*. When the fusing consciousnesses open and interpenetrate on a deeper and more intimate level, in which an essential part of the aspirations of the personality is integrated in the We, without, however, attaining the maximum of this integration, we speak of *Community*. When, finally, the most intense degree of union or of We is achieved, that is, when the consciousnesses are open to one another as widely as possible and the most inaccessible depths of the selves are integrated in the fusion (which presupposes states of collective ecstasy) we speak of *Communion*.

The intensity of fusion and the force of pressure do not by any means correspond, contrary to what might be supposed. In fact, it is in the masses precisely where the fusion of consciousnesses remains most superficial and where their deepest layers are closed to one another that the pressure of the social on the individual " selves " is strongest. On the contrary, the more the partial fusion of consciousnesses embraces and integrates deeper layers of selves, the less is the pressure of social spontaneity felt. It is less strong in the community than in the masses, it is weaker in the communion than in the community, reduced in fact to the point where it is almost imperceptible. Moreover, *intensity and volume of sociality by interpenetration do not go hand in hand.* The more intense, the less broad they are ; the broader they are, the less intense. Thus, as a rule, communions are realized only in very restricted circles (sooner in a sect than in a church, sooner in a particular trade union than in a federation of unions, etc.). Inversely sociality as masses has a capacity to be extended to the vastest totalities. This is verified in the phenomenon of the split or the schism, the danger of which is present in every communion in so far as it is a real sociality. For example, in a church, a religious sect, a magic brotherhood, a masonic lodge, etc., where sociality as communion is predominant (communion of believers in the same dogma, initiated into the same magic or symbolic rite), as soon as the communion weakens or relapses (to be replaced by sociality as community or masses), the very existence of the group is menaced. It is lost if it cannot re-establish itself as a more restricted circle of the initiated who continue to commune effectively. The split and schism then become the sole means of safeguarding unity.

Consequently, it is in the average form, as far as intensity of interpenetration is concerned, that the greatest equilibrium is established between unity and extension ; hence the community is the most stable form of sociality, the form most capable of constant realization within a group, while the communion and masses often remain in a latent state, becoming actual only under certain definite conditions.

IV. Manifestations of sociality by simple convergence, equation, and delimitation, or " relations with others ", whether inter-individual or inter-groupal, are differentiated according to the intensity of the degree of *rapprochement, separation* or a *combination of both.* " Relations with others " are the process of connection or separation between groups and individuals. To separate, as well as to join, more or less isolated consciousnesses and behaviours which communicate only by means of intermediate signs, a certain convergence is required with respect to a precise content expressed by a standard. And it is this content which becomes the object of the movement of *rapprochement* or separation. Even the individuals or groups which enter into conflict or join battle, must first converge in an identical object of desires, needs, interests, with respect to whose sharing they fail to reach an understanding. In this sense there is no hostility, struggle or conflict without convergence in an identical sign, convergence which is pre-extent to all tension, clash, delimitation or equalization.

Relations with others such as those based on sex appeal, various types of attraction, friendship, curiosity, unilateral sympathy, and love, as well as relations based on gifts, concessions of non-contractual conciliations, are examples of relations of *rapprochement*. The most striking instances for relations of separation are certain inter-groupal relations such as the struggles of classes, professions, the conflicts between consumers and producers, the struggles between nations, etc. These social relations of separation often occur between the We, within which external struggles effect a reinforcement of the partial fusion of consciousnesses and behaviours.

More widespread and current than those relations with others which involve separation and struggle are structurally mixed relations with others. It is, moreover, in them that conflicts and struggles terminate, to the extent that acceptable solutions are found. Mixed relations with others, whether inter-groupal or inter-individual, consist of a simultaneous process of *rapprochement* in one direction and *separation* in another. In such mixed relations, the approach realizes in separating, the separation realizes in approaching. Examples are exchanges, contractual relations, credits, promises of various sorts, etc.

No relations with others are possible without resting on a fusion, on interpenetration, on a pre-existing " We ", which can be slight in intensity but is always indispensable. The fact, stressed at the outset of this exposition, that relations of interdependence are necessarily bound to signs, clearly reveals the necessity of collective intuitions, at least latent or virtual ; for patterns and symbols linking consciousnesses and conducts are to signify one and the same thing to all and thus serve as means of communication. Communication by signs is impossible without that direct, intuitive union which is its foundation. Thus union, sociality by fusion, prevails over sociality by interdependence ; the " We " prevails over the relation between I, you, he, they, just as social law rising from interpenetration, as we shall see further on, prevails over inter-individual law flowing from relations with others.

V. Sociality by active partial fusion may be divided, in regard to functions, into uni-functional, multi-functional and super-functional forms. Function is only an aspect of a common task to be accomplished, and is quite distinct from aim (fixed in advance in a statute and related only to organized super-structures) ; it is the motile of collective action, the term of aspiration in sociality by fusion (the ends and values towards which it tends). The sociality is uni-functional when its activity finds expression in a single task, that is to say, is inspired by a single value and manifested in a single end (e.g., the partial fusion of workers in a factory, of the members of a trade union, etc.). It is multi-functional when various tasks are involved, being inspired by various ends and values (e.g., the partial fusion of citizens of a State or of members of an economic organization uniting producers and consumers). It is, finally, super-functional when the totality of tasks to be achieved is involved ; it is impossible to differentiate the particular aspects of this totality (e.g., partial fusion of members of a Nation or of an International Society).

Uni-functional sociality normally is integrated into multi-functional sociality, the latter into super-functional sociality which, consequently, holds primacy. On the other hand, only forms of spontaneous sociality can be super-functional, organized superstructures being, on the contrary, necessarily functional, for their rational and reflected schematism, rested on crystallized and fixed aims, can never express the totality of ends and values which are aspired to ; every aim as such is an impoverished intellectual image of ends and values. Thus the rare realizations of super-functional sociality necessarily find expression only in a plurality of organized superstructures which are irreducible to one another. Finally, a juxtaposition of the classification of partial fusions into uni-, multi- and super-functional with that into masses, community and communion, brings out the following conclusion : masses and communion, the weakest and strongest degrees of interpenetration of consciousnesses and conducts, lean towards uni-functional sociality, while the mean category of community is most favourable to multi-functional sociality.

The criterion of functionality is applicable not only to forms of sociality but also to types of groupings. They too can be either uni-, multi- or super-functional. But within them these characterizations are unstable, inasmuch as it depends on the variable actuality of corresponding forms of sociality.

VI. While uni-functional sociality always serves a particular interest and super-functional sociality only the common interest, multi-functional sociality can, according to circumstances, serve a particular, as well as a common interest. Interpenetrations serve the common interest when they succeed in balancing conflicting interests in a horizon broad enough not to hurt other equivalent kinds of interests which can arise. Thus it must be recognized that the common interest does not mean an identical interest of all, because such identity of interests does not and cannot exist, even within the same union, same group or same individual, torn as they are by perpetual conflicts among opposing and equivalent interests (e.g., interests as producers, consumers, citizens, etc.). The common interest is simply an unstable equilibrium of opposing interests, and there are as many multiple and equivalent aspects of the common interest as there are possibilities of balancing opposing interests of different kinds. Such equilibria being essentially variable, the multi-functional interpenetrations might serve one aspect of the common interest, but do not always succeed. Often they rather deserve it. In this sense, serving the common interest is a question of fact and nothing would be more false than to attribute a monopoly of representation of the common interest to a special kind of partial fusion or to a peculiar type of group (capacity to balance opposing interests within a real collective unit being infinitely more variable, while depending on the combination of different forms of sociality).

Finally, we should state that the three degrees of intensity of partial fusion, to the extent that they have a multi-functional character, have an equivalent capacity to serve the common interest, the masses and the communion being able, for example, to serve it as well as the community does.

(b) Kinds of Law corresponding to Forms of Sociality

Every form of active sociality which realizes a positive value is a producer of law, a " normative fact ". Hence microsociology of law must distinguish as many kinds of law as there are forms of active sociality. Let us leave aside, for the moment, the contrast between spontaneous and organized law which corresponds to the initial distinction made in the domain of sociality, and which will be analysed in the second paragraph devoted to layers of profundity in the reality of law. Let us here concentrate on the other kinds of law which emerge from our horizontal microsociological classification.

I. First we observe the contrast between *social law* and *individual law* (or better, inter-individual law), corresponding to the contrast between sociality by interpenetration and sociality by interdependence (intuitive union and communication by signs). " Social law " is a law of objective integration in the " We ", in the immanent whole. It permits the subjects, to whom it is addressed, to participate directly in the whole, which in turn effectively participates in jural relations. That is why social law is based on confidence, while individual law, i.e., inter-individual and inter-groupal law, is based on distrust. One is the law of peace, mutual aid, common tasks, the other the law of war, conflicts, separation. For even when individual law partly draws together subjects as in the case of contracts, it simultaneously separates them and delimits their interests. All law being a linking of the claims of some with the duties of others, an " imperative-attributive regulation ", in social law claims and duties interpenetrate each other and form an indissoluble whole, while in individual law they only limit and crash against each other. In social law, distributive, in individual law, commutative Justice predominates.

Being based on confidence, social law can never be imposed from without. It can regulate only from within, in an immanent way. Social law is, then, always autonomous, inherent in each particular " We ", favourable to the jural autonomy of interested parties. On the other hand, subordinative law is not real social law, but rather an amalgamation, a combination of integrative law and of individual law to which the first is enslaved. This can be either the effect of the predominance of mystic (magical and religious) over jural beliefs in the interpenetration involved (e.g., the " charismatic " power of the venerated chief, whose individual rights enslave the social law of the believers)— in this case we are dealing with spontaneous subordinative law— or it may be the result of the fact that the organized superstructure rests not on unorganized subjacent sociality and the spontaneous social law born thereof, but on relations of individual law coming from without (e.g., the law of property in the organization of capitalist enterprises, the law of dynastic succession in the superstructures of political autocracies, etc.) ; in this case we are dealing with organized subordinative law.

Every legal power is a function of social law, because it is, at first, only an external manifestation of the irreducibility of the " We ", of sociality by fusion and interpenetration, in regard to sociality by simple interdependence and delimitation. This primary power, which must be distinguished from the power of the group (representing a unifying synthesis, a balance among the various powers out of various interpenetrations which occur within the bosom of the group), is always impersonal, objective, immanent. It never constitutes domination, and it is not projected beyond the multiplicity of the members who constitute a " We ". On the contrary, individual law, the law of separation and equation *par excellence*, never in itself constitutes a power. But when, for the reasons just cited, social law is enslaved to individual law, the latter gives rise to a power of domination.

Jural tenets produced by social law are more intense and rigid than those produced by individual law. The latter is more elastic and mobile. Individual law favours all sorts of alienation and exchange. Social law and individual law are, moreover, irreducible to each other, as are the " We " and the I, you, he, they. Since, however, sociality by interpenetration prevails over sociality by interdependence (the " We ", the intuitive union being virtually present underneath every communication by signs, every relation with others), social law has primacy over individual law, for it presents the virtual base of every delimitive jural regulation.

II. Just as sociality by interpenetration is differentiated into masses, community, and communion according to degree of intensity, the corresponding social law may be distinguished into social law of the masses, social law of the community, and social law of the communion.

A. *Social law of masses.* The masses being weakest in fusion and strongest in pressure, the social law which integrates them is the least intense in validity and the most in violence. In fact, since the validity of all law depends on the measure of its underlying guarantee, i.e., on the firmness and stability of the normative fact on which its obligatory force is based, law integrating masses can hardly claim firm validity ; whatever integration it achieves is superficial. All the more brutal, however, are the spontaneous reactions of reprobation and blame attending its infraction. Here the violence of reaction knows no limit and often goes to the point of extermination in cases of the slightest violation of law. On the other hand, the correspondence between claims and duties which is characteristic of all law and which assumes, in social law, the particular form of interpenetration, develops with special difficulty in law integrating masses. Here the claims of the whole predominate over its duties to a point where the attributive element disappears almost completely, obliterating behind an almost exclusive imperativeness. Moreover, rights (the attributions of claims, " droits subjectifs ") of members integrated in the masses cannot affirm themselves under such conditions. In this sense, it may be said that social law of masses is characterized by exclusivity of " objective law " (prescriptions) and well-nigh complete denial of " subjective rights ". It is a result of all this that the law integrating masses is of all forms of spontaneous social law the nearest to the subordinative law of domination. In this sense, it is the least " social ".

B. *Community social law.* The community being the mean degree of partial fusion and pressure, social law rising from it should, in principle, be marked by intermediate degrees of validity and violence. The validity of community law, however, can appear remarkably intensified by two fundamental factors. First, the community is the best balanced form of sociality by interpenetration and consequently normally constitutes a particularly stable social link, realized within a group most easily. This habitually gives to the " normative fact " of the community, to the guarantee on which rests the mentioned law, a firmness and efficacy much greater than might be expected ; taking into account solely the factor of mean intensity of interpenetration is here insufficient. In the second place, the community represents generally a sociality most favourable to the generation of law, since it is there that jural beliefs have a tendency to be differentiated from moral beliefs and mystical ecstasy (religious and magical), such as often predominate in the communion. This again increases the validity of community social law by the efficacy of the spontaneous guarantee which the community gives to the obligatory force of its integrative law. And there diminishes concomitantly the violence of the spontaneous reaction to infractions, the brutality of reprobation, which has a tendency to be here moderated sensibly beyond the average level. To these considerations must be added the fact that, in community social law, the interpenetration of claims and duties, of the attributions and of imperatives, is so balanced that claims and duties of the whole, on the one hand, and of the members, on the other, appear more or less equivalent. It may be concluded that community social law is normally the most remote from the law of subordination and domination. One arrives at the same result observing that the atmosphere of a community is a *milieu* particularly favourable to an equilibrium between " objective " social law and " subjective " social rights.

C. *Communion social law.* The communion being the strongest degree of partial fusion and the weakest degree of pressure, the social law flowing from it should, in principle, be the most intense in validity, the least in violence. Here, too, however, important factors intervene to modify these characteristics. The validity of common law is often weakened by the communion's short duration, by the instability of the deep interpenetrations ; they are generally realized only in exceptional circumstances and decline quickly. Moreover, working in the same direction is the fact that the communion often has a charismatic, mystic character ; it is a *milieu* more favourable to religious and moral than to jural beliefs. That is why the efficacy of communion law is less well guaranteed than might be supposed in regard to the depth of fusion. Sociality as communion being generally a normative fact less sure and firm than that of the community, the violence of spontaneous reaction to an infraction of communion law increases, all the more so since there the reprobation is inspired more by shocked moral and religious beliefs than by infraction of jural convictions. On the other hand, the interpenetration of claims and duties takes place in communion law to the benefit of duties. The whole and the parts have reciprocal duties, while claims are shifted to the background. In this way the regulation which integrates a communion easily loses its jural character. This is also attested by the fact that in communion law as in that of the masses, " objective " social law absolutely predominates over " subjective " rights, although for different reasons. In effect, if the rights of the whole are exaggerated in the law of the masses, rights in general are weakened in communion law.

To sum up, it seems incontestable that community law is, compared to those of the masses and communion, the most delimited from meta-jural elements.

III. Sociality by interdependence and delimitation (relations with others, communication by signs) is subdivisible into relations of separation, *rapprochement*, and mixed relations. Hence the corresponding individual (or rather inter-individual) law is divisible into individual law of separation, individual law of *rapprochement* and individual law of mixed structure.

A. *Inter-individual law of separation.* Individual law of separation, which is born of conflicts, struggles, battles, and competitions and which rules them, is *par excellence* a law of war. Many writers (particularly R. Ihering) have believed that all individual law had such an origin and was nothing more than the jural procedure which formalized conflicts and assured the loyalty of parties in them. This would seem to be confirmed both by Roman jural procedure (*legis actio*) and by the procedure of the most archaic peoples who " imitate as exactly as possible the series of acts primitively executed by individuals in combat. Likewise, the formalities of arrest are inspired by primitive attack, being a substitute for it " (cf. G. Tarde and H. Maine). Individual law of separation, while a very widespread type of individual law, is not the only form of it. The reason is that, since it is not limited by the law of *rapprochement* nor moreover by *mixed individual law* (such as contractual law and others), and since it virtually, at least, is not based on social law, it would easily transform itself into the " law of the strongest " and thus dissolve all jural regulation in violence. This may be stated not only in regard to various sorts of law of war properly so called, but also for another kind of law of separation, that of individual law of alienable property, to the extent that it takes the form of *jus utendi et abutendi* (*dominium*). This law keeps away all other subjects from the acquired property, the delimitation here being a removing of subjects which are disjoined from each other by the recognition of spheres which are impenetrable for the *alter ego*. The appropriation of alienable things having, in archaic societies, a magical basis and consisting in the penetration of things by the *mana* of the subject-owner, this disjunction can be observed there with particular clarity as impossibility to break a magic circle (see below). Moreover, in this domain, if there were no limitation by law of *rapprochement* and contractual law as well as, finally, by social law virtually present, law of separation would be transformed into a simple competition of forces (magical, economic or physical).

Inter-individual law of separation is characterized by the fact that, in the delimitation of claims and duties, it is the claims which predominate and are disjoined, while the duties hardly take form. In short, in this law the attributive element which appeals to separation dominates over the imperative element scarcely perceptible.

B. *Inter-individual law of " rapprochement "*. Individual law of *rapprochement* is a rather rare form, because most relations with others having this character are passive rather than active. They are, consequently, sterile from the viewpoint of law (e.g., relations based on sex appeal, various attractions, curiosity, friendship, unilateral sympathy, and love). It is possible, however, to pick out cases in which *rapprochement* is a predominant but not unique element of the " relations with others ", an element stopped by a certain degree of remaining separation. Hence, it becomes active sociality and secretes law. Such are relationships based on gifts, unilateral concessions, non-contractual conciliations, etc. When valuable gifts are offered in order to initiate a relationship, when concessions are made without return and without implying future counter-obligation, when interests are adapted without reciprocal promises, we have active relations of *rapprochement*. These relations possess a jural character and are even capable of engendering new law to the extent that they take a typical and socially guaranteed form. Individual law of *rapprochement* thus born and which creates a jural atmosphere, a link between the subjects entering relationship (donor and recipient, he who makes and he who accepts concessions), is characterized by the fact that the imperative element predominates over the attributive, and that the delimiting function is reduced to its minimum. This is, so to speak, the most pacific type of individual law. But it is sufficient that a gift be accompanied by the principle of " give and take " (which, according to Mauss, is the character of all gifts in archaic society), or that unilateral concessions become reciprocal, etc., to transform the individual law of *rapprochement* into mixed individual law.

C. *Individual law of mixed structure, equilibrating separation and " rapprochement "*. This form of individual law is the most widespread and current. It is the form generally thought of when inter-individual and inter-groupal law is contrasted with social law. Its classic manifestation is contractual law, to which should be added the larger category of the law of transactions, credit, promises, and all kinds of obligations. The jural bond established by a contract consists simultaneously of (*a*) a convergence of wills of the contracting parties with a view to establishing a mutual obligation valid in the future (*rapprochement*) and (*b*) the opposition of two or more wills seeking exactly opposite aims and establishing opposing duties (to give something or to receive it, etc. : separation). Again, the contracting parties are in a harmony of rights and interests in so far as execution of the contract is concerned (*rapprochement*) and in a conflict of rights and interests in so far as material clauses and manner of carrying them out are concerned (separation). That is why it is impossible to characterize unequivocally, as has often been erroneously attempted, the contractual relationship, whether as a *consensus* of wills and duties (Durkheim), or as their conflict and delimitation (Tönnies). The secret of contractual bonds, as well as of exchanges in general, various sorts of obligations and the like, lies in the intercourse of *rapprochement* and separation.

It is in this form of inter-individual law that a delimitation of claims and duties constituting the closest approach to an equivalence of the two is achieved. That is why, of all manifestations of sociality by interdependence, it is the relations equilibrating separation and *rapprochement* which most easily become normative facts productive of inter-individual and inter-groupal law ; they give to this law an efficient guarantee since normative facts are raised to types or models.

IV. Social law of the masses, community and communion criss-cross with social law of uni-functional, multi-functional and super-functional fusions and, on the other hand, with particularistic law and common law, i.e., law serving the common or the particular interest. The only reservation which must be made is that social law of super-functional fusions is always common law, social law of uni-functional unions always a particularistic one. Despite this reservation, there is a multiplicity of forms of spontaneous social law (schematically speaking, not less than twenty-four), beginning with particularistic social law of the uni-functional masses and ending with common social law of the super-functional communion. Between these two are to be placed, e.g., common law of the multi- or super-functional masses, particularistic law of the uni- or multi-functional community or communion, common social law of the multi- or super-functional community and so on.

All that can be said about the spontaneous hierarchy which arises among these various kinds of unorganized social law is that super-functional law has a tendency to prevail over multi-functional law, and the latter over uni-functional law. Moreover, common law has a tendency to prevail over particularistic law. To this we must add the fact that community law, being the most efficacious, has a tendency to prevail over masses and communion law. It might be concluded by saying that, in principle, it is common social law of the super-functional community which normally tends to acquire jural primacy. But in real life the degrees of actuality and virtuality of all these forms of fusion and social law are extremely variable. Moreover, this variability is intensified by the possibility of reversal in the relationships between activity and passivity. Consequently the jural equilibria which may come about among these various kinds of law within a given group at various moments of its existence cannot be determined in advance.

If, within the spontaneous life of law, we take into account the forms of individual law as well as the forms of social law, at least twenty-seven kinds of law within each group can be cited. These are constantly in movement, in competition, in struggle. Sometimes they are hierarchized, sometimes they are equated. Always they seek an equilibrium which continually arises and dissolves. This " microcosm of kinds of law ", which we have tried to expose by means of horizontal microsociological analysis, becomes infinitely more complex when organized sociality and the kinds of law corresponding to it are taken into consideration. Such analysis is the task of jural microsociology which is concerned with strata of depth and reveals what might be called the vertical pluralism of kinds of law studied as functions of superimposed layers of jural reality.

SECTION II : JURAL SOCIOLOGY AS A DESCRIPTION OF DEPTH-LEVELS

(*The Layers of Law*)

Each kind of law thus far identified represents a scale of graduated levels. Whether we consider social or inter-individual law, law of the masses, community or communion, uni-, multi- or super-functional law, the life of law, like all social life, unfolds itself through a series of superimposed strata, moving from a more or less rigid schematism and external symbolism to an increasing dynamism and immediacy (in a descending direction), and inversely from spontaneity and flexibility to reinforced crystallization and conceptualization (in an ascending direction). From this viewpoint, it is possible to discover in all law a vertical pluralism which has, moreover, a double aspect. On the one hand, there is unorganized law always present just below organized law, these two levels of depth of jural reality corresponding exactly to the two superimposed strata of active sociality : spontaneous sociality and reflected sociality. On the other hand, there is law *fixed in advance, flexible* law formulated *ad hoc* and *intuitive* law—levels of depth relating specifically to jural reality and distinguished according to the modes of acknowledgment of all law.

These two vertical classifications, often confused with one another, do not, in fact, correspond at all, because unorganized law and organized law may both be acknowledged in three different ways—in advance, *ad hoc* and immediately. They always remain *positive law*, being based on " normative facts " which guarantee them, and being acknowledged by the three procedures indicated. Thus, we shall show that the two aspects of vertical classification criss-cross, leading to a recognition of six levels of depth within any kind of law. These are : (1) organized law fixed in advance, (2) flexible organized law, (3) organized intuitive law, (4) unorganized law fixed in advance, (5) flexible unorganized law, and (6) unorganized intuitive law. We shall begin by analysing separately the two aspects of jural microsociology concerned with depth, and then go on to compare one with the other and both with the kinds of law previously distinguished in respect to forms of spontaneous sociality.

I. *Unorganized and Organized Law. Their different relations.* All organized law is always superimposed on an unorganized subjacent law, and all unorganized law always has a tendency to cover itself with a more stable and colder crust of organized law. Between these two basic layers of jural reality, however, there remains perpetual tension whose degree of intensity is extremely variable. This tension arises from the fact that organized law, in its reflected schematism, can never entirely express unorganized law which is more dynamic and richer in content ; it is able to subsist without the organized crust, while the reverse is impossible. Moreover, jural constraints, properly so-called precise measures predetermined and established by groups against delinquents (to be distinguished from social guarantees which are manifest in spontaneous reactions of reproof), normally are realized through the agency of organized superstructures ; a fact which even further intensifies the disparity between organized and unorganized law.

In the domain of social law, unorganized law plays an incomparably greater rôle than in the domain of inter-individual law ; in the latter, the liquidity of relations with others must be reduced to typical patterns connected with organized super-structures to have jural significance. On the contrary, social law is valid without any intermediary, inside every concrete interpenetration, whose specificity it manifests *hic et nunc*. In social law conflicts and compromises between the organized and spontaneous levels of the life of law play a leading rôle. Thus, in order to achieve greater clarity, we will confine our analysis to this domain.

The character of organized social law depends on relations which are arranged between it and spontaneous social law. If guarantee is not given that organized sociality from which that law arises can remain open to the penetration of spontaneous sociality, organized law becomes separated from spontaneous law by an abyss. The result is that organized law is transformed into a law of subordination and the organization which it rules becomes an association of domination.

The law of subordination which is not, properly speaking, social law at all, not a law of integration within a " We ", can spring from two different sources : either from a discrepancy between organized and spontaneous law or, as has been indicated above, from the charismatic character of power based on mystical and not on jural beliefs. When these two sources of the law of subordination unite, the violence of the law of domination reaches its maximum (e.g., jural regulation in totalitarian regimes and Oriental theocracies).

If the organized superstructure is so laid out as to involve every possible guarantee of penetration by spontaneous sociality, then law arising from the organized superstructure is rooted in unorganized law ; this leads to an organized social law of democratic tendency, setting up organizations of collaboration. The intensity of the compulsions sanctioning this law is in principle reduced in such cases to a minimum, for, leaving aside all other factors, the violence of the constraints is directly proportionate to the measure of conflict between organized and spontaneous law. It is obvious that between the maximum of transcendence of organized law over spontaneous law, leading to the most violent domination and compulsion, and its minimum, leading to democratic collaboration and the most tempered sanctions, there intervenes a whole scale of intermediate forms of organized social law. On the other hand, inasmuch as organized social law is superimposed on spontaneous law (whether of the masses, community or communion), the kinds of organized law are further differentiated and complicated. We must study each kind by itself.

(a) *Organized law of masses.* The least intense fusions (masses) and the most intense fusions (communions) represent, however, the least favourable *milieu* for the affirmation of organized superstructures. The reason is that here the measure of unification of superstructures does not correspond to the measure of unification of their spontaneous infrastructures : it is much more intense than that of the masses, much less intense than that of the communion. That is why masses in particular organize themselves sporadically and why their organized superstructures find difficulty in maintaining themselves. Furthermore, meeting here greater resistance from spontaneous sociality, the organization detaches itself, isolates itself more easily. The better to maintain itself, it often reinforces the " distance " which separates it from the infrastructure, imposes itself from without, intensifies the transcendence, the violence of compulsions, in short, readily tends towards an organization of domination and towards subordinative law. And even if organized law of masses does not become subordinative law, that is to say, even if it flows from superstructures of collaboration, while remaining rooted in spontaneous law, it is always accompanied by particularly intense compulsions. This for a triple reason : being but slightly effective, it must rely upon reinforced threats ; since the democratic organization, when it arises, is more unified than its infrastructure, it cannot proceed except by authoritarian centralization (whence " regal democracy ") ; finally, the force of organized compulsion here meets and amalgamates with the intense pressure of violent spontaneous disapprobation characteristic of all unorganized social law of masses.

(b) *Organized community law.* Since the average unification characteristic of the community corresponds best to that of its organized superstructure, the community is the most favourable *milieu* both for the affirmation of organized sociality and for its maintenance, as well as for the maintenance of its roots in spontaneous sociality. This is all the more the case since every organization, being from the jural viewpoint a web of " subjective " social rights giving and distributing competences, the spontaneous community law, that is the balance of " objective " law and " subjective " rights which marks it, expresses itself with less difficulty in the organized sphere than any other spontaneous law. Since, at the same time, spontaneous social law of the community possesses the greatest validity and stability, and since its infringement provokes moderate spontaneous disapprobation, it follows that organized community law has a tendency to affirm itself as the least authoritarian and to be accompanied by the least violent compulsions. Again, democratic organizations rooted in communities develop more easily than any others into

G

decentralized, federalist, pluralistic democracies, which still further softens the character of the compulsions accompanying this organized social law.

(c) *Organized communion law.* The unification of the spontaneous communion being stronger than that of its organized superstructure, the latter here finds anew great difficulties in maintaining itself and in keeping itself rooted in the subjacent infrastructure. Moreover, communions tend to become narrow in scope and split, while their organizations tend to expand or maintain the *status quo*. That is why organized sociality superimposed on communions is often hardly able to affirm itself (e.g., in archaic society, where the communion predominates, organization is at a minimum), and when it manifests itself it has difficulties in keeping rooted in spontaneous sociality (e.g., the organization of the Church is often a sort of embarrassment to the faithful). The absolute predominance of " objective " law over " subjective " rights within the spontaneous communion presents one more obstacle to its adequate expression in superstructure and in organized law. The organized law of a communion having consequently greater difficulty in being penetrated by the spontaneous law, has a tendency, like the law of the masses, either to become subordinative law ; or, should it remain democratic, it assumes centralized and authoritarian forms. This all the more so, inasmuch as, despite the minimum pressure exercised by the spontaneous communion, its unorganized law, due to its instability and its limitations by mystic-religious beliefs, is habitually guaranteed by very intense disapprobations. The latter, joining with reinforced organized sanctions, give organized communion law a much more violent character than might have been expected. It becomes milder only in those rare cases where the organization from which it arises happens to be exactly adapted to the narrow circle of the communion (e.g., in certain Protestant sects such as the Independents, the Anabaptists, the Quakers, and the like). But even when its centralist character disappears, organized communion law retains the tendency to be linked with powerful repressive sanctions.

II. *Law fixed in Advance, Flexible Law found* ad hoc, *Intuitive Law.* All spontaneous law, like all organized law, may be acknowledged in the three different ways we have mentioned and which we must now describe in greater detail, following the six depth layers of the reality of law.

(a) *Organized law fixed in advance.* This, the most rigid and superficial level of jural reality, is represented by law related to a precise organization and at the same time acknowledged by statutes, " laws ", the practice of courts, cases, etc. The static character of such law has a double origin : the relative immobility of the organized as opposed to the spontaneous, and fixation by a technical procedure of acknowledgment having as its goal the prevention of doubt, the creation of a congealed pattern favourable to jural security, the extent of whose rigidity is otherwise variable.

(b) *Flexible organized law found* ad hoc. The relative immobility of all organized law is here diminished by the method of finding, which takes account of concrete events and cases, as does the law governing the internal functioning of all organizations, e.g., the law of all administrations and public services, particularly discretionary and disciplinary law, the law of *police juridique,* etc.

(c) *Organized intuitive law.* The relative rigidity of organized law can be still further limited by the intuitive method of acknowledging. This is the case when the organized normative fact is directly acknowledged by the interested parties themselves without benefit of any formal technical procedure. Intuitive law plays a rôle on the organized level of social life especially in the effective application of laws both flexible and fixed in advance, by filling out gaps in them and by modifying their meanings. It is also chiefly this kind of law which drives towards the revision and reform of law in the sense of an increasing adaptation to normative facts, the most mobile element in the reality of law. Finally, it works very intensively during revolutions by stemming the tide of belated law (whether predetermined or flexible) which is doomed to destruction. But in such cases, organized intuitive law is joined by spontaneous intuitive law, for revolution from the jural viewpoint appears above all in the guise of a revolt of spontaneous against organized law, a revolt which ends in the crystallization of a new organized law.

(d) *Fixed spontaneous law.* The flexibility of unorganized law may be very strongly diminished by the relative rigidity of the procedure for acknowledging such law. This means that spontaneous law often finds itself determined in advance by formal techniques which to a certain extent halt its drive. Such is the case with customary law, the law of non-judicial precedents, law having doctrine as a formal source, law fixed by social declarations (solemn promises, party programmes), etc. In this list the rigidity of technique of acknowledgment are in order of diminishing degree because, in passing from customs to social declarations, there is a whole scale of nuances running from sheer traditionalism to the boldest innovations. The law remains unorganized, but it is formulated in advance by more or less rigid propositions. Obviously, this law is more dynamic than organized law fixed in advance, but comparison of static and dynamic elements with those of the other two kinds of organized law (flexible or intuitive) is more difficult, because here everything depends on the precise character of the formal source, on concrete situations and on unstable equilibria.

(e) *Flexible spontaneous law, found* ad hoc. Here the dynamism of unorganized law is subject to but very few checks. An example is spontaneous law acknowledged by the free examination of a judge, the law of " standards and directives " in Anglo-Saxon jurisprudence, spontaneous law acknowledged by the recognition of a new state of affairs coming from the injured party itself (e.g., concessions by employers in labour law, or by a group of States in international law, etc.).

(f) *Intuitive spontaneous law.* Here is the most profound and dynamic level of jural reality. The mobility of unorganized law is no longer subject to interference by the method of acknowledgment, which is itself in full flux. Intuitive spontaneous law, based on the direct apprehension (with no formal procedures) of unorganized normative facts, by the interested parties themselves, plays quite a rôle by facilitating the movement of juridical life. But it does not become effectively preponderant except during epochs of revolutions and disturbances.

This description shows that, except for the extreme cases of organized fixed law and intuitive spontaneous law, the extent of static and dynamic elements in any kind of law cannot be predicted in advance and will depend upon concrete cases. Consequently, even if one desired to regard the antithesis between flexibility and rigidity as a criterion of judgment of value, it would be impossible, with respect to most kinds of law, to establish a hierarchy from this point of view. But this is not all. No estimate based on a value judgment is possible here, because from the point of view of juridical reality neither the mobility nor the rigidity of law is endowed with any special positive value. Such value depends on the variable content of the various kinds of law and on their concrete equilibrium. This is why, in opposing unorganized law, and in distinguishing within each of these types fixed, flexible, and intuitive law, we do not attribute to any of these types a positive value greater than that of any other type. Unorganized law always has a tendency to organize itself, and perfection in law consists in an equilibrium between organized and spontaneous law, in a mutual interpenetration. It would be no less false to say that intuitive law is in itself better than flexible law than to say that flexible law is better than predetermined law. Here, too, everything depends on content, on concrete equilibriums, on the fact of interpenetration adapted to circumstances. Intuitive law can be, not better, but worse than fixed law, e.g., the intuitive law of the white population of the United States at the moment of the emancipation of the slaves, an intuitive law which even to-day remains partly slavish. Flexible law can lead to the worst arbitrariness of administration and of judges, if it is not hedged about by the limitations of rigid law. The practice of German courts under the National-Socialist regime is the best proof of this. Finally, fixed law can hinder normal juridical life and may have no relation to concrete cases—*summum jus, summa injuria*—if it be entirely cut off from flexible and intuitive law. All these kinds of law, then, are equal from the point of view of values, and the qualification of good or bad can be applied only to the tensions, compromises, and interpenetrations which occur among them. Thus our microsociology of law remains faithful to the principle of all sociology, entirely eschewing evaluation.

As we have noted, the six layers of law distinguished by the vertical microsociology criss-cross with the multiple kinds of law differentiated by horizontal microsociology. Schematically speaking (only for the purpose of illustration) this would give not less than 162 (27 × 6) kinds of law which clash and balance with varying degrees of intensity and actuality inside every framework of law corresponding to each group, to each real collective unit. Obviously, we give this number only to help conjure up a picture of the true "jural microcosm" which, in principle or at least virtually, is to be found in every active group, even small. It is this microcosm which forbids hasty generalizations and oversimplifications about the jural character of various groupings (e.g., State, trade unions, churches, etc.) and about the regularities which guide the transformations of systems of law corresponding to the types of inclusive societies.

CHAPTER III

DIFFERENTIAL SOCIOLOGY OF LAW

(JURAL TYPOLOGY OF PARTICULAR GROUPINGS)

In taking up the problems of differential sociology of law we pass from the microphysical to the macrophysical aspect of jural reality. This is the field of the jural typology of particular groups on the one hand, and of all-inclusive societies on the other. The corresponding types of jural reality will not now be " kinds of law " but " frameworks of law ", jural orders (for particular groupings) and " systems of law " (for all-inclusive societies) ; these frameworks and systems constitute, as we have shown, a microcosm of kinds of law.

SECTION I : CLASSIFICATION OF SOCIAL GROUPINGS

Just as the systematic sociology of law had to begin with a classification of the forms of sociality, differential jural sociology must begin with a classification of the types of groups or real collective units, as functions of which the reality of law will be studied. Every group, every real collective unit, represents a synthesis, a balance of forms of sociality, a unity which, at the same time, is integrated in the broader whole of the all-inclusive society. What characterizes a particular group is the element of unifying synthesis which is not, however, total. Centripetal forces predominate over centrifugal, the unity of the group mind predominates over the plurality of integrated forms of sociality, but on condition that the particular group does not break entirely away from the all-inclusive society, that it remains within a broader whole.

There is no observable society which does not include a multiplicity of particular groups. Every all-inclusive society shows us a complete web of real collective unities, a macrocosm of groups, each of which constitutes a microcosm of forms of sociality. Even archaic society, which was thought in its very primitive stages to have been uniform and amorphous, in reality manifests a great complexity of particular groups. Magical brotherhoods, age and sex groups are in struggle with the clan. The group of the living opposes itself to the group of the dead, who also participate in social life. Thus, even the ancients represented their society as comparable to a living body, that is to say, composed of many cells, the unity of the all-inclusive society expressing itself in the multiplicity of particular groups. Present-day inclusive societies are to an even greater degree composed of an almost infinite plurality of particular groups : families, communes, municipalities, States, countries, regions, and public services ; sects, congregations, religious orders, monasteries, parishes and churches ; trade unions and employers' organizations (with their federations), chambers of commerce, co-operatives of consumers and producers, associations of mutual insurance ; classes, professions, producers, consumers, political parties ; learned societies and welfare organizations ; clubs, sport teams, tourist associations ; and so on, without end (cf. the valuable description of R. Maunier in *Essais sur les groupements sociaux,* 1929). All these groups criss-cross and delimit each other, unite and oppose, organize or remain diffuse, form massive blocs or scatter. The network of social life in its macrophysical aspect remains essentially complex, and is characterized by a basic pluralism.

Particular groups being the constituent elements of every all-inclusive society, the latter gives them its historic characteristics. Groups of the same kind integrated, for example in archaic, capitalist, fascist, or other societies, vary not only as functions of the instable equilibria constituted by the forms of sociality immanent in them, but also as functions of definite historic epochs or cultural spheres (Oriental, Occidental, etc.), to which belong the inclusive social types. The family or occupational group, for example, can be a very different structure in one concrete situation from what it is in another. In archaic society, the family is identical with the clan, which is itself identical with the church and the political group, and the occupational group is identical with the magical brotherhood, as in other inclusive types it is identical with caste or, again, with a free association or a public service, and so on. In the bosom of the family, even differentiated from other groups, there sometimes predominates the domestic family, sometimes the conjugal family, sometimes the household proper. Types of groups are more concrete, more subject to historical and geographical mutations than are forms of sociality, and hence classification is more difficult and delicate than it is for their component elements. Moreover, if the description of groups can acquire full validity only when one takes into account the types of all-inclusive societies in which they are integrated, points of support are necessary for this study itself, i.e., one must lean upon a general classification of groups.[1]

This classification must be based on a series of precise criteria, most of which criss-cross. These criteria would seem to be as follows : (1) scope, (2) duration, (3) function, (4) attitude, (5) ruling organizational principle, (6) form of constraint, (7) degree of unity.

I. *Particular and Inclusive Groups.* Real collective units divide according to scope into particular groups and all-inclusive groups. It is within the latter that super-functional sociality is realized. Actually, all-inclusive groups are to be found in the Nation, the international society, and Humanity (this last distinguished from the international society by the predominance of passive sociality) ; in backward societies inclusive groups are found in the Tribe, the City, and the Empire. One can distinguish all-inclusive societies from all-inclusive groups in the sense that the former represent " total social phenomena " while the latter are only groups of super-functional character. That is why the types of all-inclusive societies are more concrete than the Nation, the international society, and Humanity, which can be treated more *in abstracto* as general types, just as can the groups which are part of them. All other real collective units are particular groups ; e.g., the State, the city, the Church, the family, as well as trade unions, professions, classes, etc., are only limited partial groups because they do not represent more than one sector of the all-inclusive group. In the bosom of all these groupings, there can be realized only functional sociality.

II. *Temporary and Durable Groups.* All-inclusive groups alone are essentially durable. Partial groups can, on the contrary, be equally well temporary or durable, although the latter form is more widespread. As examples of temporary groups, we might cite (*a*) crowds, (*b*) meetings, (*c*) demonstrations (these being

---

[1] We cannot accept any of the various stimulating classifications of groups given in the sociological literature, because it seems to us that all these valuable efforts do not distinguish between forms of sociality and real collective units. Likewise, they do not sufficiently clarify the criteria of the classification. At the same time this problem outstrips our direct subject matter. Thus, the author apologizes for being forced to leave out a critical survey of different classifications and to explain in brief only his own conception. An instructive survey of American classifications of groups can be found in *The Concepts of Sociology* (1932), pp. 135–68, by Earl Edward Eubank. A valuable description of institutionalized groups in America is that by F. S. Chapin in *Contemporary American Institutions* (1935). The most important classifications developed in this country are by W. G. Sumner and Cooley for the earlier period, and by R. MacIver, Ellwood and Chapin for the more recent epoch. About German and French classifications see my consideration in *Essais de Sociologie* (1938).

often externalizations of lasting groups), (*d*) conspiracies and plots, (*e*) bands, (*f*) sport teams chosen for a single match, etc. The majority of particular groups are durable, but in varying degree, dissolution being more or less impeded by obstacles.

III. *Groups according to Function.* All partial, durable groups can be divided into six types, depending on the general nature of their functions and independent of whether uni-functional or multi-functional sociality predominates in their equilibrium. These types are (*a*) kinship groups, whether based on mystic or blood parentage (clan, conjugal and domestic family, group of parents, group of children, etc.) ; (*b*) locality groups, connected by proximity (commune, municipality, county, region, State or " political society ", bloc of neighbourhood locality groupings) ; (*c*) economic activity groups (professions, trade unions, co-operatives, classes, castes, factories, enterprises, industries, etc., in short, all groups participating in the production, distribution and organization of consumption, the totality of which constitutes " economic society ") ; (*d*) groups of non-lucrative activity (political parties, learned societies, philanthropic societies, sport associations, clubs) ; (*e*) mystic-ecstatic groups (churches, congregations, religious orders, sects, magical brotherhoods, etc.) ; (*f*) friendship groups or groups of table-companions, admirers and followers of one leader, etc.

IV. *Divisive and Unifying Groups.* Kinship, economic activity, and mystic-ecstatic groups are to be differentiated among themselves according to their attitude as divisive or unifying groups. Divisive groups have a combative attitude and unifying groups a conciliatory attitude. For example, sex and age groups in archaic society, groups of children as opposed to the parents, are divisive groups, while the clan, conjugal family and domestic family are unifying groups. Likewise, trade unions and employers' organizations, separate associations of producers or consumers and castes are divisive groupings, while factories, enterprises, industries, social insurance societies, national or regional economic organizations, are unifying groups. Among the groups of non-lucrative activity, political parties are divisive groupings and philanthropic and learned groups are unifying. Among mysticoecstatic groups, the magical brotherhoods, sects, religious orders are divisive groups, the churches are unifying groups. What sets locality groups apart from all others is the fact that they are always unifying groups and never divisive, whereas groups of economic activity as well as of mystic-ecstasy can be either unifying or divisive. This distinction, moreover, must not be confused with the opposition between the common interest and a particular interest arising from forms of sociality. Thus, unifying groups can serve a particular interest (e.g., factories, enterprises, etc., and under certain conditions the State itself) and divisive groups can serve the common interest (e.g., political parties, trade unions, etc.).

V. *Unorganized and Organized Groups.* The majority of groups, even the transitory, have a virtual capacity for organization. In fact, as we know, this capacity is connected with the predominance of active over passive sociality, the latter being incapable of expression in organized superstructures. Normally, active sociality plays a preponderant rôle in that equilibrating synthesis of forms of sociality which every group is, for action is necessary to form a group, to constitute its unity and to maintain it. We can cite only one exception : in groups of friendship and adoration passive sociality is habitually predominant and normally prevents organization. Obviously, the fact that a majority of groups can organize does not at all imply that they do so effectively. Numerous groups remain unorganized despite this capacity (e.g., social classes, professions, industries, the bloc of economic activity groups, economic society under actual circumstances). The possibility of their organization depends on the situation in the all-inclusive society in which they are integrated. On the other hand, certain types of groups organize themselves with greater difficulty than others, e.g., transitory as compared with durable groups, mystic-ecstatic groups and kinship groups as compared with locality and various sorts of activity groups. In mystic-ecstatic groups, organization finds an obstacle in the predominance of religious and magical over jural beliefs and of the communion over the community and masses. In kinship groups, the obstacle to organization arises from the great limitation of active by passive sociality. That is why the domestic family, into which an element of economic activity enters and wherein active sociality plays an important rôle, is incomparably better suited to organization than the conjugal family or the household. Moreover, the respective rôles of different forms of sociality within one type of group being unstable and dependent on essentially variable concrete circumstances, the measure of the capacity of a group to organize itself cannot be determined in advance. Nor can the fact be overlooked that once organized, a group maintains within its framework important layers of the subjacent spontaneous life ; the organized superstructure never expresses a group entirely, and is only one form of sociality among a plurality of other forms within the group's unifying synthesis.

VI. *Groups with Conditional and with Unconditional Constraint.* If the guarantee which surrounds all law is a fact of spontaneous sociality, if the measure of the violence and the moderation of compulsion (including the relation between repressive and restitutive constraint, as distinguished by Durkheim) are determined by the obstacles or facilities for realization which organized sociality meets from spontaneous sociality, the contrast between conditional and unconditional constraint arises from the unity of the group itself. That is why the distinction between conditional and unconditional constraint is connected with that between different types of groups and can furnish a criterion for their classification.

The majority of groups, whether organized or not, have available for the maintenance of their unity only conditional constraint, because their members may more or less freely retire from the group and thus escape measures of compulsion. There are, however, certain groups from which free exit is forbidden and whose members have no legal possibility of withdrawing from such compulsions as may be imposed. These are groups which dispose of unconditional constraints.

The gravity of the compulsion has nothing to do with this distinction. In fact, conditional constraints may assume a violent and repressive form (e.g., corporal punishment and imprisonment by the guilds and universities in the Middle Ages ; boycott and expulsion in modern trade unions ; punitive war, as foreseen by the Covenant of the League of Nations). But by quitting the group in question, it is possible to avoid the application of these sanctions. Inversely, unconditional constraints may be as mild as possible and purely restitutive (e.g., small fines, payment of damages and interest in civil law), which does not negate the fact that it is legally impossible to escape them since they are imposed by groups free exit from which is forbidden.

It is primarily locality groups based on proximity which have a tendency towards the organization of unconditional constraint, while economic activity or non-lucrative groups, as well as mystic-ecstatic groups, in principle at least, have a tendency towards merely conditional constraint. Nevertheless, in addition to locality groups, there are others which can resort to unconditional constraint. Thus the family, conjugal as well as domestic, possesses even to-day some kind of unconditional compulsion in so far as minor children are concerned. On the other hand, mystic-ecstatic groups have at certain historic moments taken the form of organizations possessing unconditional constraints (certain magical brotherhoods in archaic societies, the Catholic Church in the Middle Ages). Finally, even economic activity groups may sometimes use this type of constraint (e.g., hereditary castes in India, the fourteenth- to sixteenth-century guilds, compulsory trade unions in contemporary totalitarian States). That is why, in order to achieve a precise definition of the political group or State, one of whose criteria is the *monopoly of unconditional constraint*, it is also necessary to turn to a second criterion, that of *the bloc of locality groupings*, because it is only the combination of these two characteristics which effectively distinguishes the State from other groups.

VII. *Unitary, federalist and confederated groups.* Every group being a synthesis and an equilibrium, and achieving some degree of unity, a classification of groups according to the extent of their unity is necessary. This is possible, however, only with respect to organized groups, because in them alone does the degree of unification show itself in a way which may be grasped in the reflected pattern fixed in advance, according to which the competences of the organization are combined and hierarchized.

The organized group is unitary when its organization represents either a direct synthesis of forms of sociality, or when sub-organizations existing within it play only a subordinate rôle, the central organization dominating them (e.g., all kinds of decentralization). The group is federalist when its organization represents a synthesis of sub-organizations, a synthesis so worked out that the central group and the sub-groups are equivalent in the formation of the unity. The group is confederated when its organization is a synthesis of sub-organizations so worked out that the sub-groups predominate over the central group.

Every group whose organization is sufficiently rooted in subjacent spontaneous sociality may, in its inner functioning, be characterized as a " complex collective personality ", an equilibrium between a central personality and partial personalities, a synthesis between a unique subject and a relation among a multiplicity of persons. Thus the above definitions may also be formulated as follows. In the unitary group, the equilibrium between the central personality and the partial personalities is achieved in the complex collective person for the benefit of the central person. In the federalist group, the same equilibrium is achieved with equivalence between the central person and the partial persons. Finally, in the confederated group, the equilibrium is achieved in favour of the partial persons over the central.

It would be entirely false to believe that this distinction is applicable only to States (and to relations among States) which have long been differentiated (but without agreement on the criteria) as unitary, federal, or confederated States. This distinction applies to all organized groups, kinship, economic or non-lucrative activity or mystico-ecstatic, which may be either unitary, federal, or confederated. Typical groups of economic activity having a federal character are federations of trade unions in a specific industry, labour exchanges, co-operatives, mutual insurance companies, etc. Others of confederated character are the French " Confédération Générale du Travail ", the " American Federation of Labour ", etc.

The majority of criteria on which this classification of groups is based criss-cross with each other, which leads to a great multiplication of their types. Moreover, we must consider the fact that the types which we have established are very broad and often require differentiation into sub-types (e.g., such divisive groups as the sect, profession, social class, political party, are sociologically quite distinct one from another, each demanding special study) and that they differ from each other as functions of situations in the all-inclusive society. Thus the conclusion is necessary that only vast " sociographic " investigations, describing empirically the innumerable plurality and variety of particular groups in an all-inclusive society at a precise historical moment, can give a complete and living picture of them. Every general classification of types of groups is doomed to remain schematic and abstract, being really nothing more than a programme of concrete sociographic investigations to which it serves only as a point of support. These very reservations, however, justify and emphasize the utility of the study of types of groups tested particularly in application to problems of differential sociology of law which studies the frameworks of law or jural orders appropriate to each of the types.

On the other hand, these considerations show that it is impossible from the sociological viewpoint, as well as from the viewpoint of values, to establish an *a priori* hierarchy among the various particular groups, because their relations vary as double functions of the structure of the all-inclusive society and the mobile equilibrium of different forms of sociality constituting each group. At the same time, every group may sometimes realize positive, sometimes negative, values of various kinds, depending on concrete and unforeseen circumstances. Thus, the sociology of groups must rebel with the utmost rigour against the widespread prejudice according to which the bloc of locality groups, that is, the State, predominates *a priori* over the bloc of groups of economic activity. In reality their relations, their equivalence or the pre-eminence of one of these blocs over others, depend on the extent of their organizations, as well as on their variable capacity to represent an aspect of the common interest ; finally, these relations depend on variations in the collective jural beliefs of the societies in which they are integrated. Only super-functional groups (Nations, international society, Humanity) have a tendency always to predominate over functional groups. And one may add that among partial groups it is the enduring ones which prevail over the transitory. It is impossible to establish any other *a priori* hierarchy of groups.

SECTION II : DIFFERENTIATION OF FRAMEWORKS OF LAW AS FUNCTIONS OF TYPES OF GROUPS

Every group in which active sociality predominates and which realizes a positive value (like every form of sociality which satisfies these requirements and of which the group in question represents a unifying synthesis) affirms itself as a " normative fact " engendering its own jural regulation. As we have already indicated, the normative fact of the group is the source not of kinds of law but of their particular equilibrium within a framework of law, a specific jural order. This framework of law, while it is a microcosm of kinds of law, may nevertheless in most cases be considered primarily as a synthesis of different kinds of *social law*. This for two reasons, first, because inter-individual law ordinarily is born from the external relations between groups (inter-groupal law which, like inter-individual law, may take the form of law of *rapprochement*, law of separation, or a mixture of the two), or between individuals belonging to different groups. Secondly, because the regulation by inter-individual law in developed jural life is in the end concentrated around two particular frameworks, that which corresponds to the politico-territorial-State group (especially for organized individual law) and that which corresponds to Economic Society (especially for spontaneous individual law). As an exception, we can here cite only the rôle, as a source of inter-individual law, played in the Middle Ages by canon law, the legal framework of the Catholic Church (cf. *infra*, Chapter IV, section 4). In all other frameworks of law corresponding to various types of groups, one can establish only the germs of inter-individual law, which we shall leave aside for the sake of greater clarity and simplicity in our exposition.

I. *Respective Capacities of Different Groups to engender Jural Frameworks.* Not even all groups which meet the conditions cited above are equally favoured by their structure for the constitution of frameworks of law. In the first place, transitory groups lack the stability necessary to this end. Crowds, meetings, conspiracies, etc., represent a chaos of kinds of law rather than a balanced jural order. Secondly, groups which remain unorganized set up frameworks of law only with the greatest difficulty, unless it be groups enjoying extraordinary endurance, such as the Nation, the International Society, spontaneous Economic Society, industries, and the like.

Among the groups distinguished according to functions, those of kinship give rise to jural frameworks only with a certain difficulty because of the rather passive nature of the conjugal family, combined with the predominance therein of moral over jural beliefs. The domestic family alone, being linked to economic functions, shows itself capable of serving without obstacles as the normative fact for a true legal code.

As sources of jural frameworks mystic-ecstatic groups are subject to the influence of contradictory factors. On the one hand, the predominance in their equilibrium of religious or magical beliefs, as well as of the element of the communion, is unfavourable from the jural viewpoint. On the other hand, the unusually strong and steady cohesion rising from these very mystic beliefs facilitates the unifying synthesis which constitutes these groups and, by the same token, shows itself favourable to the engendering of an orderly framework of law. That is why the legal code emanating from the Church (sticking to Christianity, we have ecclesiastical law and the more broad canon law) develops sometimes with greater facility and intensity (e.g., the case of the Catholic Church with its insistence on the external unity of the visible church), sometimes with greater difficulty (e.g., the case of the Eastern Orthodox Church with its sacrifice of external unity to collective mysticism and of the Calvinist

Reformed Church with its exclusive reliance on the inner conscience of the faithful).

Locality and activity groups (economic or non-lucrative activity) show themselves equally capable of engendering frameworks of law. Nevertheless, since locality groups, being founded on proximity, are more stable than activity groups, they often show a capacity to secrete legal codes with more precise contours and to express themselves more rapidly in organized superstructures than do the second type of groups. It is probably the recognition of this nuance which has led numerous jurists to the quite erroneous conclusion that locality groups, and more precisely their totality, the State, are alone capable of producing or, at any rate, of formulating law. Here a grain of truth has produced a serious mistake which has long weighed heavily on research. We will also have occasion to insist forcefully on the independent validity of legal codes secreted by economic groups, and on the possibility of their equivalence with the framework of State law in the event of conflict between the two.

The differentiation among collective units into groups of division and unification, into unitary, federal, and confederated groups, finally into groups possessing conditional or unconditional constraints, would seem to us to influence in no way the extent of their capacity to engender frameworks of law.

II. *Frameworks of Political, Economic, and Mystic-ecstatic Law.* The internal structure of jural frameworks obviously varies according to the nature of the groups engendering them. It is here essential to distinguish groups according to function, according to the measure of unity, and finally, according to scope. Particularly interesting from the first point of view is the differentiation of frameworks of law into those of locality groups, groups of economic activity, and mystic-ecstatic groups. Jural frameworks engendered by locality groups are characterized by territoriality, while those of the two other types are marked by extraterritoriality. Consequently, the former tend more towards rigidity, the latter towards elasticity, flexibility and mobility. This is seen clearly in the fact that the sphere of subject matters concerned in territorial jural regulation can be foreseen and determined in advance, while jural frameworks corresponding to economic groups in particular often impose themselves unexpectedly on an undetermined sphere of subjects (e.g., collective bargaining, industrial arrangements).

Moreover, in frameworks of " economic law " and " mystic-ecstatic law " (e.g., canon law), non-jural beliefs are reflected more intensely than in frameworks of territorial legal codes. This may be shown especially for canon law, where intense mystic and moral elements are involved and where, as a result, the law of communion predominates. In frameworks of economic law, corresponding especially to worker-producer groups, the influence of common effort, collective work, favouring the preponderance of community law, manifests itself. Finally, in jural frameworks corresponding to consumer and, even more, to unemployed groups, law of masses predominates. Since the community is the form of sociality most favourable to the validity of law, frameworks of law corresponding to worker-producer groups affirm themselves in economic life with more ease and force than all others, and take the initiative in the development and organization of the economic jural codes which compete with State law.

III. *Unitary, Federal, and Confederated Frameworks of Law.* The synthesis of kinds of law does not take place in an identical manner in unitary, federal, and confederated jural frameworks, each of which shares all the characteristics of corresponding types of groups. Thus, the law of the communion and of the masses plays a rôle only in the unitary jural framework, while in the federal and confederated frameworks the law of community necessarily dominates. But the favourable effect upon jural efficiency is offset by the fact that federal and confederated frameworks of law are particularly " formalistic ", capable of acknowledgment only by procedures fixed in advance and admitting little or no flexible and intuitive law. Moreover, these types of jural orders affirm themselves on a more superficial level than do unitary frameworks, which admit simultaneously *all* methods of acknowledgment, thus gaining in intensity what they lose in precision.

In the light of such contradictory factors it would be false to affirm as some (e.g., Proudhon) have done that federal and confederated frameworks contribute more to the primacy and efficiency of law than do unitary orders. On the other hand, while a combination of unifying groups (i.e., groups with a conciliatory attitude), tends towards unitary framework of law, a combination of divisive groups (i.e., groups with a combative attitude), tends rather towards a federal or confederated framework. Since divisive groups (classes, professions, trade unions, etc.) are especially widespread in the sphere of economic activity, the order of economic law finds its expression with special ease in federal or confederated forms. On the other hand, locality groups are always unifying groups, and hence, when combining, tend towards a unitary framework of law. The federal framework applies here with greater difficulty, and the confederated framework of law appears only by exception.

To sum up, one may state that the confederated jural orders are particularly characteristic for economic activity groups, and unitary orders for locality groups, with federal frameworks of law possible for both types but less hindered in economic society.

IV. *Divisive and Unifying Frameworks of Law.* The jural frameworks corresponding to divisive groups and unifying groups differ in the degree of effectiveness, which is connected with the unequal complexity of the synthesis of kinds of law they produce. In fact, the jural orders of a sect, social class, profession, group of producers, etc., represent an equilibrium simultaneously more simplified and more intense in its acting force than the frameworks of law of a church, business group, industry, all-inclusive economic society, etc. Compared to the legal code of a unifying group, " class law ", " proletarian law ", " bourgeois law ", " middle class law ", etc., are, from this viewpoint, particularly characteristic, In the struggle, the clash between " proletarian law " and " bourgeois law ", we have not only a conflict between two different orders of law regulating the internal life of two respective classes, but also a conflict between divergent visions of jural values, between aspects of justice ; hence, the force of collective conviction, the greater simplicity of the unifying synthesis and the greater effectiveness of these jural frameworks.

On the contrary, the legal codes of unifying groups are based on a complex synthesis pervaded by the spirit of compromise. The force of conviction here finds itself singularly weakened, and with it the degree of efficiency of the jural framework in question. However, it does not at all follow therefrom that divisive jural orders have greater validity than unifying orders. Other factors intervene with a contrary effect. In reality, unifying groups easily acquire broader scope when integrating divisive groups and balancing their conflicts by means of a superimposed jural framework. If, moreover, these unifying groups succeed in representing an aspect of the common interest, their jural frameworks acquire in the form of " common law " additional title to prevail over the particularistic frameworks of law of divisive groupings. Finally, it must not be forgotten that all-inclusive groups, whose orders of law predominate over all others, are unifying groups—those which are broadest of the type—i.e., groups in which super-functional sociality and a corresponding jural regulation are acting. The reciprocal efficiency of jural frameworks of divisive and unifying groups thus depends on a multiplicity of variable factors, among which intensity is only one, and, hence, not to be regarded as decisive.

V. *National and International Frameworks of Law.* Up to now we have been analysing only the jural typology of partial groups. Obviously, all-inclusive groups also engender their specific jural orders. Here we must consider the frameworks of law of Nation and of International Society, because Humanity (in which passive forms of sociality predominate) shows itself sterile from the jural viewpoint. National and international orders of law have this in common, that they are characterized by their super-functionality. This implies first of all that neither can express itself except in a plurality of functional jural frameworks (in their national and international aspects) : e.g., political law, economic law, ecclesiastical law, and so on. This implies further the fact that the jural frameworks of Nation and International Society, by virtue of their structure, remain in a spontaneous form, effecting their unifying syntheses in the domain of unorganized law only by means of several independent frameworks of organized law (e.g., the organized jural framework of the League of Nations, the International Labour Office, etc.). Finally, national and international legal orders possess jural primacy over partial frameworks integrated within them (e.g., that of the Nation prevails over that of the State or Economic Society). These orders rule the relations and the conflicts among the latter, i.e., they decide about the hierarchy or equality.

On the other hand, national and international jural frameworks possess the characteristics of unifying orders expressed in a particularly intense way. Hence they lend themselves more than any other framework of law (e.g., political or economic) to acknowledgment by flexible and intuitive procedures. That is why the synthesis of different kinds of law develops here more towards flexible and intuitive law than towards any other kinds. *Ad hoc* acknowledgments and direct intuitive acknowledgments of interested parties who grasp the normative fact of the Nation or of International Society, here play a preponderant rôle ; but custom, convention, doctrine, unilateral recognition, and so on, fixing in advance the spontaneous framework of national and international law, intervene also. We must now clarify the problem of the specificity of national and international legal orders, as well as of their relations.

In the unifying synthesis making up the framework of national law, community law normally plays a leading rôle, while in the framework of international law the reciprocal rôle of law of masses and of community law is much more unstable, with a general and undeniable tendency towards the predominance of masses law. It is exactly while the international legal order is dominated by law of masses that it is less effectively valid than national law. If we took into account only the capacity to produce a jural framework, we should have to recognize the primacy of national over international law. But other factors intervene here, as we have already had occasion to mention. In addition to stability and degree of efficiency, factors of scope and of degree in the capacity to embody Justice and represent the common interest also intervene in the problem of the interrelations of legal frameworks. From this point of view, the international legal order has primacy over a national one, whose functions it defines and delimits. Since the factors making for primacy are, however, contradictory and reciprocally opposed, everything depends on their unstable equilibrium. The relations between national and international law are variable and shift as functions of the cohesion of the nation or international society (of the extent of the predominance in their frameworks of community and masses law). These factors diminish or increase the effect of scope and of the special qualities of international society. All that can be said *a priori* is that, in cases of equal degree of efficiency, the framework of international law possesses primacy over the national.

In breaking ground for the jural typology of groups (which, in any case, like the classification of groups, remains and must remain on the level of a schematic programme for concrete investigations to which it can offer only points of support), we have been compelled throughout our analysis to show the impossibility of establishing any preconceived hierarchy of jural frameworks. With the sole exceptions of the predominance of all-inclusive legal orders over partial, of frameworks of common law over those of particularist law, and of enduring orders over transitory, relations among the various frameworks of law are seen to be essentially unstable ; they permit reciprocal pre-eminence or equality depending on a multiplicity of divergent factors and their unstable equilibria. In particular, contrary to the deep-rooted prejudice in favour of the primacy of State law, we have shown that frameworks of economic and canon law—not to speak of international law—possess all the characteristics which, in concrete circumstances, enable them to compete with the political legal order in regard to which they can affirm themselves as equals or superiors.

This conclusion, which would seem to follow from the viewpoint of an objective analysis of types of groups, may, however, appear to be in flagrant contradiction with the " principle of sovereignty " ; several sociologists sometimes insist on the latter with even greater energy than some jurists, because for them it is tied to the problem of the unity of all real society. Thus in order to clarify the results of our analysis, let us re-examine the relationship between jural frameworks from the point of view of the principle of sovereignty, considered as an element of social reality.

SECTION III : " SOVEREIGNTY " AND THE RELATIONS OF VARIOUS JURAL ORDERS WITH THAT OF THE STATE

If, from a purely sociological point of view, one were to interpret the principle of sovereignty as the preponderance of unity over multiplicity, of centripetal over centrifugal tendencies, in every real collective unit or group, we should have to acknowledge that every group possesses sovereignty over the forms of sociality composing it. In fact, the group as reality cannot exist without affirming itself as a whole, irreducible to constituent elements, over which it causes the unity and cohesion which are proper to it to prevail. Likewise, we would have to recognize in this sense that all-inclusive groups are sovereign with respect to partial groups integrated within them. This would lead to the statement that every jural framework is sovereign over the kinds of law synthesized in it, that multi-functional legal orders are sovereign over uni-functional, and finally, that super-functional frameworks of law (those of the Nation and International Society) are sovereign over all others (e.g., over those of the State, of the Economic Society, etc.).

These simple statements should be sufficient to establish a distinction between power and sovereignty and to differentiate within the latter between *relative* and *absolute* sovereignty. In fact, sovereignty thus conceived is not one with power but is merely a qualification of power. Generally speaking, social power is the manifestation of the irreducibility of the whole in regard to its component elements. Now, the first expression of power relates not to groups but to diverse forms of sociality by interpenetration and partial fusion, i.e., to the masses, community and communion, which exercise a power over members to the extent of the varying degrees of pressure to which the members are subject. This power, or rather these powers, on a micro-sociological scale, cannot be described as " sovereign " for the twofold reason that in spontaneous sociality (owing to the " reciprocity of perspectives ")[1] there can be no question of a primacy of the whole over the participants, and that organized sociality possesses in itself no primacy over spontaneous sociality.

Thus sovereignty, as a particular quality of power, appears only when we pass from the microsociological to the macro-sociological scale. We have seen that this sovereignty of groups has varying degrees, because all sovereignty, except that of all-inclusive societies, can be only a relative sovereignty. Conse-quently super-functional groups such as the Nation and Inter-national Society can alone possess absolute sovereignty.

The social power of a relatively or absolutely sovereign group is only a function of the jural framework of the group, more precisely of the order of its social law ; this to the extent that the above-mentioned power is based on law rather than on mystic-religious beliefs (charismatic power). One may also say that normally the sovereignty of any social power is a jural sovereignty, the sovereignty of a framework over the kinds of social law which it equilibrates or the sovereignty of one legal order prevailing over others. That is why sociological analysis leads to the conclusion that the fundamental problem of sovereignty is that of *sovereignty of law,* and that this jural sovereignty, if one takes it in a superlative sense, always belongs only to all-inclusive, super-functional groups. Thus under-stood, the principle of sovereignty merely confirms our conclusion as to the impossibility of establishing a preconceived hierarchy between the framework of political law and that of economic law. Their essentially variable relations are precisely ruled by the sovereign jural order of the Nation and of International Society which alone possess absolute jural sovereignty ; these latter alone can establish at given moments either the predominance or equivalence among functional and partial frameworks of law which are embraced within them.

The problem would seem to be complicated, however, by the

---

[1] See my article " Masses, Community, Communion " in the *Philosophical Review* (August 1941), and my *Essais de Sociologie* (1938).

fact that the principle of sovereignty was worked out precisely in that historic epoch when the jural framework of all-inclusive societies gave marked primacy to the State order. It was at the epoch of the formation of the modern territorial State, struggling on two fronts against organizations which, without being locality groups, claimed a State character : the Church and the Holy Roman Empire externally, feudalism internally. The territorial State, in affirming its " sovereignty ", defended generally its monopoly of unconditional constraint, that is to say, its external independence of all organizations claiming State character, and its internal supremacy over all groups making the same claim, i.e., a claim to dispose of unconditional compulsion. The monopoly of the latter, which is an effective badge of the State, and which, in conformity with hallowed terminology, we may call " *political sovereignty* ", in no sense implies by itself *jural sovereignty*, which is quite another matter.

In fact, the State's monopoly of unconditional constraint was exercised and is always exercised within the limits of the State's jural competence ; the latter always depends on the legal order of the inclusive super-functional society which constantly modifies the competences of the State and of the other functional groups, sometimes broadening, sometimes narrowing them. These all-inclusive societies, although exclusively enjoying jural sovereignty, do not at all dispose of unconditional constraint.

The tendency to attribute to the State both political sovereignty and jural sovereignty (competence over competences) is simply an optical illusion. It is produced by the historical simultaneity of the extension of State competences, derived from the legal order of the all-inclusive societies which gave the competences to the State, as well as from the accidental fact of relative primacy of political law in a certain epoch. But this primacy was not at all definitive. This jural pre-eminence of the State did not flow at all from its specific nature as a bloc of locality groups endowed with a monopoly of unconditional constraint. It was only a historical accident.

The same optical error took place in an inverse sense at the beginning of the twentieth century when some jurists, observing the tendency towards a greater limitation of the State's jural competences (by international and trade union organizations), hastened to proclaim that " the principle of sovereignty is dead ". They did not notice the fact that the reversal of pre-eminence among various orders of law was only a confirmation of the jural sovereignty ; for the monopoly of unconditional constraint by the State exercised within the variable limits of its competences is not dependent on the extent of the latter.

To sum up, we may conclude that the principle of sovereignty, while indispensable from the sociological and jural viewpoints of the harmonizing of different frameworks of law in struggle, as well as from the political viewpoint of the specificity of the State, implies no pre-established hierarchy of groups and corresponding jural orders. It leaves, on the contrary, a door wide open to perpetual reversals and variations in their relations.

It might, however, be objected that these considerations affect only diffuse, unorganized sovereignty of law, and ignore the problem of jural sovereignty concentrated in an organ capable of expressing it consciously and deliberately. Would not every sufficiently developed society be characterized by such concentration and organization of the sovereignty of law ? To which we reply that the problem poses itself effectively only when the frameworks of political and economic law are recognized as juridically equal by the subjacent jural order of Nation and International Society. Then, to formulate and express jural sovereignty, the necessity arises for organizations of arbitration with a jurisdictional character ; it is a form of supreme court competent to interpret the spontaneous sovereign law of Nation and International Society. On the other hand, in epochs when jural orders of all-inclusive societies accord legal pre-eminence to one partial group (e.g., in the Middle Ages to the Church, in the sixteenth to nineteenth centuries to the State), it is the partial groups which become organs competent to interpret and represent the sovereignty of law. This fact, however, does not mean at all that jural sovereignty may be attributed to partial groups, because in any case true jural sovereignty remains diffuse within all-inclusive super-functional societies.

Even in an epoch when sovereign jural frameworks of Nation and International Society accord legal pre-eminence to the State, its relations with the various frameworks of non-State law may take various forms.

From this viewpoint, we can establish four different types of frameworks of social law, completing the jural typology of groups which we undertook in the second section of this chapter.

I. *Frameworks of pure and independent social law* which, in cases of conflict, are superior to or equivalent to the legal order of the State, such as national super-functional law, international law, the law of the Roman Catholic Church (ecclesiastical and canonical), and of other Churches in cases of separation of Church and State, and finally, economic law in cases of autonomously organized economy which transforms it from particularistic law into common law.

II. *Frameworks of pure social law subjected to State tutelage*, i.e., not disposing of unconditional constraint and being autonomous, but, in cases of conflicts, bowing before and giving way to the State legal order. Externally this is expressed by the relegation of such frameworks in the field of " private law ", since the very distinction between public and private law, as we have seen, depends on variable decisions of the State. Such is the case to-day with jural frameworks of kinship groups, non-lucrative activity groups, and even the majority of economic activity groups which, under the existing regime, affirm themselves as particularistic. They are innumerable.

III. *Frameworks of autonomous social law annexed by the State*, i.e., put to its service either by incorporation within it as " decentralized public services " or by simple elevation to the privileged domain of public law. In cases where such annexation concerns locality groups of limited scope (municipalities, borough councils, counties, etc.), that is to say, the frames of local self-government law or of the law of landowners' associations (e.g., holders of riparian rights, mine owners, etc.), the annexation is least striking, given the fact that the State is a bloc of locality groups. The very decentralization of State organs performing purely technical functions (teaching institutions, transport, post office, hospitals, etc.), likewise takes place under the form of autonomous jural orders annexed by the State. More striking is the case of State annexation of economic activity groups (e.g., professional organizations), non-lucrative groups (insurance and mutual aid societies), and, finally, under the Cæsaro-Papal regime, of mystic-ecstatic groups. For all these groups have non-territorial character, and do not come into the network of the State (the bloc of locality groups) except by virtue of their envelopment by the unconditional constraint which the State monopolizes. In totalitarian States, the regime of compulsory and obligatory trade unions, imposed from without on the interested parties in order to dominate them, is particularly characteristic from this viewpoint.

IV. *Frameworks of social law condensed in democratic State law*, whose characteristics we already know.

It is obvious that each of these frameworks, like all those which have been distinguished as functions of types of groups, represents an unstable equilibrium of different kinds of law, in particular of the law of the masses, the community and the communion. It is no less clear that, depending on concrete historical circumstances and variations in the sovereign jural frameworks of the Nation and International Society, the frameworks of law subject to tutelage or annexation by the State move sometimes towards a pure and independent order of social law, sometimes in a reverse direction towards the legal order of the State. It is these movements of the intermediate frameworks of law which make manifest sometimes the pre-eminence of the domestic-political group, sometimes the pre-eminence of the State, sometimes that of Economic Society, or finally the jural equality of several of these groups. But here our analysis has reached a new problem : that of the legal typology of all-inclusive societies.

CHAPTER IV

DIFFERENTIAL SOCIOLOGY OF LAW (*continued*)

(LEGAL TYPOLOGY OF INCLUSIVE SOCIETIES)

The infinite complexity, the richness of aspects and contents of every inclusive society—every manifestation of " total social phenomena "—prevents their fixation in sociological types, unless one takes as a point of support some particular social activity. Thus, the classification of types of inclusive societies will give very different results according as one evisages it from the viewpoint of economic, religious, moral, jural or other phenomena. Numerous attempts which have been made at classification and an exhaustive discussion of them by S. R. Steinmetz may be found in *L'Année Sociologique* (1900), vol. III. To this should be added the analysis of doctrines of " eras of civilization " advanced by Gräbner, Schmidt, and Koppers, and of the " cultural morphology " of Frobenius and Spengler, which Mauss succinctly but penetratingly criticized in his note " On Civilizations ", in *Prem. Sem. Internationale de Synthèse* (1930). If all these attempts fail to give satisfactory results, above all it is (aside from the influence of evolutionist prejudices) because of the monistic efforts to establish a unique typology valid for studying together all aspects of social reality.

Recognizing the impossibility of such an attempt and taking account of the essentially pragmatic character of all classifications of types of " total social phenomena ", classifications which admit multiple variants depending on the aim pursued, we shall limit ourselves to outlining some schematic types of inclusive societies with reference to the study of jural phenomena. These types are constructed more as illustrations of the direction which such studies should take. They claim neither to give definitive results nor to be exhaustive, and certainly not to replace the concrete history of law and culture in general, which alone are capable of expressing the full reality of different inclusive societies with their individualized particularities.

We shall establish seven different types of inclusive societies from the point of view of repercussions on systems of law. In making this division we have been guided chiefly, on the one hand, by the criterion of pre-eminence within the equilibrium of frameworks of law of one particular group over all others, and, on the other hand, by the criterion of the degree of mysticism and rationalism in the conceptions of law and power characteristic for various societies—a criterion especially developed by Max Weber (cf. *Wirtschaft und Gesellschaft*, 1922). Weber, from this viewpoint, distinguished between " charismatic ", " traditional " (especially patrimonial) and " rational powers " ; he distinguished as well between systems of law penetrated entirely by the supernatural (magical or religious), relatively rationalized systems (whether of procedures, i.e., " formal rationalization ", or of content, i.e., " material rationalization " (*Zweck-rationalisation*), often linked with patrimonial absolutism or survivals of theological conceptions), or finally entirely rational (simultaneously formal and material), secularized by the aid of a formal logic immanent to the law. Weber also pointed out that law assumes various characters, depending on whether it is formulated and applied by prophets and divines, by jurisprudents (who may have been formed by courtroom practice or in theological schools), by owners of patrimonial power, or finally, by a bureaucracy of jurists trained in special schools. What was lacking in Weber's very suggestive and profound views was an integration of these partial and, so to speak, dispersed aspects into types of inclusive societies established as functions of the equilibrium of particular groups.

We will seek to avoid in our classification this basic defect, while trying to utilize Weber's valuable contributions. At the same time, there is not in archaic society a differentiation of groups according to the types which we have distinguished, inasmuch as locality groups hardly appear and the clan is simultaneously family, State and Church (being limited exclusively by the magical brotherhoods). Thus, Durkheim's characterization, emphasizing the structure of archaic society based on a series of identical segments (in contrast to all other types) remains more or less valid. We will take account of it, all the more since it is precisely the jural typology of backward society which has been best studied by the Durkheim school, whose contributions we shall utilize.

Taking all these points into consideration, we arrive at the following jural types of inclusive societies : (1) legal systems of poly-segmentary societies, having a magical-religious basis ; (2) legal systems of societies given homogeneity by the principle of theocratic-charismatism ; (3) legal systems of societies given homogeneity by the pre-eminence of the domestic-political group —relatively rationalized systems ; (4) legal systems of feudal societies based on the juridical pre-eminence of the Church— semi-mystical and semi-rationalized systems ; (5) legal systems of societies unified by the pre-eminence of the city and the empire —more rationalized systems ; (6) legal systems of societies unified by the pre-eminence of the territorial State and autonomy of individual will ; (7) legal systems of contemporary societies in which the groups for economic activity and the territorial State are struggling for a new jural equilibrium—transitory systems.

It is obvious that for each of these types one could give a number of historical illustrations and geographic variants, and that the distinction of an entire series of sub-types would become necessary if one were to go into details. Not less obvious is the fact that none of these types (except the last, which we have deliberately left vague) is to be found in a pure expression in history, because sociological types straddle one another and combine with each other in varied ways. It is simultaneously the force and limitation of sociological types that they remain to some extent abstract and general, supplying points of support for the historian's efforts at individualization.

I. *Legal Systems of Poly-segmentary Societies, having a Magical-religious Base.* Inclusive archaic society is the tribe (*phratry, curia*) formed by the repetition of a series of identical segments called clans ("*genos*", *gentes*). The clans and tribes have a religious basis ; their emblems are totems, symbols of their gods, in which they participate and with which they commune in a mystic way. The kinship group is not differentiated here from the mystic-ecstatic group, for kinship and the exogamy which arises therefrom is here principally a link with the same totem. The locality group is not clearly defined, the clan is not always a " village community ". The religious group here absorbs locality groups, as it does for those of economic activity, at least to the extent that the latter has a domestic character. Under these conditions, it would be tempting to reduce all jural regulation to a single framework of common social law of clan and tribe having a religious basis—founded in taboos derived from the Holy and excluding every type of inter-individual law, all elasticity, alienability, mobility, even all particularistic law.

If it seems indisputable that jural sovereignty, diffuse in the tribe and penetrated by the transcendent supernatural, accords pre-eminence to totemic clans and to their law, archaic society, nevertheless, cannot at all be reduced exclusively to clans, as modern ethnography has shown. It is infinitely more complex, abounding in fraternal associations, age and sex groups, men's houses, clubs, secret societies, etc., sometimes limited to single clans, sometimes spreading over entire tribes. Their basis is also a belief in the supernatural, not the holy transcendent supernatural which requires submission, but the magical, immanent, flexible supernatural, which can be ordered about and even created (*Mana*, pointed out by Codrington for Melanesia, has been found under various names in the most diverse primitive societies).

The collective magical *Mana*—basis of the particularistic social law of the brotherhoods—partly releases the latter from the grip of religious taboos. The connection of magic with all risked effort and labour (Malinowski) favours concentration within the brotherhoods of certain economic activities (e.g., the blacksmith's craft) and military art. The limitations which the activity and law of the magical brotherhoods put upon the power of the clan benefited the individuals who might possess different degrees of individual *mana*, permitting them to affirm their " prestige ", to occupy higher ranks in the brotherhoods, to appropriate alienable objects, to contract, and to trade. The works of Frazer, Mauss, Huvelin, Lévy-Bruhl, Malinowski, and Granet have shown the diverse aspects of the repercussions of magic on law and economy in primitive societies, repercussions of which remnants are found in very ancient Roman, Greek, Germanic, Chinese, and Hindu law.

Certain institutions represent an amalgamation of competing influences of both religion and magic, such as penal law which protects the inviolability of human life, and the formation of the State and royal power by the victory of the magical brotherhood over the clan—victory which transforms the chief of the former into a priest-king subjected to Religion. What is certain is the fact that the legal system of archaic society rests on the double base of Magic and Religion ; they are sometimes opposed to each other, sometimes interpenetrating. But always the common sacred law of the totemic clan possesses primacy over the particularistic law of the brotherhoods as well as over the interindividual and inter-group law, both being inspired by magical *Mana* (cf. my article " Magic and Law " in *Social Research*, 1942, and my *Essais de Sociologie*, 1938, pp. 173–273).

The magical-religious basis of the jural system of poly-segmentary society leads to the following characteristics : (*a*) all power has here a character either theocratic (in the clan) or charismatic (magical eminence inherent in the holder of power in the brotherhoods, and, after the establishment of the State in the kings) ; (*b*) acts formulating, applying and sanctioning law have a mysterious character (oracles, law prophecies, " revelations " of law in the name of God or *Mana*, " ordeals " and " combats of God ", magical purifications and religious sacrifices, charms, curses, bonds through magical things and formulas, etc.) ; (*c*) any appropriation of a thing consists of its penetration by a supernatural force (religious in the case of inalienable property, especially land, magical in the case of alienable, especially property of mobile things) ; (*d*) finally, there predominates in social law the law of the communion, and in individual law the law of *rapprochement* (e.g., the gift) or separation (struggle) and not law of mixed structure (e.g., contract).

The French sociologist, P. Fauconnet, in his well-known work *Responsabilité* (1920), brought out sharply and penetratingly the connection of this institution in archaic societies with magical-religious beliefs. He emphasized that not only were conscious individuals and groups held responsible, but also children, madmen, corpses, animals, and even tools. The situations generating responsibility consisted in supernatural contamination by contact with an act violating a rite or a ban, whether the contact was connected with the infringement by causal link or not. Thence, among other forms, collective responsibility, which imposed punishment in regard to family or locality connected with the guilty, etc. The responsible subject, Fauconnet concluded, is, in such a society, the point of discharge of wrath of the outraged collective mind, the scapegoat. The function of responsibility here would be to " make possible the realization of punishment by furnishing it with a point of application ". It must be added, however, utilizing the path-breaking work of L. Lévy-Bruhl on primitive mentality, that, inasmuch as the idea of causality is entirely different in the primitive mind from ours, and that, being ignorant of secondary causes, primitive peoples seek mystic primary causes, causality in this sense would not at all seem absent from situations generating responsibility in archaic societies. This mystic causality may be attributed to conscious as well as to unconscious agents, children, madmen, corpses, tools, animals, and the like.

The works of Mauss and Davy on exchanges, gifts, the germs
of contractual relations, have clarified the institution of the
" potlatch " discovered by F. Boas in the American north-west
(see p. 154) and whose existence and rôle have been confirmed
in different regions (Melanesia, Papua, Polynesia, South America,
Africa).

The potlatch is a discounted gift which presupposes not only the
obligation to give but also that to accept and to return, a primitive
form of exchange which mobilizes and redistributes property. It is
also a form of challenge which gives rivals an opportunity to outdo
each other in showing off their treasures and which takes place in
connection with a feast, birth, marriage, invitation, inauguration of
a tomb, installation of a chief (Bouglé).

It is, above all, groups, clans, tribes, and magical brotherhoods which mutually obligate, trade with, contract with, affront
and oppose each other in that sort of festival-market which is the
potlatch. Thus, the first form of obligation and contract is
inter-groupal rather than inter-individual.

M. Mauss has brought out the fact that the functions of the
potlatch are not simply jural and economic, because it also has
the character of exchanges of names, blazonings, feasts, ceremonies, dances, rites, military services, etc. At the same time,
Mauss connected this institution with that of the gifts, and
through it with the action of magic, because the *mana* of the
giver is implied in the thing given ; this threatens the recipient
should the latter not return an equal gift implying his *mana*
(everything appropriated being a " magic appurtenance ").
Thus, the *mana* involved in the things exchanged enables each
to avenge the other if need be. The principle of " give and
take ", of a " gift for gift ", which underlies the law of obligation,
is manifested most plainly in the potlatch, for whatever is exchanged in a potlatch is penetrated by magical forces which
stimulate the circulation of gifts. " The circulation of goods
follows that of men, rites, ceremonies, dances, in a whole formed
by *mana* " immanent to men, groups and things and connecting
them with each other (Mauss).

G. Davy has described how the individual may profit from
a potlatch by the generosity of his gifts, to gain both magical and
economic prestige, to raise himself to higher social rank in the
clan or brotherhood. Therefore, the potlatch appears to be a
powerful factor of inter-individual, economic, jural, and even
political differentiation. Also, Davy tried to establish a parallel-

ism between the development of the potlatch-contract favourable to inter-individual law and the concentration of political power in the hands of a chief (birth of the State and of Royalty). This last process takes place especially, as we have said, through the channel of magical brotherhoods ; here the ascents to superior hierarchical rank, promotions to the post of chief based on both personal *mana* and wealth, are particularly frequent.

All we have exposed shows clearly that even the archaic system of law, despite the undifferentiated state of certain species of groups, represents a complex of different frameworks of law seeking an equilibrium and admitting a certain place to inter-individual and inter-groupal law. This situation is confirmed by the conflicts and compromises between Religion and Magic, Totem and Mana, the rigid and the elastic supernatural, jural primacy belonging, however, to the social law of the clan with its religious basis.

II. *Legal Systems of Societies given Homogeneity by the Theocratic-charismatic Principle.* All-inclusive societies can unify themselves by eliminating their segmentation into clans in various ways. (1) One is to superimpose on the identical segments and their tribal combination a new unity, that of the State-Church incarnated in a King-Priest-living God, which presupposes a particular combination of religion and magic and leads to theocratic-charismatic power ; the chief of State, who represents God and acts in his name, being qualified for this function by his own qualities, generally of magical character (charisma). (2) Another way of unification is through the absorption of dissolved segments in the domestic group, which represents an identity of the kinship group (now based on blood, particularly male filiation) with the economic activity group, often likewise connected with the locality and neighbourhood group. The all-inclusive society is here led to homogeneity by the predominance of the domestic-political group over all others, which can give rise to a patriarchal State. (3) Finally, a third way is the elimination of the segments by a " synoecism ", a junction and interpenetration of segments which have partially become domestic groups, in a " city " or "*polis* " with a territorial basis, to which primacy is accorded. Historically speaking, these three types can be interwoven with each other as well as combined in diverse fashions.

Historical instances of the first type are widespread and varied in the Orient, beginning with the Egyptian Empire (down to

H

the end of the IVth dynasty and after the XVIth), Babylon,
Assyria, the Hittite kingdom, Persia, China during the imperial
epoch (after 300 B.C. and especially after the Emperor Wan),
Japan, Peru before the discovery, India and Tibet, winding up
with the Islamic Khalifate under the Ommeyad and Abbassid
dynasties (eighth to twelfth centuries A.D.).   The unity in these
theocratic-charismatic empires, which correspond to the transition from tribal to national religion, is quite superficial, because
it depends on the personality of the chief or on the hereditary
supernatural qualities of his dynasty.   It is the son of the " King
of the Sun " (Ra, in Egypt, the Son of Heaven (China), the
descendant of the prophet of Allah (Mohammed), etc., who alone
embodies this unity.   At the same time, the enormous expansion
of the framework is brought about by the predominance of the
mass-element over that of community and communion, the
subjects of Oriental empires being, despite their theocratic character, an amorphous body.   Under this vascillating unity, there
continue to exist the ancient segments or domestic-patriarchal
groups and various brotherhoods.   Some of these societies, before
having been homogenized by the theocratic-charismatic principle, went through a long feudal period (e.g., China and Japan)
or, on the other hand, became feudal between two periods of
unification (e.g., Egypt under the Vth-XIth dynasties).

What characterized the legal systems of these societies was,
on the one hand, their rigidity, related to their divine and
mysterious origin (e.g., in principle, Islamic law is in its entirety
included in the Koran), and on the other hand, arbitrariness of
application into which enter religious and moral motives as well
as the direct inspiration of the chief or of priests and judges acting
in his name.   To the extent, however, that it was necessary to
give a more precise basis for the concrete application of these
legal systems, there were recourses on flexible patterns, models of
conduct (the " *hadith* " which constitute the " sunnah " in Islamic
law), or the opinions of theological jurists (the " *fikh* " in Islamic
law).

It is interesting to observe that such a jural regime does not
exclude the existence of civil courts parallel with those of the
temple, e.g., in Babylonian law as given in the Hammurabic Code
(2000 B.C.) or in Egyptian law, which admits the function of the
hequa het aat and of the *sab*, judges, and which worships a special
goddess of civil justice, " *Maat* ".   The possibility of such distinctions derives from the fact that everybody linked with the

theocratic-charismatic chief, whether priest or layman, acquires a share in the latter's supernatural powers.

Even more important is the fact agreed upon by all historians of the law of these types of society (e.g., J. Pirenne, *Histoire des Institutions et du Droit Babylonien, les Lois Assyriennes et les Lois Hittites*, 1928), that theocratic-charismatic systems of law do not bar a notable development of law of exchanges with pronounced individualistic character, implying a law of obligation, contract, credit, and presupposing the alienability and divisibility even of landed property. The Hammurabic code leaves no doubt on this score, and observation of customary Islamic law shows generous borrowings from Roman and Hellenic law. It seems impossible to explain this fact except by the persistence and growth, under the cover of theocratic-charismatic unity, of broad layers of independent social and jural life, partly inspired by magic, partly surmounting it through a certain rationalistic trend connected with economic calculation ; but in any case these regulations are not directly integrated in the general legal system. The latter is concerned only with common social law, here assuming the character of masses law and hence achieving only a very limited primacy.

III. *Legal Systems of Societies given Homogeneity by the Pre-eminence of the Domestic-political Group—relatively rationalized systems.* The kinship group based on masculine filiation, involving economic activity and more or less attached to the soil, can win pre-eminence in the all-inclusive society over clans, tribes, brotherhoods, etc. The domestic group thus becomes the germ of a State, and may be described as domestic-political, sometimes serving as a model for a true patriarchal State. The social structure described in the Old Testament, in the *Iliad* and *Odyssey*, as well as the Slavic *Zadruga*, are different instances of the pre-eminence of the domestic-political group under its patriarchal form. Some traits of this type may also be studied in the " Roman family ", which, however, was integrated in a very different species of all-inclusive society, as well, finally, as in the *latifundia* peopled by the *coloni* of the Roman Empire (later period). The German *Hausgenossenschaften*, which appear through the *Marks* (clans becoming " village-communities " which annually distribute parcels of collective landed property among the families), the *Gau* (county) and the *Sippenschaft* (tribe), suggest domestic-political groups without any proper patriarchal character. To the extent that the primacy of the domestic-political group is connected with private landed property the chief may become the monarch of a patriarchal State, of which the Roman *latifundia* represent a sketch. As historic instances, one may cite the Frankish monarchy (sixth to ninth centuries), to some extent the Russian monarchy in the Muscovite period, and, finally, the patriarchal implications of the Egyptian, Chinese, and Islamic theocracies.

The system of law corresponding to the predominance of the domestic-political group in an all-inclusive society is characterized by the following traits : (A) Subordination in the political field of social law to the individual right of the chief as landowner. (B) There is confusion between legislation and administration on the one hand, and economic management on the other. Thus, for instance, the " capitulary *de villis* " of the Frankish epoch is still to some extent a set of instructions given to the managers of the king's properties rather than a collection of " laws ", the statutes—*leges barbarorum*—being nothing but codifications of existing customary law. At the same time, officials bear, quite characteristically, the titles of personal employees of the king having to do with his court and domain ; they are called " seneschal " or intendant, marshal-overseer of the stables, cupbearer and treasurer, finally " count of the palace " who later becomes special guardian of the administration of justice and *major-domus* who rises above all other officials.

(C) The most important part of the life of law remains free from the intervention of the patriarchal State, being concentrated in popular custom, whether codified or not, and law is mainly applied by the popular benches (*mallus* in the Frankish epoch) in which only elders hold sittings. To the extent that the kings or their officials (sometimes as presidents of the popular courts) intervene in trials, they introduce the patriarchal and intimate spirit of family life, judging more in terms of equity (the *Sühne* of Germanic law, characteristic of justice within the *Sippe*) than in terms of predetermined rules.

(D) The domestic-political group being a restricted and stable one, it generally realizes in its midst the sociality as community rather than as mass or communion. That is why, when the unification of an all-inclusive society takes place under the primacy of this group, i.e., in a patriarchal manner, the community begins to play a more important rôle in the life of law—a rôle favourable to its development. This influence, however, is strongly limited by the fact that, in the domestic-political group, the community has only a semi-active, semi-passive character (passivity, as we are aware, leading to sterility from the jural viewpoint). Another obstacle lies in the submission of community law to the individual right of the patriarchal chief.

(E) The same rise of the element of the community—limited it is true—in regard to jural life comes about with the decline of the influence of religious and magical beliefs in law. Even when the chief of the domestic-political group plays the rôle of priest of the family gods, this is but a secondary function which easily passes into the hands of a special sacerdotal class, servitors of the superior tribal and national gods. Thus the system of law corresponding to a society equilibrated by the patriarchal principle is characterized by a certain degree of rationalization and secularization, affecting, it is true, content rather than formal procedures. This debut of rationalization, however, touches barely, if at all, the most important levels of law (e.g., customary law, which remains exterior to patriarchal unification).

IV. *Systems of Law of Feudal Society with Semi-rational, Semi-mystical Basis.* The feudal type of society is an extremely complex equilibrium between different types of groups and their corresponding jural frameworks, an equilibrium the principles of which cannot be reduced to a single principle. On the one hand, there is the pre-eminence of the bloc or hierarchized federation of patriarchal groups, founded on the combination of privilege and personal devotion to a suzerain lord (vassalage), giving birth to a series of superimposed " fiefs ". On the other, there is the pre-eminence of a mystic-ecstatic group which, under Christian influence, has taken the form of a Church quite distinct from all other groups and incarnating, in the Middle Ages, the super-functional union under its aspect of *corpus mysticum.* These two blocs share primacy.

But, beside this twofold supremacy in competition, there are independent functional and extra-territorial activity groups (sometimes taking a fraternal form) which in the economic sphere are manifested in merchant associations, guilds, *corps de métiers,* regencies, and precentorships (the union of all these associations is at the basis of " cities ", " communes "). In the non-lucrative sphere, these groups appear in the " estates " of the nobility (in the case of " knightly orders " in the form of fraternal societies), the clergy, the commons, the villeins and the serfs, and in monastic orders, religious and charitable brotherhoods, universities, etc.

What is certain is the fact that the " State " in feudal society has no proper territorial character (neither in the form of the Holy Roman Empire nor in that of the totality of leading lords of a region, barely connected with the feudal king). Moreover, the State is not only without any jural primacy over all these groups and is rather inferior to them, but it hardly contrives to exercise unconditional constraint in the extremely limited sphere of competence assigned to it. If one insists on the definition of the State as a junction of a bloc of locality groups and a monopoly of unconditional constraint, it would seem beyond dispute that feudal society is one without a State, one in which the State is dead ; since what we call the State has in that society neither of the two required characteristics. Under these conditions, the distinction between public and private law, which always arises from the State, is not applicable to the most important jural orders of feudal society.

That is why it would be erroneous to say, as historians and jurists often have said, that the system of feudal law is a mixture, a confusion of public and private law. The specific nature of this system is precisely the fact that these categories are inapplicable. Even more false would be a reduction of the system of hierarchized fiefs, relations between lords and vassals, to an amalgamation of real and contractual law. The bond of personal devotion between vassal and lord which is established by " homage and faith " on one side and by " investiture " on the other, has a form reminiscent of the contract only in a very external sense. At bottom, this bond is not related with sociality by inter-dependence and equality and does not arise from inter-individual law. The act of " infeudation " is one of integration in a pre-existing whole, an uninterrupted chain of interpenetrated " allegiances ". Thus, it rests on a sociality by fusion in the We, and arises from social law as do the majority of other feudal jural institutions. From this viewpoint, the act establishing vassalage may be compared to collective bargaining and all other contemporary forms of " contracts of adhesion " which are contracts in name alone. From this point of view, the jural system of feudal society may be characterized by the very sharp preponderance of different orders of non-State social law over individual law, but the majority of manifestations of this social law have the character of hierarchical law of domination. This character comes either from the enslavement of social law to individual law through the patrimonial principle (one of the bases of feudal power) [1] or directly from the supernatural element which transcends the jural in the monistic *corpus mysticum* whose visible incarnation is the Church. This last reinforces the subordinative structure of its law by appealing to the tradition of Roman law (whence the " Roman-canonical doctrine "). Only in the free associations of economic activity and their unions in city-communes does social law under the feudal regime appear to be an equalitarian social law of collaboration.

The system of law of mediæval society is characterized by extraordinary particularism and pluralism. The feudal order of law (itself divided into seigneurial or domanial law and feudal law proper), the order of canon law, the order of municipal law (of which franchises sketched only the general outline), the order of merchant and craft guild law, customary popular law applied to villeins and serfs, represent independent systems of law to which must be added also royal law and Roman law (in the regions of " written law ").

As a parallel, the administration of justice, the power to punish, is scattered among innumerable groups. Every feudal lord has the double power of judging the inhabitants of his fief and his vassals. The Church has its own courts with very wide jurisdiction competing with the secular courts. The free cities possess their own judicial organs connected with the municipalities, merchant and craft guilds. The universities have their courts. (In Germany, we must also note the secret punitive societies, the *Fehmgerichte*.) Moreover, the requirement according to which nobles have a right to be tried " by their peers " is applied, in the last analysis, to all classes of feudal society. This produces in all secular courts a multiplication of assizes made up of notables from the *milieu* of the defendant (experts in the relevant customary law), and only placed under the presidency of a representative of the lord, the city, etc. The material jurisdictions of these diverse courts often criss-cross and compete, their conflicts often being resolved by the fact that the points at issue have been submitted to them by the interested parties themselves, which lends to the courts the colour of courts of arbitration.

[1] The fief, penetrated by the act of infeudation and wherein are super-imposed the rights on the land of several subjects forming a network, obviously is something quite different from property in the Roman or modern sense. One may here be tempted to speak of a law of " organic " property and to apply the Germanic formula of " the common hand " (*Gemeinschaft zur gesammten Hand*) ; in feudal landed property there remains, however, an element which indisputably comes from individual law on patrimony.

It can be indicated, however, that there was one group whose courts had a particularly broad jurisdiction which, from the tenth to the thirteenth centuries, tended to expand simultaneously with the tendency to the pre-eminence of the jural order which this group engendered. This was the Church. Church courts were universally competent *in ratione personae*, that is to say, in all criminal and civil matters concerning the clergy, as well as the *miserabiles*, widows, orphans and crusaders. These courts, moreover, had the power to act *ratione materiae*, that is, in all matters having to do with faith, marriage conflicts, most questions relating to wills, inheritance, adultery, infanticide, usury. The jurisdiction of ecclesiastical courts, competing with secular jurisdiction, extended to promises and obligations, and especially to violations of contracts. The latter jurisdiction depended on the plaintiffs, who generally appealed to ecclesiastical courts. In fact, canon law applied by Church courts was better elaborated and more human than the law applied by secular courts (except, perhaps, those of the municipalities), and their procedure was less formalistic. " Less eager for gain than the justice of the lords, Church justice enjoyed general popularity " (Calmette, *Société Féodale*, 1923).

The Church also claimed that " the negligence of secular judges is enough to authorize a party to a dispute to appeal in any sort of question to ecclesiastical justice ". If we add that the Church had a very broad right of asylum and that it intervened with the secular powers on behalf of all who sought refuge with it ; that it was the Church which initiated the " peace of God " (exempting certain people from the violence of armed conflicts) and the " truce of God " (suspending hostilities during certain days : Friday evening to Monday—and for certain holy periods) ; that the Church represented, finally, the visible incarnation of the *corpus mysticum*, integrating, according to the conception of the Middle Ages, the whole plurality of autonomous groups in a superior unity, it may be declared without hesitation that jural primacy in the feudal legal system was attributed by collective beliefs to the Church and its canon law.

One cannot cite against this conclusion the struggle which, from the eleventh to the fourteenth centuries, split the partisans of the Pope and those of the Emperor, the Guelphs and Ghibellines. For the famous conflict over investitures between Pope Gregory VII and Henry IV was not over the question of the jural primacy of the Church, which nobody denied earlier

DIFFERENTIAL SOCIOLOGY OF LAW

than the fourteenth century, but over the rôle of the Church in the chain of secular feudal rights over fiefs. The Pope claimed for the Church the right to break the chain of feudal allegiances in its favour. It was only an enlargement of the quarrel which led to exaggerated claims from the point of view of the legal system of that epoch. The partisans of Popes Alexander III, Innocent III, and Boniface VIII came to demand *dominium mundi* for the Church, that is, its transformation into a World State. The partisans of the Emperors of the Holy Roman Empire supported by the jurists of the Bologna School (who were nourished in Roman law) came to negate even the jural primacy of the Church, both parties finding themselves in conflict with contemporary positive law.

The primacy of canon and ecclesiastical law should not be interpreted as supremacy of the mystical over the rational element in the jural system of feudal society. In fact, canon law was a complex combination of jural rules borrowed from Roman law based on rational logic, as well as from Holy Writ and the Church Fathers. On the other hand, secular feudal law itself was penetrated with mystical elements, the chief one being the " faith " involved in relations between lords and vassals and in the consecration of knights. The same must be said for the customs of various circles of the population, for example, the survival of certain forms of trial by ordeal. Thus, we may say of canon and ecclesiastical law, as of feudal law in general, customary law and even the law of merchant and craft guilds (the two latter were connected with religious brotherhoods), that they were jural codes with mixed bases, semi-mystic and semi-rationalist. Only the tradition of Roman law revived after the twelfth century by the University of Bologna (the Glossators school), afterwards growing constantly stronger, as well the law of municipalities, represented a purely rationalistic element in the system of feudal law.

The feudal system of law showed its mixed and pluralistic character from another point of view too. If in the Church (at least at the outset of the Middle Ages) communion law predominated, and in the cities, merchant, and craft guilds community law (also affirming itself in the internal law of knighthood and within all social estates), in the relations between lords and the inhabitants of their domains either mass law or extra-legal violence predominated.

V. *Systems of Law of Societies unified by the Pre-eminence of the*

City and the Empire—more rationalized systems. Unification of the
jural order of the all-inclusive society may come about through
the supremacy of a specific territorial group, the city, the town,
symbolizing the locality and neighbourhood principle which first
limits and later gradually dissolves groups based on kinship and
religious beliefs (*genos, gentes ; curias, phratries, etc.*) ; thus was
established a direct contact between the central power and *patres
familias* (*singuli singulas familias incipiunt habere*) and later with
each individual citizen.   Unification of this kind is illustrated
by the Greek *polis* (seventh to fifth centuries B.C.) and the Roman
civitas (fifth to first centuries B.C.).   The affirmation of the jural
primacy of the city over all other groups is marked by the following characteristics : democratization and secularization of law,
differentiation of law from religion and ethics, opposition between
public and private law and, finally, legal individualism.   Democratization proceeds hand in hand with the reinforcement of the
territorial principle.   The inclusion of the plebeian in the city,
with equality before the law, first, then later with equality of
rights (the reforms of Solon, Cleisthenes and Pericles in Greece ;
the law of the " Twelve Tables ", the reforms attributed to
Servius Tullius, the series of laws culminating in the *lex Hortensia*
in Rome), are accompanied by the replacement of groups based
on birth and mystic creed (passing through a stage of classes
qualified to vote by their wealth) by new groups based on domi-
cile.   The rôle at Rome of the *comitia tributta* which gradually
displaced the *comitia curiatta* is typical of this development.

The secularization and rationalization of the legal system of
the city are related to its very structure.   Despite the absence of
opposition between city and Church, the locality and neighbourhood group dominates religion because in the city the community
prevails over the ecstatic communion.   Furthermore, the more
territoriality, and with it democratization, advances, the more
does the influence of religious belief decline, the " gods of the
city " losing influence over law.   It is precisely in order to free
law from secret mysteries, to wrest it from the hands of priests
and arbitrary oracles, to make it common knowledge, changeable
by the human will and reason, that there takes place a struggle
between the *demos* and the *eupatrides*, between the plebs and the
patricians ;   a struggle whose first outcome, the legislation of
Solon and the Twelve Tables, constituted an obvious revolt
against the religious conception of law as an unchangeable and
indisputable revelation.   " What the votes of the people ordered

in the last analysis is the law," the Twelve Tables already proclaim. The *themistes*, sprung from a shadowy tradition, are
replaced by *nomoi*, promulgated openly and resting on a purely
rational base (cf. Glotz, *La Cité Grecque*, 1928, and Fustel de
Coulanges, *La Cité Antique*). Prætors and " prudents " (jurisconsults) in Rome, *dicastes* and *heliastes* (juries) in Greece, all
purely secular agents, entirely replace pontifical jurisdiction.
Judicial procedure drops formalism which is linked with magic,
utilizes rational formulas which become more and more flexible.
Roman law, particularly, became the classic example of a purely
secular law, founded on a quite perfect autonomous " jural
logic " (*ratio scripta*). It is entirely distinct from religion and
ethics set off against the *fas* as well as the *mos*.

The principle of the *persona* as the centre of jural life, a principle
introduced by the Romans and having as its primary significance
the mask,[1] received in Roman law a double meaning : that of
the subject of the " jural mask "—the subject of law—as distinct
from the moral agent and religious being, and that of the commanding will belonging to the *persona* as separated with and
opposed to other *personae* (conceived as simple and absorbing
unities). The *persona* was considered as the unique and exclusive
foundation of all jural links, of every obligatory force of the law.
On a small scale, this *persona* is the *paterfamilias* with his *dominium*,
while on a grand scale it is the *civitas* with its *imperium* and *potestas*,
whence the reduction of all law either to subordination or
co-ordination. The equilibrium between *imperium–potestas*, guaranteeing the *dominium* of private persons as well as the limitations
imposed thereby on the *imperium*, is the major inspiration of the
Roman legal system, which thus shows its penetration by an
increasingly emphasized jural individualism. The pre-eminence
of the locality and neighbourhood group over all others, as well
as the junction in the family (which alone constituted a limitation
of the power of the State) of kinship and economic activity groups,
favoured jural individualism (associations and brotherhoods,
hetairiai and *thiasoi* in Greece, *sodalitates* and *collegia* in Rome
never played a considerable rôle in economic or jural life). The
familia had an absolute chief in the *paterfamilias*, whose will inside
the homestead was at first without any limitation ; this was his
private domain where—until a much later period—the law of
the city did not penetrate.

[1] Cf. on this question the very penetrating sociological analysis of Mauss, " Une
catégorie de l'esprit humain : la notion de personne, celle de ' moi ' " (*Huxley Memorial
Lecture, London,* 1938).

The isolated will of the *paterfamilias* made law in the family, just as the will of the city made law in the latter, and an agreement of equal wills of two or more *patresfamilias* established an obligation (if not delictual) among them. As a consequence, all jural rules were reduced either to law of commandment or of isolation, with the law of integration excluded.

Here is the primary source of an important jural distinction, characteristic of the legal system of the city and unknown either to the theocratic-charismatic legal system or to that of patriarchal and feudal law. This is the dichotomy of public and private law. Its origin lies in the primacy of the law of the city over the internal law of families, of the *imperium* over the *dominium*. The private power founded on the patrimony is here sharply distinguished from public power founded on the city ; on the other hand, *privatorum conventio juri publico non derogat*. The principle of the mentioned primacy expressed in the very term *respublica*, and showing itself in the contrast between *ordo judiciorum privatorum* and *persecutiones publicae*, *dikai* (private actions) and *graphai* (public actions), could not admit a private law with sources entirely heterogeneous to the city. Thus arose the notion of *civil law* in which *private law* was integrated as a part—*jus civile* linked with the quality to be a citizen of the city ; nevertheless, this law remained opposed to *jus publicum*. That private law was regarded as a sector of *jus civile* indicates that it was available only by virtue of membership in the city, which alone guaranteed *dominium*, *connubium* and *commercium*, the capacity of owning property, marrying legally, and concluding contracts and obligations.

Through *jus civile*, the city intervenes in private law and modifies it, not so much directly by means of law and prætorian edicts, however, as by indirect means : interpretations by prudents, juriconsults, custom and court practice. (That is why *jus civile* may be contrasted with *leges* as well as with the *jus honorarium*, the law embodied in prætorian edicts.) Thus, the differentiation between civil and public law, as well as the primacy of the latter, does not lead directly to the centralization of all sources of law in legislation and to jural statism.

This last was simply the effect of the substitution of the city-regime by that of the *principate* and later by the *Empire*, characterized by the development of an imperial bureaucracy, of excessive centralism, of Cæsarian absolutism and, finally, by the predominance of the mass element over that of the community in the whole of the all-inclusive society. It was in this epoch (to which we owe the Code of Justinian, A.D. 534) that Roman private law was definitively universalized and rationalized (civil law being identified with the *jus gentium*, because all free subjects of the Roman State had received full rights of citizenship). On the other hand, Roman public law was deformed by the penetration of theocratic elements borrowed from the Orient and became the source of all statist conceptions of law.

VI. *Entirely secularized and logicized Systems of Law of Societies unified by the pre-eminence of the Territorial State and the autonomy of Individual Wills (primacy of State law and contract).* The type of all-inclusive society whose thoroughly rationalized jural system rests on the supremacy of the law of the territorial State and on the freedom of individual contracts, corresponds to the classic capitalist regime characteristic of Western life from the sixteenth to the end of the nineteenth centuries. This system was in full course of formation under the *ancien régime* when the territorial State, in the form of an absolute monarchy supported by the bourgeoisie (the third estate), had begun to affirm its " indivisible and inalienable " sovereignty against feudalism and the guild system, internally, and against the Holy Roman Empire and the Pope, externally. " One king, one law " was the leading watchword of this regime which tended towards dissolution of " intermediate bodies " lying between the individual and the State, as well as towards affirming the equality of all citizens before the law. Only a law sufficiently general and fixed in advance whose applications could be calculated in advance and which would leave freedom of movement to the will of the individual (*laisser faire, laisser passer*), could satisfy the needs of the nascent bourgeoisie and its great industrial and commercial enterprises. It was at this epoch that Roman law was adopted in its entirety in Germany, and other regions where it had not been applied earlier. On the other hand, the appearance on the scene, thanks to the Reformation, of several competing Christian Churches, made acute the problem of the limitation of the power of the State to the benefit of individual freedom.

But it was not until after the French Revolution, after the Declaration of the Rights of Man and Citizen and the Napoleonic Civil Code, after the radical elimination of the last vestiges of feudalism, the dissolution of the estates and guilds, the suppression of the monarchy and its theocratic survivals in favour of " national sovereignty ", after the geometrical and deductive spirit of the eighteenth century had penetrated into the legal system, after, finally, the triumph of the synthesis of liberty and equality as the basis of all power, that this type of jural regime achieved its most complete expression.

The system of law founded on this basis is too well known for us to have to expatiate on its characteristics. Let us observe simply some differences with the antecedent systems. The family group has been reduced to a contractual relation and domestic society has been eliminated from it in favour of the household. Civil law has been oriented towards economic life, from which slavery and serfdom have been excluded. All property—landed almost as much as other forms—has become mobile and property has been transformed into a right of values. The modern State of vast extent has become independent of the city. There have been introduced the principles of the division of powers, of representation, and of officialdom. The law of the State has become sovereign, binding the judge and reducing custom and judicial practice to secondary rôles. Finally, and as a compensation for legal centralization, there are affirmed, parallel with the most complete freedom of will and contractual liberty, public " subjective " rights of citizens which directly limit the power of the State and enjoy the guarantee of either administrative or constitutional courts.

This system favours only State law and the rights of individuals. It disfavours or entirely ignores groups of non-territorial character (the development of communal and municipal autonomy does not contradict this tendency, because this concerns precisely *local* self-government agencies belonging as territorial groups to the State). If the State cannot dissolve economic activity groups, which multiply with the development of industry, it permits them to exist only on the margin of official law and endeavours to see in them nothing but simple contractual relationships or legal fictions. Thus, inter-individual law overtakes social law ; the latter manifests itself as organized law principally in the condensed form of territorial law of the democratic State and, as unorganized law, it is driven into the shadow of the jural order of the Nation, scarcely visible and generally ignored.

VII. *Transitional System of Law of Contemporary Society.* In this system the different kinds of social law, whether pure or annexed by the State, take their revenge. Since economic activity, even if one leaves aside the development of trade unions, is concentrated in enterprises—vast organizations of domination, within which rules a subordinative economic law that eludes popular sovereignty and has no relation to contract—and since there can be no equality of jural wills between the economically powerful and the economically feeble, the system of the " Declaration of Rights " and the Napoleonic Code is quickly sapped by the very forces which brought about its elaboration. The rigidity of the system of the sovereignty of State law and contract, since it appeals only to organized law fixed in advance, precipitates its ruin by provoking sharp conflict with spontaneous and flexible social law engendered by economic society.

The development of organized capitalism (joint-stock companies, cartels, trusts),[1] of trade unionism, of collective labour agreements, simultaneously breaks up the principles of national sovereignty and the autonomy of will, as well as freedom of contract. The aforementioned institutions express themselves in organized social law which competes with the framework of State law. At the same time, industrial property, separated from ownership (possession), undergoes a change in character and is enveloped by a multiplicity of superimposed or juxtaposed owners (possessors) combined in a whole which leads either to a federalization of property (joint property of co-operatives, etc.) or to the recrudescence with renewed force of quasi-feudal fiefs (relations between finance and industrial capital, between large and small industry). In both cases the network of inter-penetrating ownerships and the jural frameworks which rule them undermine the authority of the State and deprive it of the legislative monopoly to which it had laid claim. On the other hand, organizations of international society, such as the League of Nations, the International Labour Office, and the Permanent Court of International Justice, sometimes very strong as in the decade after the First World War, sometimes very feeble as in the last years before the war of 1939, but always based on economic and political requirements of prime importance, raise the problem of the limitation of the legislative authority of the State from the outside.

Even the jural pre-eminence of the State (within which the community element gives way more and more to the mass element) is challenged anew. Anarchy reigns in economic society where, in the place of contractual relations which have become inapplicable, unforeseen institutions arise and where the element

---

[1] See the forthcoming volumes of the International Library of Sociology and Social Reconstruction : A. B. Levy, *Corporations and their Control* (2 vols.) ; Andrew Neugroschel, *The Control of Industrial Combinations.* Cf. also in the same Library, Rudolf Schlesinger, *Soviet Legal Theory,* Its Social Background and Development.

of the communion (in struggling classes and trade unions) and the element of the masses (in enterprises, still more in the aggregation of unemployed, and finally in the whole economic society) stand opposed to each other. In the face of this unbalanced situation, two new competitors raise their heads : the autonomous jural organization of economy on the basis of industrial democracy and totalitarianism of different kinds.

It should not be thought that the rise of contemporary totalitarian States, fascist and other, contradicts the fact of the overthrow of relations between the State and the various other groups. It is the growing struggle of competing aggregations of big capital and of trade unionism which provokes the desperate effort of the State to integrate them within itself, in order the better to enslave them as organs of the State by the semblance of a " corporative organization of industry " imposed from outside. This of course can succeed only by virtue of a personal dictatorship displaying all the traits of charismatic power, based upon a revival of mystic beliefs in an unexpected field, which repel all jural beliefs and crush all control of law over political and social life. These mystic beliefs, moreover, are acting only in the " chief's escort " (the fascist " élite ") in which communion predominates, while in the population and in the entire nation the mass element predominates. As for the community, most favourable to jural life, it is no longer able to survive.

The reverse tendency of contemporary all-inclusive society is to enforce the community element in economic society by integrating groups of producers and consumers in the whole according to the principle of parity. This integration is based on a framework of common, pure and independent social law, equivalent in validity to the State law. It presupposes the autonomous organization of economic society in a vast federated association of collaboration. The organs of industrial democracy, beginning with factory councils and running up to a National Economic Council ; " directed economy " subjected to the control and rule of interested parties themselves ; federated and mutualized industrial, agricultural and financial property—all are different aspects of the same future organization. Its realization alone could lead both to the elimination of employers and a new jural equilibrium between the bloc of locality groups—the State—and the bloc of economic activity groups, i.e., to a pluralistic democracy which, by that very fact, would be a socialist regime.

The territorial State thus materially limited in its jural competences but disposing of unconditional constraint would then be effectively counterbalanced by a jurally equivalent independent economic organization. Not exercising unconditional constraint, this organization would find its resistive power in the federated property on which it would rest. Conflicts between the two organizations would be regulated by a supreme court of arbitration acting in the name of the super-functional Nation and of its spontaneous and flexible framework of social law which rules the relations and the equilibria among the functional groups integrated in the all-inclusive society.[1]

The strengthening of State power and authority which may be observed to-day even in the American and British democracies under the influence of sharp economic and international crises, are not decisive counter-indications of the tendency towards pluralistic democracy. In fact, it is difficult to state definitely whether the recent phase of State interventionism is not simply a temporary intensification of power in order to support the development of the autonomous collaborative groups of economic activity which will one day be called on to limit the State itself (the State to-day aiding these groups in their struggle against industrial feudalism and employer autocracy) ; or whether, on the contrary, there are tendencies towards a directed economy with an authoritarian basis, and finally, new types of totalitarianism and tyranny.

The sociology of law, like all sociology, is concerned neither with predicting nor with evaluating the future. Various tendencies and legal systems are at grips with each other in the transitional society of to-day. The only thing which appears to us beyond question is the fact that the tendency towards pluralistic democracy is the most favourable to jural culture, to the safeguarding of the autonomy of social control through law contrasted with other spheres of control and regulation. Certainly the legal system of a pluralistic and socialistic society would be more flexible and mobile, less formalistic and rigid, but it would remain in essence a jural regulation, a field which cannot be reduced to mystic-ecstatic beliefs and pure technique. On the other hand,

[1] See the more detailed description of this tendency in present-day society in my article, " The Problem of Social Law ", *International Journal of Ethics* (1941, October), and my books, *Le Temps Présent et l'Idée du Droit Social* (1932), and *Expérience Juridique et Philosophie Pluraliste du Droit* (1935), pp. 235-95 ; in the same text see my appreciation from this point of view of the principles inspiring the " New Deal " policy.

if a new authoritarian system should emerge from to-day's struggles, it would seem indisputable that the jural sphere would largely lose its influence, giving way to regulations and collective beliefs of other kinds which will produce regimes to be regarded, from a jural point of view, as a degeneration.

CHAPTER V

GENETIC SOCIOLOGY OF LAW

Genetic sociology of law must renounce the evolutionist pre-judice which believes that the " germ " of an uninterrupted unilinear development of jural institutions may be found in primitive society and which confuses problems of the legal typology of societies with that of their origin. The two problems proper to genetic sociology of law are (*a*) a study of regularities as tendencies of change within each type of legal system, and (*b*) a study of the factors of such regularities of transformation in the life of law in general.

Section I : Regularities as Tendencies of Change

Regularities in change which can be established for social life apply only on the macrosociological scale, being connected with inclusive structures and relations between groups ; they are inapplicable on the microsociological scale. On the other hand, these regularities are not " laws " of evolution whether static or dynamic, because of the extremely high degree of indeterminate-ness which characterizes social reality and particularly jural reality (connected with collective symbols and values). Regular-ities in this field are only " chances " (Weber), " probabilities ", " tendencies ", whose realization is limited by a wide margin of unpredictability. That is why we speak of " regularities as tendencies ". Finally, as we have said above, regularities as tendencies can be established only for one type of all-inclusive society.

The passage from one type to another always implies dis-continuity ; the hiatus is here so pronounced, the types which can substitute in a given society being capable of such extreme vari-ations, that it would be hazardous to seek here even probabilities.

The general regularities of transformation of jural institutions which some sociologists have believed they could observe may be reduced to the following : the movement from the pre-dominance of statute to that of contract (Spencer and H. Maine) ; the broadening and generalization of the circle of persons bound by the same jural order (Tarde) ; the progressive substitution of restitutive law for repressive law and the parallel growth of the rôle of the State and the contract (Durkheim) ; the multiplication and ever more intense interweaving of particular groupings and their codes, leading to a strengthening of the rights of individuals (the latter gain enfranchisement through the struggle among groups and their reciprocal limitation, cf. Bouglé, *Les idées égalitaires*, 1899) ; the increasing rationalization and logicization of law (Weber). Truth to tell, all these regularities are valid only for legal changes in certain types of society, most particularly the primitive one. The question is further complicated by the fact that every all-inclusive society and every system of law corresponding to such a society is a microcosm of jural frameworks and kinds of law, so that contradictory movements may take place within the same type, as we have already tried to establish in criticizing Durkheim's thesis.

By observing the regularities as tendencies which have to be stated separately for each type of legal system, it seems possible to us to reach the following conclusions which must be regarded only as working hypotheses ; this is all the more so since no type except the primitive and the contemporary has been submitted to sociological study deep enough to entitle us to speak of regularities more or less surely established.

For primitive society it is possible to add to the regularities enumerated above, a tendency towards the victory of magical brotherhoods over the clan, a victory which gives birth to the first form of State and the concentration of political sovereignty in the hands of a chief (Davy), as well as to a movement towards the weakening of the element of communion in favour of the element of community.

For the theocratic-charismatic system of law we can observe first of all a tendency to render the charismatic element " habitual ", prosaic, traditional (" *Veralltäglichung des Charismas* " as described by Weber). This is shown by the strengthening of the hereditary or elective principle in the succession of chiefs, and by the growing bureaucratization of law and administration, mystical elements becoming more and more conventional. At the same time, the conflict between the masses element, predominant in the subjected population, and the communion element, on which the unifying power is based, tends to decline through the formation of more limited groups (e.g., groups of officials or of theologian-jurisprudents, patriarchal groups, etc.), in which the community element is more pronounced. Finally, all these traits drive the theocraticocharismatic system towards a strengthening of the rôle of standards, patterns, customs, doctrines, statutes, in short, of law fixed in advance as opposed to law which springs from mysterious sources and the chief's direct inspiration.

Regularities of change which may be observed in the patriarchal system are a tendency towards the formation of conjugal and more limited domestic families, and the breaking up of the patrimony by its division among heirs. This leads to an opposition between the law belonging to family groups proper and the law of the domestic-political group in which the territorial element and hence also the political element proper are stronger. At the same time, the active element grows within the domestic-political group, whose law, having become thereby more effectively valid and more formally acknowledged, begins to limit the law of kinship groups in which intuitive and customary law predominates.

Owing to the extreme complexity of the feudal system of law, regularities as tendencies in its changes move in diverse and even contradictory directions. If the law of the hierarchized federation of lords and vassals shows a tendency towards the increasing limitation of the circle of subjects bound by such regulation, there is a tendency towards universality in the law both of the Church and of municipalities ; finally, State law moves towards territorial limitation and, within those confines, tends towards generalization. If the equalitarian and fraternal element progressively shrinks in feudal relations proper, it shows a trend towards intensification in guilds and municipalities, while in State law the growth of authoritarianism is accompanied by a levelling tendency in regard to subjects. Church law shows a tendency towards affirming jural supremacy, but the decline in intensity of the religious communion, which tends to relax towards the mass element, facilitates the resistance and final triumph of territorial law. Regularities as tendencies in the feudal legal system drive it in diverse directions ; besides the issue towards the absolutism of the territorial State as in the Occident, or of a charismatic theocracy as in the Orient (China, Japan, Egypt), an issue in the direction of a universal federalism of equivalent and equalitarian associations would appear not to have been excluded.

In the legal system of the ancient city we may observe regularities as tendencies towards the universalization of law, the broadening of the sphere of individual law limiting social law, the progressive and parallel growth of the State and contracts. Plato, Aristotle, and Polybius believed they could see in political law a cyclical movement from monarchy to aristocracy, thence to democracy (in its various forms) and finally to tyranny, which led back to monarchy and repetition of the cycle. This cyclical regularity is partly true with the twofold reservation that it is limited solely to the legal type of the city and that Cæsarism has very little relation to the initial monarchy.

The legal system founded on the pre-eminence of the territorial State and autonomy of individual will is characterized by the following regularities. First, a progressive march towards equality of rights, passing from equality before the political power to equality before the law, thence to equality of civil rights and finally to equality of political rights, including the right to liberty. Second, there is a trend towards rational " natural law " anticipating the reforms of positive law (the growing rôle of " utopia " in law). Other tendencies are a movement towards mobility and alienability of all private rights, shown especially in the growing pre-eminence of " laws of credence " over real law (E. Levy) ; an increasing difficulty for law of credence and for law of the State to penetrate into the inner life of economic groups ruled by an autocratic law on the margin of official law. There is, hence, a successive deepening of the disequilibrium between the legal order of the State and the jural framework of economic society.

In the contemporary legal system, which is to-day in full transition, there are, as we have already indicated, contradictory tendencies towards pluralistic democracy and towards totalitarianism. Obviously, no regularity of movement can be determined in advance. Other regularities manifest indisputable parallel decadence of statutory law of the State and of contract, an increasing return to particularization of jural regulations valid for limited circles of interested parties ; progressive strengthening of the framework of social law to the disfavour of the framework of individual law ; the growing rôle of law acknowledged *ad hoc* and of intuitive law to the disfavour of law acknowledged in advance ; the growth within law acknowledged in advance of the influence of custom, social declarations, tribunal and other practices, collective agreements, decrees, etc., all at the expense of State legislation ; the ever-sharper struggle between the jural frameworks of the various classes and professions.

SECTION II : FACTORS, INTRINSIC AND EXTRINSIC

Factors must be clearly distinguished from *causes* in the true sense of the word. This distinction holds for both natural and social sciences. For example, in explaining the blasting of a rock, the resistance of the rock, the dynamite and the fire are factors, while the cause is the force and expansion of gas. With respect to social phenomena, the study of causality, on the one hand, and of the factors, on the other, is complicated for the following reasons : (*a*) the cause of social facts always lies in " total social phenomena " (according to Cooley in America and Mauss in France) ; if the various aspects of society are to be explained, they must be integrated in the inclusive whole from which they have been more or less artificially detached ; (*b*) total phenomena, which alone are real social " causes ", represent qualitative types of all-inclusive societies and hence causal explanation is valid in sociology only within the particular type in question ; (*c*) the various social factors being only abstract aspects of a single whole which manifests itself in a qualitative inclusive type, they are interwoven with one another and affect each other mutually. If, for example, the ecological basis, economics, religion, magic, morals, and dominant mode of knowledge, are factors of the transformation of jural reality, this jural reality is in turn a factor of the transformation of each of these phenomena, and generally each of them is in the same situation from this viewpoint.

On the other hand, in each qualitative type of all-inclusive society, the rôle of different factors in the change of a social phenomenon (e.g., law) is not the same. This is not simply because the importance of a factor depends on the feature of the whole wherein lies effective causality, but also because the rapidity of movement of different social phenomena is not identical in different types of society or at different moments of existence of the same type. Thus, for example, religious and moral beliefs sometimes rush forward, sometimes remain behind jural beliefs ; jural reality sometimes lags behind economic, sometimes it outstrips it, etc. In principle, obviously " social factors " gain in importance in regard to a relatively background phenomenon and lose in importance when they lag behind this phenomenon.

Moreover, it should be noted that a distinction must be drawn between the *internal factors* of the movement of jural life, which consist of the conflicts and tensions between various kinds of law,

levels of depth, modes of acknowledgment, types of jural frameworks, and the *external factors* which are social phenomena other
than law. Since the intrinsic factors of change were described
in our exposition of the microsociology of law and of jural
typology, we may here limit our analysis to a study of extrinsic
factors.

I. *The Ecological Basis of Society and Law.* The material
substratum of society, principally demographical and geographical, i.e., the volume and density of population, the manner
of its distribution on the earth and even the character of the
latter, are unquestionably factors both of the general movement
of social life (the object of study of social morphology in the strict
sense) and of the movement of its particular aspects : economics,
law, religion, morality, etc. (the objects of study of the morphology of economics, law, religion, morality, etc., called by
Halbwachs social morphology " in the broad sense of the
term ").[1]

Durkheim, Mauss, and Halbwachs devoted important studies
to the repercussions on law of the volume and density of society,
never failing to emphasize that " material density " itself is subject to the influence of " moral densities " (especially of jural
beliefs, symbols and values), because it is profoundly transfigured
by collective human action and is penetrated by patterns, symbols,
ideas and values which the collective mind attributes to it.[2]
Durkheim believed he could prove that in societies which are
both extensive and very densely populated restitutive law (corresponding to organic solidarity) predominates over repressive law
(corresponding to mechanical solidarity). Mauss, by means of
a particular example involving seasonal variations in Eskimo [3]
societies, tried to show how the legal system of primitive tribes
was different in winter from what it was in summer. " Winter
law ", he argued, was connected with intensely concentrated
cohabitation, reminiscent of the clan, and was penetrated by
religion and collectivistic tendencies. " Summer law ", regulating the life of small, scattered families, had a more secular
character and was also more favourable to individualism. Halbwachs pointed out the different effects of scope and density of
population as well as of modes of agglomeration (countryside,
scattered villages, medium cities, concentrated cities) on the

[1] Cf. on this subject, M. Halbwachs, *Morphologie sociale* (1938).
[2] Cf. on this subject also L. Fevre, *La terre et l'évolution humaine* (1926).
[3] " Les variations saisonnières des sociétés esquimaux " in *Année Sociologique*, vol.
IX (1906).

organization of justice, structure and functioning of courts, relations between judges and those subjected to their courts and, finally, political regimes.

All these views, very instructive in themselves, require nevertheless more precision and concretization ; moreover, they must be connected with the different qualitative types of inclusive societies. In fact, the influence of the morphological basis on law and, inversely, of the legal system on the morphological basis, varies in different types of society and at different historic moments in the life of any particular type. Vast investigations are required, therefore, to establish the effective importance for jural life of the " material density " of societies of various structures. It seems beyond question that it was very great in primitive and patriarchal society, great also—if not decisive—in the theocratic-charismatic empires (where vast scope is combined with minimal density of population and striking instability and inconsistency of subdivisions), as well as during the broad migratory movements which preceded the Middle Ages.

The ecological factor does not, however, act so surely with respect to the city and feudal systems of law, and still less with respect to the present-day system of bourgeois law which seems to influence the material basis of society (particularly relations between births and deaths, urban-rural migrations and regional and international migrations) rather than to be dependent on them.

The only general conclusion which seems to be acceptable is that, as Halbwachs showed, the morphological basis would seem to exercise more intense influence on law and economics than on religion or, we may add, on morals or knowledge. Law, more than religion and morals, is linked with external reality, with collective forces proper, with people and things in so far as they find their place in the spatial *milieu* whose resistance to collective creative activity is particularly strong in the field of law. This leads us directly to the problem of the relation between law and economics, i.e., to an analysis of the rôle of another factor in the transformation of jural reality.

II. *Economics and Law.* No factor of the life of law has thus far been analysed or discussed so attentively as economics. The reason is that it appears unquestionable that there are particularly close ties between jural life and economic life. The English sociologists, Hobhouse, Ginsberg and Wheeler, in their book, *The Material Culture and Social Institutions of the Simple People*

(1930), even sought to establish by statistical methods a functional correlation between law and economics, by establishing for primitive society a very high coefficient of correlations, which could certainly also be done for other types of society, particularly bourgeois society in its contemporary transitional stage.

The fundamental problem, however, does not lie in this intense correlation, which nobody denies and which can be observed without recourse to statistics, but in the question of whether economics always leads and dominates jural reality (Marx) or whether law is the " logical form " and economics only the " matter " constituted by this form, a relationship which would bar any unilateral or reciprocal influences from both sides, since the two would be only aspects of the same thing (cf. R. Stammler, *Wirtschaft und Recht*, 1896, 3rd ed., 1924) ; or, finally, whether, depending on the type of society, economics sometimes leads law and law sometimes leads economics, their influence always being reciprocal (Weber, *Wirtschaft und Gesellschaft*, and Stammler's *Uberwindung der materialistischen Geschichtsauffassung*, 1907 ; B. Horwath, *Rechtssoziologie*, 1934).

The Marxist conception of the primacy of the economic factor is based on a doubly disputable premise. In the first place, it presupposes that law is simply an ideological projection, an epiphenomenon of the productive forces, which means that law has no social reality of its own. Secondly, it entirely identifies economics with the total social phenomenon (Marx wrote that " the totality of the relations of production is what we call society ", and his recent interpreter, H. Cunow, *Die marxistische Geschichts- Gesellschafts- und Staatstheorie*, 1923, 2 vols., plentifully elaborated this identification). Now, if the first premise is as arbitrary as it is anti-sociological, the second is simultaneously too narrow and too broad. It is too narrow in its conception of society, too broad in its conception of economy. Finally, the Marxist thesis comes down to a tautology : if economics and social reality are identical, the unilateral dependence of law on productive forces is obvious, since the cause of modifications of a social phenomenon cannot lie anywhere but in the whole of society, from which follows precisely the Marxist interpretation of economics, considered not as a factor, but as a cause.

Stammler's conception, representing a reaction from Marxism, exaggerates in the opposite sense. Stammler transforms effective positive law, with all its empirical content, into an ideal, logical form of society which cannot be influenced by economics, since the latter is only the tangible, sensible material of society formed by law. After denying the possibility of considering either law or economics as factors, Stammler, nevertheless, makes law structurally immutable and gives it both axiological and genetic primacy over economics. Profoundly contradictory from the methodological viewpoint, Stammler's thesis also collides with hard facts : such as the innumerable conflicts between jural and economic structures ; such as the existence of sectors of social reality in which jural regulation is inapplicable and which are sterile from the jural viewpoint (e.g., forms of passive sociality and groups in which passivity predominates) ; such as the sometimes more, sometimes less intense rôle of the legal system in different types of inclusive society. Moreover, Stammler confuses economics with all activity which satisfies needs, forgetting that what marks economic activity is the *limited character, the scarcity of the means of such satisfaction* and forgetting also the fact that collective activity is infinitely broader than economic activity. Moreover, he confuses social reality with its organized superstructures which alone effectively presuppose pre-existing law : the spontaneous law on which they are more or less based. Finally, despite his exaggerated struggle against Marxism, Stammler shares one of the basic prejudices of that doctrine : the identification of concrete society with economics which, in reality, is only one of its sectors. He does not notice that law may rule activities which have no direct connection with economics.

Thus, the sole acceptable theory is the conception which states that in various types of inclusive society, it is sometimes economics which, by overtaking the reality of law, serves as its factor, and sometimes law which, by leading economic reality, conditions the latter. For instance, in bourgeois and contemporary society, economics indisputably moves more rapidly than law ; since law has lags, changes in it are greatly influenced by economics. But not less indisputably in feudal society we can observe a greater mobility of the legal system than of economics ; here law dominates economics, sometimes fixing it within rigid confines (seigneurial law, guild monopolies), sometimes pushing it towards free competition and the accumulation of goods (Roman law and the law of free municipalities).

In patriarchal society, on the contrary, law and economics have an equivalent influence on each other, while in primitive society and, to a large extent, in theocratic-charismatic empires, law, economics, religion and magic are not yet sufficiently differentiated from each other, so that beliefs in the supernatural are dominant over law as well as over economics.

To be precise, we must not overlook the fact that economics can serve as a factor, not only of inclusive legal systems, but also of the constitution of particular groups which engender their own jural frameworks. Thus, groups of economic activity arising in various types of society are obviously under a particularly intense influence from the ruling economic regime, which is more or less reflected in the autonomous jural codes produced by these groups.

III. *Religion, Morality, Knowledge, and Law.* Religion, morality, and knowledge, as collective mentalities, beliefs and behaviours, have in common with law the fact that they, too, are particularly linked to the symbolic and spiritual levels of social reality. Their rôle as factors of changes in jural reality varies, however, with the type of society, and moreover, not each of these factors has the same influence on law.

Religion and, more broadly, beliefs in the supernatural (including magic) have played a preponderant rôle in the life of the law of primitive and theocratic-charismatic societies. In other types of society the rôle of religion varies according to the intensity of belief and to the structure of the Church, as well as according to its relations with other groups. The subjection of the Church to the ancient city, for example, greatly reduced the rôle of religion as a factor of law. The independence of the Church and its jural pre-eminence in the Middle Ages considerably increased the influence of Christianity on law (despite its detachment from mundane life). The struggle of various Christian Churches after the Reformation, while weakening their direct domination over jural life, strongly contributed to the affirmation of the rights of man and citizen which limited the public power. While the separation of Church and State at the beginning of the twentieth century (earlier in the United States) led to the complete secularization of the legal system, at the same time it reinforced the autonomous jural framework of the Church. Finally, the very character of a religion and the content of its dogmas affect the intensity of its influence on law. Thus, tribal and national religions are linked with law more than universal religions. Among the latter Judaism and Islam are linked more closely with law than is Christianity. Within Christianity, Catholicism is more active in law than Protestantism and especially than Eastern Orthodoxy. Thus, the rôle of religion as a factor of jural life is subjected to a series of concrete variations which act sometimes in various directions.   Determination of this rôle requires a complex analysis which takes account of all the circumstances involved.

In developed societies, where religion, morality, and law are sufficiently distinct from each other, the connections between jural reality and effective morality are particularly intense.   In fact, since law is only a logicization of moral values whose heat it tempers by generalization and determination of its exigencies (permitting the establishment of a correspondence between the duties of some and the claims of others) it varies in the more direct way as a function of mutations of morality.   It does not at all follow, however, that the change of morality and that of law are absolutely synchronized in a society.   There are, on the contrary, constant conflicts and, in principle, it is law which generally tends to lag behind morality.   The latter, in going ahead of law, is habitually a very important factor in eventual mutations of law.   Morality, by its structure, is incomparably more dynamic, more revolutionary, more mobile, more directed towards the future (from which it anticipates the direction) than is the law. The latter is more attached to traditional practices than to acts of innovation, more dependent on intellectual representations, economic realizations, and the balance of forces than is morality.

Did not ancient morality rebel for centuries against the jural institution of slavery before the latter began declining?   Did not the morality of Christian societies outlaw serfdom and private wars before the Middle Ages?   Has not contemporary morality long called for the elimination of the economic exploitation of man by man and for the legal organization of an international society which would outlaw war, while in the reality of law these phenomena persist?   When conflicts between the law and the morality of a society become particularly sharp, the pressure of the moral factor on law is shown in the utopias of " natural law ", that is in appeals to morality against a laggard law, appeals to which " ideologies ", seeking to justify existing law, offer resistance (cf. Mannheim).   It is, however, necessary to note that the reverse situation is also possible : the overcoming of a current morality by an advanced law which can become in this way a factor in moral mutations.   This, of course, comes about only at exceptional moments, during revolutions or major reforms in which legislative measures and the intuitive law which inspires them surpass, at a bound, not only the old law but even the morality which helped demolish it.   Such anticipations of law over morality, however, have great difficulty in maintaining themselves and generally provoke deep reactions.

Knowledge as a social phenomenon may act as a factor of change in the reality of law under two aspects. First, collective intellectual representations being, in combination with moral values, a constituent element of all law, their variations provoke a mutation of jural beliefs and behaviours. For example, it is enough that there occurs a variation in ideas of causality, matter, society, the personality, etc., for jural institutions like responsibility, property, inheritance, obligations, etc., to undergo very profound changes (cf., for examples along this line, my *Expérience Juridique*, 1935). Secondly, knowledge acts as a factor of law-changes in another more concentrated and more limited way. It intervenes in the modes of acknowledging law, it influences the formal sources of the latter. Even the orientation and intellectual training of judges, jurisprudents, lawyers (e.g., the jurisprudents in Rome, the legists of the Middle Ages, the judges, attorneys, and professors of law to-day) are important factors in the movement of jural reality. The more a legal system is rationalized and secularized, the stronger becomes such influence of knowledge on the reality of law.

The rôle of law as a factor of knowledge is, on the other hand, very limited. Here there are simply various legal limitations on freedom of thought, limitations which sometimes decline, sometimes increase.

IV. *Collective Psychology and Law*. As the most profound layer of social reality, penetrating all its manifestations and aspects, the collective mentality is virtually present underneath all the factors just enumerated. Collective psychology indirectly influences law through religion, morality, knowledge, and even through economics and the morphological basis of society. But we must also take into account the states of collective mind as direct factors of the life of law.

We have already touched on this question in its microsociological aspect, because masses, community and communion are primarily manifestations of different states of the collective mind. We have described their direct effects upon law. Likewise, the diverse unifying syntheses of forms of sociality which constitute particular groups, presuppose the existence of corresponding collective minds, the measure of whose cohesion in a group-mind and the principles of its unity are reflected directly in the characteristics and the degree of validity of the jural frameworks.

We also need to take into account the states of larger collective mentalities corresponding to all-inclusive societies as factors of the corresponding legal systems.[1]

Most important here are the differences in the dosage of intellectual, emotional, and volitional elements on the one hand, of imagination, memory, and intuition on the other, in the collective psyche of all-inclusive societies. It is inter-relations of these elements which vary in the psychology of the different types of societies. The predominance of diverse forms of collective emotionality on the one hand, of social memory on the other, characterize, for example, the jural psychology of primitive societies and theocratic-charismatic empires, while the jural psychology of the ancient city and bourgeois society is characterized by a predominance of intellectual elements and, particularly, of concepts ; this mentality is oriented towards the pre-eminence of " security " over " justice ". On the other hand, contemporary jural psychology, perhaps like those of all epochs of transition and change, is marked by a predominance of collective volitions and imaginations, combined with a new emotional wave ; this state of mind drives towards the pursuit of justice at the expense of security. The field of study about which I am speaking still remains entirely virgin. As with so many other problems of sociology of law, we must await the outcome of extensive investigations of which we have here tried to indicate no more than the possible directions.

[1] On the pluralism of collective minds in group-minds and, moreover, in the psyche of all inclusive societies, see my *Essais de sociologie,* Chapter II, " The Problem of Collective Consciousness in Durkheim's Sociology ", pp. 115–69.

SOCIOLOGY OF LAW AND PHILOSOPHY OF LAW

In the Introduction and all the way through our exposition, we have tried to point out the character of the sociology of law as a kind of sociology of the human spirit. We have also insisted on the mutual interdependence between this part of sociology and philosophy. To conclude our book, it seems to us desirable to return to this subject for more precision.

The spiritual realm is the particular subject of philosophy, which is concerned with the study of values, ideas and the acts which grasp and embody them from the viewpoint of their objective validity and their veracity ; obviously these problems entirely transcend the scope of sociology. Thus, to the extent that the sociology of law and the philosophy of law impinge on the same spiritual sphere—the objective ideas and values inspiring law—they treat it from two essentially different points of view. The first views it as a function of social reality ; the second views it in itself, intrinsically, and with relation to other sectors of the human spirit, envisaged in its objective validity. But after we have recognized this there immediately arises the question whether the distinction between sociology of law and philosophy of law implies the total separation, the absolute mutual independence of the two disciplines, or whether there is not rather an indispensable collaboration and mutual assistance.

As we have stressed in the Introduction, philosophy of law entirely cut off from sociology of law would be nothing more than a sort of dogmatic rationalism ; such a philosophy has long since been surpassed. Philosophy of law of this type would find itself in a vacuum of deductive constructions, vainly seeking to derive content from form, multiplicity from unity, the real from the ideal, irreducible antinomies from an initial harmony. At every step it would run counter to the results of sociological and historical investigations. Conversely, a sociology of law having no contact with philosophy would be deprived, as we have seen, of the points of support necessary for the construction of its specific object : the social reality of law which is neither an immediate datum nor a matter of perception. This construction assumes the differentiation between the subject of sociology of law and the subject of the sociology of morality, of religion, of æsthetics, of knowledge, a differentiation which can be made only through philosophy. Isolated from the latter, sociology cannot profit from autonomous reflection on ideal structures, on the objective values which are embodied in social facts. It would be driven towards an exaggerated realism, tending towards naturalism or behaviourism, and would lose the law, that is, the proper subject of its study ; generally, the study of the problem of social control, as well as the differentiation of its kinds would appear impossible.

In view of the sterility, dogmatism, and impotence to which a philosophy of law and a sociology of law deprived of mutual contact would be doomed, their reciprocal dependence and maximum possible collaboration would seem indispensable. Out of this requirement, however, immediately arise new problems which might seem very disturbing. We have stressed them in the Introduction. In the first place, if sociology of law and philosophy of law are founded upon each other, have we not a vicious circle ? Next, aside from the logical contradiction, how shall we avoid the dangers of having the philosophy of law narrow the sphere of the sociological observations by intervening in the construction of the jural fact, and of having the investigations of sociologists destroy the objective validity of jural values (to be systematized and verified by philosophy) by revealing their infinite variability of aspects ?

We have mentioned in the Introduction that an answer to these questions can be given only through the theory of *immediate jural experience*, infinitely variable in both spiritual and sense data and alone making it possible to grasp the full reality of law. It is this experience which serves as a common basis for the philosophy of law and sociology of law, as well as for the jurisprudence, the dogmatic-normative science of law. All these disciplines reflect on the same experience after it is accomplished ; this experience is subjacent to each of them : its immediate data are all utilized by these disciplines for further elaboration, each of the latter doing this in its own way and under a particular light.

We cannot pause here to take up the idea of the integral experience of the immediate, which includes experiences both spiritual and sensible, and which is virtually present in every consecutive, symbolic or conceptualized experience, for example, scientific experience and, particularly, sociological experience. Nor can we pause to discuss the methods of actualizing integral experience, i.e., the return to the immediate, which is always furthest from us, most difficult of access, and which pre-supposes a long and difficult labour of reflective approach. Nor, finally, can we pause to examine the procedures for verifying the objective validity of the spiritual data of these experiences. Invoking doctrinal precedents found in the philosophies of W. James (and partially Dewey), Bergson, Rauh, Husserl and Scheler, we have tried to describe the philosophical procedures of " inversion " and " reduction ", conducting step by step from conceptual constructions to the immediate date, in our books, *Expérience Juridique et la Philosophie Pluraliste du Droit* (1935), *La Morale théorique et la Science des Mœurs* (1937), *Les Tendances actuelles de la Philosophie allemande* (1930). In a book, *Ethics and Sociology*, now being prepared for publication, we hope to develop this subject at greater length. In these writings may also be found precise details on the specific nature of the jural experience as contrasted with the moral experience, and on the relation of both to corresponding sociological and philosophical disciplines. Here we must limit ourselves to summing up some of our theses mentioned already in the Introduction and concerning the character of the jural experience and the tasks of the philosophy of law.

Immediate jural experience, which lies midway between moral experience and the experience of logical ideas, as well as between spiritual experience and sense experience, consists of collective acts of *cold recognition* of tangible social situations which realize positive values. In these collective acts of intuitive recognition there is actually experienced one of the infinite aspects of justice in the process of its realization in different manifestations of the social : forms of sociality, types of groups, types of all-inclusive societies. The jural experience and its immediate data vary simultaneously as functions of the variations of " recognized " values (moral and others) ; of the intellectual ideas which limit them ; of the *rapport* between these two elements, as well as the proportion of the experience of the sensible and of the experience of the spiritual, and the degree of actuality and virtuality with which they are grasped in the various layers of depth of the experience of law. The spiritual data of this experience grasped in their embodiment in tangible facts, reveal only particularized and localized sectors of the infinite whole of justice which can never be grasped in its entirety. That is why the philosophy of law, which is concerned with the study of spiritual jural values in an effort to verify their objectivity by integrating them in an open system whose image it seeks to reconstruct, has a primary interest in seeing to it that the broad investigations of sociology of law do not overlook any of the innumerable variations of jural rules, behaviour patterns, symbols, principles and values. The more such variations sociology establishes and describes, the richer becomes the image of justice which philosophy seeks to reconstruct. Consequently, there is no reason for fearing encroachments or conflicts between the philosophy of law and the sociology of law, provided that the two cling to a *radical empiricism* with an *intuitional basis* ; such a conception does not at all exclude the objective validity of the spiritual data concerning which it affirms only an infinite variety of localized and particularized aspects capable of being grasped only when embodied in tangible facts.

What are the tasks and the rôle of the philosophy of law so conceived ? Its *first task* is to lead back from constructed and symbolic jural experience to immediate jural experience in its various layers. In actualizing step by step the immediate jural data by means of reflection, data which are hidden from us by concepts, patterns, symbols and behaviours (the point of departure), the philosophy of law has as a *second task*, the pointing out of the specific nature of jural experience as contrasted with other kinds of integral experience : moral, religious, æsthetic, intellectual. The *third task* of the philosophy of law is to distinguish, within jural values which have really been grasped or embodied, between illusions—subjective projections of the collective mentality and objectively valid ideal structures. The method of accomplishing this task is to find the indispensable place of the concrete jural values in the image of the whole of justice, in which they, when objective, complement each other by constituting a plurality within a unity.

It is easy to state that if the philosophy of law, in achieving the third task, affirms itself absolutely independent of sociology of law, it remains, on the contrary, in constant and mutual contact with the latter when it tries to accomplish the first two tasks. It is no less obvious that the philosophy of law, thus understood, deduces nothing and prescribes nothing. It provides no judgments of value, but merely theoretical judgments about jural values which have really been grasped or embodied, whose objective validity it only verifies and whose specific nature it defines.

This does not at all prevent the results of the philosophy of law, combined with those of sociology of law, from being utilized, however, to establish, for a given epoch or a given type of society, a technique for the improvement of law, " a jural policy ". This would have for its subject the facilitating (by taking into account the " regularities as tendencies " involved in the system of jural reality in question and by leaning on the concrete objective values embodied therein) of the more complete realization of such values in the social life of law and in the complex web of diverse equilibria that constitute it.[1]

[1] I cannot finish this book without expressing my gratitude to Mr. Herbert Solow of the New School for Social Research, who contributed essentially to giving it an acceptable English expression.

INDEX

International Library of Sociology

Edited by
John Rex
University of Warwick

Founded by
Karl Mannheim

as The International Library of Sociology
and Social Reconstruction

*This Catalogue also contains other Social Science
series published by Routledge*

Routledge & Kegan Paul   London and Boston

68-74 Carter Lane London EC4V 5EL
9 Park Street Boston Mass 02108

Contents

● *Books so marked are available in paperback*
All books are in Metric Demy 8vo format (216 × 138mm approx.)

GENERAL SOCIOLOGY

Belshaw, Cyril. The Conditions of Social Performance. *An Exploratory Theory. 144 pp.*

Brown, Robert. Explanation in Social Science. *208 pp.*

Cain, Maureen E. Society and the Policeman's Role. *About 300 pp.*

Gibson, Quentin. The Logic of Social Enquiry. *240 pp.*

Homans, George C. Sentiments and Activities: *Essays in Social Science. 336 pp.*

Isajiw, Wsevold W. Causation and Functionalism in Sociology. *165 pp.*

Johnson, Harry M. Sociology: *a Systematic Introduction. Foreword by Robert K. Merton. 710 pp.*

Mannheim, Karl. Essays on Sociology and Social Psychology. *Edited by Paul Keckskemeti. With Editorial Note by Adolph Lowe. 344 pp.*

   Systematic Sociology: *An Introduction to the Study of Society. Edited by J. S. Erös and Professor W. A. C. Stewart. 220 pp.*

Martindale, Don. The Nature and Types of Sociological Theory. *292 pp.*

● **Maus, Heinz.** A Short History of Sociology. *234 pp.*

Mey, Harald. Field-Theory. *A Study of its Application in the Social Sciences. 352 pp.*

Myrdal, Gunnar. Value in Social Theory: *A Collection of Essays on Methodology. Edited by Paul Streeten. 332 pp.*

Ogburn, William F., and **Nimkoff, Meyer F.** A Handbook of Sociology. *Preface by Karl Mannheim. 656 pp. 46 figures. 35 tables.*

Parsons, Talcott, and **Smelser, Neil J.** Economy and Society: *A Study in the Integration of Economic and Social Theory. 362 pp.*

● **Rex, John.** Key Problems of Sociological Theory. *220 pp.*

Stark, Werner. The Fundamental Forms of Social Thought. *280 pp.*

FOREIGN CLASSICS OF SOCIOLOGY

● **Durkheim, Emile.** Suicide. *A Study in Sociology. Edited and with an Introduction by George Simpson. 404 pp.*

   Professional Ethics and Civic Morals. *Translated by Cornelia Brookfield. 288 pp.*

● **Gerth, H. H.,** and **Mills, C. Wright.** From Max Weber: *Essays in Sociology. 502 pp.*

Tönnies, Ferdinand. Community and Association. *(Gemeinschaft und Gesellschaft.) Translated and Supplemented by Charles P. Loomis. Foreword by Pitirim A. Sorokin. 334 pp.*

SOCIAL STRUCTURE

Andreski, Stanislav. Military Organization and Society. *Foreword by Professor A. R. Radcliffe-Brown. 226 pp. 1 folder.*

● **Cole, G. D. H.** Studies in Class Structure. *220 p.*

Coontz, Sydney H. Population Theories and the Economic Interpretation. *202 pp.*

Coser, Lewis. The Functions of Social Conflict. *204 pp.*

Dickie-Clark, H. F. Marginal Situation: *A Sociological Study of a Coloured Group. 240 pp. 11 tables.*

Glass, D. V. (Ed.). Social Mobility in Britain. *Contributions by J. Berent, T. Bottomore, R. C. Chambers, J. Floud, D. V. Glass, J. R. Hall, H. T. Himmelweit, R. K. Kelsall, F. M. Martin, C. A. Moser, R. Mukherjee, and W. Ziegel. 420 pp.*

Glaser, Barney, and **Strauss, Anselm L.** Status Passage. *A Formal Theory. 208 pp.*

Jones, Garth N. Planned Organizational Change: *An Exploratory Study Using an Empirical Approach. 268 pp.*

Kelsall, R. K. Higher Civil Servants in Britain: *From 1870 to the Present Day. 268 pp. 31 tables.*

König, René. The Community. *232 pp. Illustrated.*

● **Lawton, Denis.** Social Class, Language and Education. *192 pp.*

McLeish, John. The Theory of Social Change: *Four Views Considered. 128 pp.*

Marsh, David C. The Changing Social Structure in England and Wales, 1871-1961. *272 pp.*

Mouzelis, Nicos. Organization and Bureaucracy. *An Analysis of Modern Theories. 240 pp.*

Mulkay, M. J. Functionalism, Exchange and Theoretical Strategy. *272 pp.*

Ossowski, Stanislaw. Class Structure in the Social Consciousness. *210 pp.*

SOCIOLOGY AND POLITICS

Crick, Bernard. The American Science of Politics: *Its Origins and Conditions. 284 pp.*

Hertz, Frederick. Nationality in History and Politics: *A Psychology and Sociology of National Sentiment and Nationalism. 432 pp.*

Kornhauser, William. The Politics of Mass Society. *272 pp. 20 tables.*

Laidler, Harry W. History of Socialism. *Social-Economic Movements: An Historical and Comparative Survey of Socialism, Communism, Co-operation, Utopianism; and other Systems of Reform and Reconstruction. 992 pp.*

Mannheim, Karl. Freedom, Power and Democratic Planning. *Edited by Hans Gerth and Ernest K. Bramstedt. 424 pp.*

Mansur, Fatma. Process of Independence. *Foreword by A. H. Hanson. 208 pp.*

Martin, David A. Pacificism: *an Historical and Sociological Study. 262 pp.*

Myrdal, Gunnar. The Political Element in the Development of Economic Theory. *Translated from the German by Paul Streeten. 282 pp.*

Verney, Douglas V. The Analysis of Political Systems. *264 pp.*

Wootton, Graham. Workers, Unions and the State. *188 pp.*

FOREIGN AFFAIRS: THEIR SOCIAL, POLITICAL AND ECONOMIC FOUNDATIONS

Bonné, Alfred. State and Economics in the Middle East: *A Society in Transition. 482 pp.*
  Studies in Economic Development: *with special reference to Conditions in the Under-developed Areas of Western Asia and India. 322 pp. 84 tables.*
Mayer, J. P. Political Thought in France from the Revolution to the Fifth Republic. *164 pp.*

CRIMINOLOGY

Ancel, Marc. Social Defence: *A Modern Approach to Criminal Problems. Foreword by Leon Radzinowicz. 240 pp.*
Cloward, Richard A., and **Ohlin, Lloyd E.** Delinquency and Opportunity: *A Theory of Delinquent Gangs. 248 pp.*
Downes, David M. The Delinquent Solution. *A Study in Subcultural Theory. 296 pp.*
Dunlop, A. B., and **McCabe, S.** Young Men in Detention Centres. *192 pp.*
Friedlander, Kate. The Psycho-Analytical Approach to Juvenile Delinquency: *Theory, Case Studies, Treatment. 320 pp.*
Glueck, Sheldon, and **Eleanor.** Family Environment and Delinquency. *With the statistical assistance of Rose W. Kneznek. 340 pp.*
Lopez-Rey, Manuel. Crime. *An Analytical Appraisal. 288 pp.*
Mannheim, Hermann. Comparative Criminology: *a Text Book. Two volumes. 442 pp. and 380 pp.*
Morris, Terence. The Criminal Area: *A Study in Social Ecology. Foreword by Hermann Mannheim. 232 pp. 25 tables. 4 maps.*
Trasler, Gordon. The Explanation of Criminality. *144 pp.*

SOCIAL PSYCHOLOGY

Bagley, Christopher. The Social Psychology of the Child with Epilepsy. *320 pp.*
Barbu, Zevedei. Problems of Historical Psychology. *248 pp.*
Blackburn, Julian. Psychology and the Social Pattern. *184 pp.*
● **Fleming, C. M.** Adolescence: *Its Social Psychology: With an Introduction to recent findings from the fields of Anthropology, Physiology, Medicine, Psychometrics and Sociometry. 288 pp.*
● The Social Psychology of Education: *An Introduction and Guide to Its Study. 136 pp.*
Homans, George C. The Human Group. *Foreword by Bernard DeVoto. Introduction by Robert K. Merton. 526 pp.*
  Social Behaviour: *its Elementary Forms. 416 pp.*

Klein, Josephine. The Study of Groups. *226 pp. 31 figures. 5 tables.*

Linton, Ralph. The Cultural Background of Personality. *132 pp.*

Mayo, Elton. The Social Problems of an Industrial Civilization. *With an appendix on the Political Problem. 180 pp.*

Ottaway, A. K. C. Learning Through Group Experience. *176 pp.*

Ridder, J. C. de. The Personality of the Urban African in South Africa. *A Thematic Apperception Test Study. 196 pp. 12 plates.*

● **Rose, Arnold M.** (Ed.). Human Behaviour and Social Processes: *an Interactionist Approach. Contributions by Arnold M. Rose, Ralph H. Turner, Anselm Strauss, Everett C. Hughes, E. Franklin Frazier, Howard S. Becker, et al. 696 pp.*

Smelser, Neil J. Theory of Collective Behaviour. *448 pp.*

Stephenson, Geoffrey M. The Development of Conscience. *128 pp.*

Young, Kimball. Handbook of Social Psychology. *658 pp. 16 figures. 10 tables.*

SOCIOLOGY OF THE FAMILY

Banks, J. A. Prosperity and Parenthood: *A Study of Family Planning among The Victorian Middle Classes. 262 pp.*

Bell, Colin R. Middle Class Families: *Social and Geographical Mobility. 224 pp.*

Burton, Lindy. Vulnerable Children. *272 pp.*

Gavron, Hannah. The Captive Wife: *Conflicts of Household Mothers. 190 pp.*

George, Victor, and **Wilding, Paul.** Motherless Families. *220 pp.*

Klein, Josephine. Samples from English Cultures.
1. Three Preliminary Studies and Aspects of Adult Life in England. *447 pp.*
2. Child-Rearing Practices and Index. *247 pp.*

Klein, Viola. Britain's Married Women Workers. *180 pp.*
The Feminine Character. *History of an Ideology. 244 pp.*

McWhinnie, Alexina M. Adopted Children. *How They Grow Up. 304 pp.*

Myrdal, Alva, and **Klein, Viola.** Women's Two Roles: *Home and Work. 238 pp. 27 tables.*

Parsons, Talcott, and **Bales, Robert F.** Family: *Socialization and Interaction Process. In collaboration with James Olds, Morris Zelditch and Philip E. Slater. 456 pp. 50 figures and tables.*

SOCIAL SERVICES

Bastide, Roger. The Sociology of Mental Disorder. *Translated from the French by Jean McNeil. 264 pp.*

Carlebach, Julius. Caring For Children in Trouble. *266 pp.*

Forder, R. A. (Ed.). Penelope Hall's Social Services of Modern England. *352 pp.*

George, Victor. Foster Care. *Theory and Practice. 234 pp.*
Social Security: *Beveridge and After. 258 pp.*

● **Goetschius, George W.** Working with Community Groups. *256 pp.*

Goetschius, George W., and **Tash, Joan.** Working with Unattached Youth. *416 pp.*

Hall, M. P., and **Howes, I. V.** The Church in Social Work. *A Study of Moral Welfare Work undertaken by the Church of England. 320 pp.*

Heywood, Jean S. Children in Care: *the Development of the Service for the Deprived Child. 264 pp.*

Hoenig, J., and **Hamilton, Marian W.** The De-Segration of the Mentally Ill. *284 pp.*

Jones, Kathleen. Lunacy, Law and Conscience, *1744-1845: the Social History of the Care of the Insane. 268 pp.*

Mental Health and Social Policy, 1845-1959. *264 pp.*

King, Roy D., Raynes, Norma V., and **Tizard, Jack.** Patterns of Residential Care. *356 pp.*

Leigh, John. Young People and Leisure. *256 pp.*

Morris, Pauline. Put Away: *A Sociological Study of Institutions for the Mentally Retarded. 364 pp.*

Nokes, P. L. The Professional Task in Welfare Practice. *152 pp.*

Timms, Noel. Psychiatric Social Work in Great Britain (1939-1962). *280 pp.*

● Social Casework: *Principles and Practice. 256 pp.*

Trasler, Gordon. In Place of Parents: *A Study in Foster Care. 272 pp.*

Young, A. F., and **Ashton, E. T.** British Social Work in the Nineteenth Century. *288 pp.*

Young, A. F. Social Services in British Industry. *272 pp.*

SOCIOLOGY OF EDUCATION

Banks, Olive. Parity and Prestige in English Secondary Education: a Study in Educational Sociology. *272 pp.*

Bentwich, Joseph. Education in Israel. *224 pp. 8 pp. plates.*

● **Blyth, W. A. L.** English Primary Education. *A Sociological Description.*

1. Schools. *232 pp.*

2. Background. *168 pp.*

Collier, K. G. The Social Purposes of Education: *Personal and Social Values in Education. 268 pp.*

Dale, R. R., and **Griffith, S.** Down Stream: *Failure in the Grammar School. 108 pp.*

Dore, R. P. Education in Tokugawa Japan. *356 pp. 9 pp. plates*

Evans, K. M. Sociometry and Education. *158 pp.*

Foster, P. J. Education and Social Change in Ghana. *336 pp. 3 maps.*

Fraser, W. R. Education and Society in Modern France. *150 pp.*

Grace, Gerald R. Role Conflict and the Teacher. *About 200 pp.*

Hans, Nicholas. New Trends in Education in the Eighteenth Century. *278 pp. 19 tables.*

● Comparative Education: *A Study of Educational Factors and Traditions. 360 pp.*

Hargreaves, David. Interpersonal Relations and Education. *432 pp.*
● Social Relations in a Secondary School. *240 pp.*
Holmes, Brian. Problems in Education. *A Comparative Approach. 336 pp.*
King, Ronald. Values and Involvement in a Grammar School. *164 pp.*
● **Mannheim, Karl,** and **Stewart, W. A. C.** An Introduction to the Sociology of Education. *206 pp.*
Morris, Raymond N. The Sixth Form and College Entrance. *231 pp.*
● **Musgrove, F.** Youth and the Social Order. *176 pp.*
● **Ottaway, A. K. C.** Education and Society: *An Introduction to the Sociology of Education. With an Introduction by W. O. Lester Smith. 212 pp.*
Peers, Robert. Adult Education: *A Comparative Study. 398 pp.*
Pritchard, D. G. Education and the Handicapped: *1760 to 1960. 258 pp.*
Richardson, Helen. Adolescent Girls in Approved Schools. *308 pp.*
Simon, Brian, and **Joan** (Eds.). Educational Psychology in the U.S.S.R. *Introduction by Brian and Joan Simon. Translation by Joan Simon. Papers by D. N. Bogoiavlenski and N. A. Menchinskaia, D. B. Elkonin, E. A. Fleshner, Z. I. Kalmykova, G. S. Kostiuk, V. A. Krutetski, A. N. Leontiev, A. R. Luria, E. A. Milerian, R. G. Natadze, B. M. Teplov, L. S. Vygotski, L. V. Zankov. 296 pp.*
Stratta, Erica. The Education of Borstal Boys. *A Study of their Educational Experiences prior to, and during Borstal Training. 256 pp.*

SOCIOLOGY OF CULTURE

Eppel, E. M., and **M.** Adolescents and Morality: *A Study of some Moral Values and Dilemmas of Working Adolescents in the Context of a changing Climate of Opinion. Foreword by W. J. H. Sprott. 268 pp. 39 tables.*
● **Fromm, Erich.** The Fear of Freedom. *286 pp.*
The Sane Society. *400 pp.*
● **Mannheim, Karl.** Diagnosis of Our Time: *Wartime Essays of a Sociologist. 208 pp.*
Essays on the Sociology of Culture. *Edited by Ernst Mannheim in co-operation with Paul Kecskemeti. Editorial Note by Adolph Lowe. 280 pp.*
Weber, Alfred. Farewell to European History: *or The Conquest of Nihilism. Translated from the German by R. F. C. Hull. 224 pp.*

SOCIOLOGY OF RELIGION

Argyle, Michael. Religious Behaviour. *224 pp. 8 figures. 41 tables.*
Nelson, G. K. Spiritualism and Society. *313 pp.*

Stark, Werner. The Sociology of Religion. *A Study of Christendom.*
  Volume I. *Established Religion. 248 pp.*
  Volume II. *Sectarian Religion. 368 pp.*
  Volume III. *The Universal Church. 464 pp.*
  Volume IV. *Types of Religious Man. 352 pp.*
  Volume V. *Types of Religious Culture. 464 pp.*
Watt, W. Montgomery. Islam and the Integration of Society. *320 pp.*

SOCIOLOGY OF ART AND LITERATURE

Beljame, Alexandre. Men of Letters and the English Public in the Eighteenth
  Century: *1660-1744, Dryden, Addison, Pope. Edited with an Introduction
  and Notes by Bonamy Dobrée. Translated by E. O. Lorimer. 532 pp.*
Jarvie, Ian C. Towards a Sociology of the Cinema. *A Comparative Essay
  on the Structure and Functioning of a Major Entertainment Industry.
  405 pp.*
Rust, Frances S. Dance in Society. *An Analysis of the Relationships between
  the Social Dance and Society in England from the Middle Ages to the
  Present Day. 256 pp. 8 pp. of plates.*
Schücking, L. L. The Sociology of Literary Taste. *112 pp.*
Silbermann, Alphons. The Sociology of Music. *Translated from the German
  by Corbet Stewart. 222 pp.*

SOCIOLOGY OF KNOWLEDGE

Mannheim, Karl. Essays on the Sociology of Knowledge. *Edited by Paul
  Kecskemeti. Editorial note by Adolph Lowe. 353 pp.*
Stark, Werner. The Sociology of Knowledge: *An Essay in Aid of a Deeper
  Understanding of the History of Ideas. 384 pp.*

URBAN SOCIOLOGY

Ashworth, William. The Genesis of Modern British Town Planning: *A Study
  in Economic and Social History of the Nineteenth and Twentieth Centuries.
  288 pp.*
Cullingworth, J. B. Housing Needs and Planning Policy: *A Restatement of
  the Problems of Housing Need and 'Overspill' in England and Wales.
  232 pp. 44 tables. 8 maps.*
Dickinson, Robert E. City and Region: *A Geographical Interpretation.
  608 pp. 125 figures.*
  The West European City: *A Geographical Interpretation. 600 pp. 129 maps.
  29 plates.*
● The City Region in Western Europe. *320 pp. Maps.*

Humphreys, Alexander J. New Dubliners: *Urbanization and the Irish Family. Foreword by George C. Homans. 304 pp.*

Jackson, Brian. Working Class Community: *Some General Notions raised by a Series of Studies in Northern England. 192 pp.*

Jennings, Hilda. Societies in the Making: *a Study of Development and Redevelopment within a County Borough. Foreword by D. A. Clark. 286 pp.*

Kerr, Madeline. The People of Ship Street. *240 pp.*

● **Mann, P. H.** An Approach to Urban Sociology. *240 pp.*

Morris, R. N., and **Mogey, J.** The Sociology of Housing. *Studies at Berinsfield. 232 pp. 4 pp. plates.*

Rosser, C., and **Harris, C.** The Family and Social Change. *A Study of Family and Kinship in a South Wales Town. 352 pp. 8 maps.*

RURAL SOCIOLOGY

Chambers, R. J. H. Settlement Schemes in Africa: *A Selective Study. 268 pp.*

Haswell, M. R. The Economics of Development in Village India. *120 pp.*

Littlejohn, James. Westrigg: *the Sociology of a Cheviot Parish. 172 pp. 5 figures.*

Williams, W. M. The Country Craftsman: *A Study of Some Rural Crafts and the Rural Industries Organization in England. 248 pp. 9 figures. (Dartington Hall Studies in Rural Sociology.)*

The Sociology of an English Village: *Gosforth. 272 pp. 12 figures. 13 tables.*

SOCIOLOGY OF INDUSTRY AND DISTRIBUTION

Anderson, Nels. Work and Leisure. *280 pp.*

● **Blau, Peter M.,** and **Scott, W. Richard.** Formal Organizations: *a Comparative approach. Introduction and Additional Bibliography by J. H. Smith. 326 pp.*

Eldridge, J. E. T. Industrial Disputes. *Essays in the Sociology of Industrial Relations. 288 pp.*

Hetzler, Stanley. Technological Growth and Social Change. *Achieving Modernization. 269 pp.*

Hollowell, Peter G. The Lorry Driver. *272 pp.*

Jefferys, Margot, *with the assistance of Winifred Moss.* Mobility in the Labour Market: *Employment Changes in Battersea and Dagenham. Preface by Barbara Wootton. 186 pp. 51 tables.*

Millerson, Geoffrey. The Qualifying Associations: *a Study in Professionalization. 320 pp.*

Smelser, Neil J. Social Change in the Industrial Revolution: *An Application of Theory to the Lancashire Cotton Industry, 1770-1840. 468 pp. 12 figures. 14 tables.*

Williams, Gertrude. Recruitment to Skilled Trades. *240 pp.*

Young, A. F. Industrial Injuries Insurance: *an Examination of British Policy.* *192 pp.*

ANTHROPOLOGY

Ammar, Hamed. Growing up in an Egyptian Village: *Silwa, Province of Aswan. 336 pp.*

Brandel-Syrier, Mia. Reeftown Elite. *A Study of Social Mobility in a Modern African Community on the Reef. 376 pp.*

Crook, David, and **Isabel.** Revolution in a Chinese Village: *Ten Mile Inn. 230 pp. 8 plates. 1 map.*
The First Years of Yangyi Commune. *302 pp. 12 plates.*

Dickie-Clark, H. F. The Marginal Situation. *A Sociological Study of a Coloured Group. 236 pp.*

Dube, S. C. Indian Village. *Foreword by Morris Edward Opler. 276 pp. 4 plates.*
India's Changing Villages: *Human Factors in Community Development. 260 pp. 8 plates. 1 map.*

Firth, Raymond. Malay Fishermen. *Their Peasant Economy. 420 pp. 17 pp. plates.*

Gulliver, P. H. Social Control in an African Society: a Study of the Arusha, Agricultural Masai of Northern Tanganyika. *320 pp. 8 plates. 10 figures.*

Ishwaran, K. Shivapur. *A South Indian Village. 216 pp.*
Tradition and Economy in Village India: *An Interactionist Approach. Foreword by Conrad Arensburg. 176 pp.*

Jarvie, Ian C. The Revolution in Anthropology. *268 pp.*

Jarvie, Ian C., and **Agassi, Joseph.** Hong Kong. *A Society in Transition. 396 pp. Illustrated with plates and maps.*

Little, Kenneth L. Mende of Sierra Leone. *308 pp. and folder.*
Negroes in Britain. *With a New Introduction and Contemporary Study by Leonard Bloom. 320 pp.*

Lowie, Robert H. Social Organization. *494 pp.*

Mayer, Adrian C. Caste and Kinship in Central India: *A Village and its Region. 328 pp. 16 plates. 15 figures. 16 tables.*

Smith, Raymond T. The Negro Family in British Guiana: *Family Structure and Social Status in the Villages. With a Foreword by Meyer Fortes. 314 pp. 8 plates. 1 figure. 4 maps.*

DOCUMENTARY

Meek, Dorothea L. (Ed.). Soviet Youth: *Some Achievements and Problems. Excerpts from the Soviet Press, translated by the editor. 280 pp.*

Schlesinger, Rudolf (Ed.). Changing Attitudes in Soviet Russia.
2. *The Nationalities Problem and Soviet Administration. Selected Readings on the Development of Soviet Nationalities Policies. Introduced by the editor. Translated by W. W. Gottlieb. 324 pp.*

11

SOCIOLOGY AND PHILOSOPHY

Barnsley, John H. The Social Reality of Ethics. *A Comparative Analysis of Moral Codes. 448 pp.*

Douglas, Jack D. (Ed.). Understanding Everyday Life. *Toward the Reconstruction of Sociological Knowledge. Contributions by Alan F. Blum. Aaron W. Cicourel, Norman K. Denzin, Jack D. Douglas, John Heeren, Peter McHugh, Peter K. Manning, Melvin Power, Matthew Speier, Roy Turner, D. Lawrence Wieder, Thomas P. Wilson and Don H. Zimmerman. 358 pp.*

Jarvie, Ian C. Concepts and Society. *216 pp.*

Roche, Maurice. Phenomenology, Language and the Social Sciences. *About 400 pp.*

Sklair, Leslie. The Sociology of Progress. *320 pp.*

International Library of Social Policy

General Editor Kathleen Janes

Jones, Kathleen. Mental Health Services. *A history, 1744-1971. About 500 pp.*

Thomas, J. E. The English Prison Officer since 1850: *A Study in Conflict. 258 pp.*

Primary Socialization, Language and Education

General Editor Basil Bernstein

Bernstein, Basil. Class, Codes and Control. *2 volumes.*
1. *Theoretical Studies Towards a Sociology of Language. 254 pp.*
2. *Applied Studies Towards a Sociology of Language. About 400 pp.*

Brandis, Walter, and **Henderson, Dorothy.** Social Class, Language and Communication. *288 pp.*

Cook, Jenny. Socialization and Social Control. *About 300 pp.*

Gahagan, D. M., and **G. A.** Talk Reform. *Exploration in Language for Infant School Children. 160 pp.*

Robinson, W. P., and **Rackstraw, Susan, D. A.** A Question of Answers. *2 volumes. 192 pp. and 180 pp.*

Turner, Geoffrey, J., and **Mohan, Bernard, A.** A Linguistic Description and Computer Programme for Children's Speech. *208 pp.*

Reports of the Institute of Community Studies and the Institute of Social Studies in Medical Care

Cartwright, Ann. Human Relations and Hospital Care. *272 pp.*
   Parents and Family Planning Services. *306 pp.*
   Patients and their Doctors. *A Study of General Practice. 304 pp.*
Dunnell, Karen, and **Cartwright, Ann.** Medicine Takers, Prescribers and Hoarders. *About 140 pp.*
● **Jackson, Brian.** Streaming: *an Education System in Miniature. 168 pp.*
Jackson, Brian, and **Marsden, Dennis.** Education and the Working Class: *Some General Themes raised by a Study of 88 Working-class Children in a Northern Industrial City. 268 pp. 2 folders.*
Marris, Peter. Widows and their Families. *Foreword by Dr. John Bowlby. 184 pp. 18 tables. Statistical Summary.*
   Family and Social Change in an African City. *A Study of Rehousing in Lagos. 196 pp. 1 map. 4 plates. 53 tables.*
   The Experience of Higher Education. *232 pp. 27 tables.*
Marris, Peter, and **Rein, Martin.** Dilemmas of Social Reform. *Poverty and Community Action in the United States. 256 pp.*
Marris, Peter, and **Somerset, Anthony.** African Businessmen. *A Study of Entrepreneurship and Development in Kenya. 256 pp.*
Runciman, W. G. Relative Deprivation and Social Justice. *A Study of Attitudes to Social Inequality in Twentieth Century England. 352 pp.*
Townsend, Peter. The Family Life of Old People: *An Inquiry in East London. Foreword by J. H. Sheldon. 300 pp. 3 figures. 63 tables.*
Willmott, Peter. Adolescent Boys in East London. *230 pp.*
   The Evolution of a Community: *a study of Dagenham after forty years. 168 pp. 2 maps.*
Willmott, Peter, and **Young, Michael.** Family and Class in a London Suburb. *202 pp. 47 tables.*
Young, Michael. Innovation and Research in Education. *192 pp.*
● **Young, Michael,** and **McGeeney, Patrick.** Learning Begins at Home. *A Study of a Junior School and its Parents. 128 pp.*
Young, Michael, and **Willmott, Peter.** Family and Kinship in East London. *Foreword by Richard M. Titmuss. 252 pp. 39 tables.*

Medicine, Illness and Society
General Editor   W. M. Williams

Robinson, David. The Process of Becoming Ill.
Stacey, Margaret. *et al.* Hospitals, Children and Their Families. *The Report of a Pilot Study. 202 pp.*

Routledge Social Science Journals

The British Journal of Sociology. *Edited by Terence P. Morris. Vol. 1, No. 1, March 1950 and Quarterly. Roy. 8vo. Back numbers available. An international journal with articles on all aspects of sociology.*

Economy and Society. *Vol. 1, No. 1. February 1972 and Quarterly. Metric Roy. 8vo. A journal for all social scientists covering sociology, philosophy, anthropology, economics and history.*

Printed in Great Britain by Lewis Reprints Limited
Brown Knight & Truscott Group, London and Tonbridge   21972